A NOTE FROM THE AUTHOR

This is the story of my battle with myself. I mention others only in so far as I rubbed shoulders with them while I tackled the storms within my particular teacup. I was fortunate to have good men as colleagues. That band of brothers is now dispersed. Most have gone on to other things, left the priesthood or, like me, married. A few have died. All we ever wanted was to help others, to do good. Had things worked out differently for me I might well be writing this from a treadmill on Dinosaur Alley in Cork. Instead I am writing it on Aran, where storms are real and the waves are tall.

ARAN TO AFRICA

An Irishman´s Unique Odyssey

Pádraig O'Toole

CONTENTS

ACKNOWLEDGMENTS

My grateful thanks to Mícheál Muldoon, my neighbour on Aran, and Mary O'Hara, my wife, without whose urging and constant encouragement this book might never have seen the light of day.

PART I
ARAN TO AFRICA
CHASING A DREAM

"Where storms are real and the waves are tall."

1

ARAN

It must have been a few years into World War II when the first picture of my surroundings etched itself on my memory. It is of a cluster of the men of our village standing on the height south of our house and looking attentively out to sea. They were watching a raft floating in the tide being dragged through the narrow channel that separated our island from uninhabited Branach Island to the west. Suddenly they all scuttled off in the direction of the shore and soon, we children with our mothers watched two currachs approaching the raft and latching on to it. Obviously from the conversations of our elders, we gathered that they were trying to tow the raft ashore. Eventually the tide won; the currachs separated from the raft and came ashore. They had liberated a few tins of biscuits and some fishing tackle. The biscuits were shared out among the children. It was a novelty in a world where very little ever happened. So it stuck in the memory. In the following few years there were a few more such rafts and the usual hard biscuits. As the war continued, the novelty wore off.

The eldest of seven children, I was born on Easter Night, April 1938 in Bungabhla, the last village on Inis Mór. This is the largest of the three inhabited Aran Islands. It is an oblong island about nine miles long stretching southeast northwest across the mouth of

Galway Bay on the west coast of Ireland. A narrow road runs along the length of the island and Bungabhla marks the western end of that road. It is a bleak full stop among the crags. It faces the Atlantic. My first memories are of constant gales, the groaning noise of the sea and the white waves crashing on to the shore. In winter big blobs of white foam lodged against our doors and windows. A salty taste clung to our lips.

There were eleven houses in Bungabhla, each lined parallel to the road that ran along the island from east to west. On Aran all reference to direction follows the points of the compass. One travels east or west, north or south, even south west. The orientation of the wind is always described very accurately. About half the houses were thatched and the other half slated.

Our house was north of the road so that our south door faced the road and the sun. Our south door was never locked and was permanently open during the day allowing extra light into the kitchen. We seldom used our north door except at the height of the south-westerly gales.

On the left, *ti Bhid Bhilla*, the house in Bungabhla where I was brought up. In the forefront: the ruins of the house where old Máire Chubairt was born. She gave me a rosary that, years later, my monkey Ramidan stole.

We did not like the north door. It made the house and its occupants gloomy. At each end of the house there was a tank to store rain-water from the roof. We had no well or running water. Sometimes in summer we ran out of water and then we had to travel to one or other of the wells in the locality.

Bungabhla is built on top of a limestone slab. The fields are mostly man-made and enclosed by limestone walls. As children we spent our lives climbing over these walls, building them up whenever we knocked them down. Knocking down a neighbour's wall was a constant source of irritation between neighbours and we were continuously reminded to put back any stone we knocked down.

Bungabhla may have been a small village but, at that time, about thirty children and teenagers lived there. Each house was surrounded by a field which we called a 'street' – not a garden or field. The street around our house was made by my father when he returned from America in 1935. He built very sturdy walls around it and planted a few shrubs, the only shrubs in the village at the time. My mother was unusual in that she liked flowers. She devoted a lot of time to them. She went to the shore herself and fetched sand and seaweed for her flowerbeds. She tended them regularly and taught us to do likewise. It was not easy to grow flowers on the island because of the constant wind blowing there. Also, salt was always in the breeze. But my mother succeeded with her flowers when most people would have given up.

Irish was the only language spoken or understood in Bungabhla. My father had learnt English in America. But by the time we were growing up he had forgotten most of it. The only time he made use of it was when a jobber came around to buy cattle or when (very rarely) a tinker came around to sell goods or buy scrap items. The arrival of tinkers was a great novelty for us children. My mother made them tea and after much haggling she bought a few tin cans or saucepans.

My father was referred to locally as Martin Phatch Sheáin Ui Thuathail (the son of Patch, the son of Seán O'Toole). According to local tradition, Seán O'Toole—or perhaps his father— came originally from Connemara to Aran to make *poitín*, poteen in English, a potent local brew condemned by priests and fishermen's wives alike. The O'Tooles must have done well because they never returned to Connemara and made their home on Aran. I was the fifth generation.

My mother was known locally as Bid Bhilla, (pronounced Villa, Bid the daughter of Bill). She was of indigenous island stock, 'Ó Miolláin by surname. Her people had never left the island; nor had she. Her mother was called Nainín Thomáis but was known as *An Cailín Bán*, the blonde girl, and my mother took after her. I understand from stories I heard that as a teenager she was something of a tomboy - very blonde and very wild, the direct opposite of my father. My maternal grandfather, Seán Bhilla (Ó Miolláin), lived in Onaght. He was less of a distant figure than my paternal grandfather, probably because I got to know him better since he survived into my teens. I seldom talked to him but I remember being intrigued hearing him tell how he would sometimes pilot sailing ships into Galway.

"There were a few of us in Onaght that Galway people accepted to pilot ships into the port. When we spotted a sailing ship passing, we would rush to our currachs and race one another to the ship. Whoever reached the ship first boarded it and got the job. It was much needed money at the time."

I now regret I did not follow up and question him more.

THE SKELETON IN THE FAMILY CUPBOARD

The same paternal grandfather, Seán Bhilla, was, by any calculation, a cautious and sensible man. He had the contract to supply the lighthouse every fortnight. For this he had a cart and what was referred to as a jaunting car which he used to transfer the lighthouse-keeper from the Galway ferry to the currach that in due course landed him at the lighthouse.

I remember granddad as a very pious man. At that time it was customary for people to make an annual pilgrimage to honour the various saints supposedly buried on the islands. People visited a well or "bed" associated with the saint, walking around the place while reciting a certain number of 'Hail Marys'. You first filled your pockets with pebbles, each representing a 'Hail Mary'. You dropped a pebble when you finished a prayer until your pocket was empty. As children, these outings were welcome adventures. We all piled on to grandfather's jaunting car and set off to Cill Éinne, Mainistir, or wherever. Walking around reciting the recommended number of 'Hail Marys' was not all that exciting. But the bottle of lemonade we got to share at the end of the day was a rare treat.

However, what I remember best about grandfather is not the pilgrimages (and there were several) but the motor-car he kept imprisoned in a shed near his home. The shed door was permanently padlocked but we children queued up to view what was inside. Through the cracks in the door, we saw what I now recall as something like an ancient model Ford car. My mother claimed it was the first car that ever came to Aran. Granddad had bought it on one of his rare trips to the mainland. The vendor accompanied grandfather and the car back to Aran on the ferry. After driving granddad home to Onaght village and parking the car beside the house, the vendor returned to Galway on the ferry. At that time the ferry came only once a fortnight. Like me, most of the villagers had never seen a car.

Next morning, the whole village assembled to see the car start up. It never did! Perhaps, my mother mused, granddad did not know how to start it. Nobody on the island knew, though there must have been many suggestions. Anyway, grandfather built a stone shed around the parked car, padlocking it inside and never again touching it. My mother was of the opinion that granddad was cheated by one of those bad people on the mainland. The shed, a lasting monument to Grandfather's one mistake in life, was demolished only after he died – a skeleton in the family cupboard! Only that, in this case, it was in the outhouse!

Growing up on Aran, I never knew want. We did not feel lacking in anything. There was always much laughter around. We were poor and didn't know it. Around our fireside we heard of other people in the world who were poor, hungry and sick but we did not consider ourselves in need of anything except perhaps a little more money. We understood we were blessed by God, that we should always count our blessings and that we were lucky to be living here in Bungabhla away from all the distress that plagued the rest of the world. Our aim in life was to grow up, emigrate and send money home to help our parents who worked themselves to the bone for us. We had no dreams of college or education or even of wealth. We just dreamed of making ourselves and our parents happy.

As we sat around the fire in winter, my father talked about his years in Boston during the Great Depression. He did not refer to it as such because he knew of no depression, great or small. While in

Boston he worked by day as a handyman bricklayer and by night as a watchman on buildings. All night he kept warm by stoking fires in barrels and people who could not sleep came and talked to him. "Some of these were very rich" he told us. He saw their names in the newspapers. "Some lost their money and killed themselves". We thought this very sad. We heard about the other people my father mixed with in Boston, mostly other Irish emigrants, but also with Italians, Poles and *An Fear Gorm*. The latter is literally translated from the Irish as 'Blue Man', but it is known to us nowadays as 'Black Man'.

One evening, I must have been about eight, I witnessed a very sad sight in our village. Bungabhla is out of the way and nobody ever comes there by mistake or, for that matter, un-noticed. There was a *strainséar* (stranger, the name we give to someone from outside the island), well dressed and forlorn standing on the height (*ard*) south of our house. He was looking around him as if searching. Someone approached him to see if he needed help. I heard later that his people came from Bungabhla and had left for America a long time ago. They never came back or kept in touch. There was not a trace left of their house. The man looked very upset. He walked slowly up the hill and back towards Kilronan and the ferry. Though we did not know him, we felt sad for him.

I remember that it was always a struggle to keep a fire on the hearth. We had to be parsimonious about the sods of turf we placed on the fire. There is no bog on Aran and turf had to be brought over from Connemara, the Irish mainland to the north of us. It was costly. Sometimes the turf was augmented by briars my father cut over the summer. We had a few cattle and gathered all the cow dung (*scriúógaí*) which we dried. Dried dung made a good fire. Also, clearing it off the grass tidied up the field and left more grass for the few cows.

I am sure that keeping food on the table was a constant struggle but it did not affect us children. We grew our own potatoes and vegetables. Only flour was bought. There was always plenty of potatoes and my mother baked bread. For supper we ate potatoes with dried fish and a mug of buttermilk. The fish was salted and dried during the previous summer. Meat was a rare treat and only on special occasions. Nothing was ever wasted. What was not consumed by the family was given to the animals. Wasting food was considered sinful.

Apart from that, sin itself did not ever figure in our lives or conversation. God, yes! He was Goodness and Mercy. Nobody doubted the existence of *Dia Mór*, the Great God. He was so evident in nature and in the elements all round us and was a constant part of everyday language. The priest was respected, as much for the fact that he was educated as for what he represented. He was not fawned over. Only a few priests acted the *Dia Beag*, the little God, but people overlooked that failing.

An aunt of mine, Mary Bhilla, was a *Dia Beag* and pontificated a lot. When I left the priesthood, I thought it important to square it with her. On my first Sunday home in Aran after leaving the sacerdotal state, I sat on the wall outside the church, as most of the men did before Sunday Mass. I watched for my aunt's arrival – as I am sure everybody else did too. When she pulled level, I stood up and approached her. I put out my hand and proclaimed for all to hear:

"Mary, I got the permission of the Pope to leave."

She took my hand, shook it and replied in a loud voice:

"If I were him, I would not have granted you permission."

My parents prayed to God daily. But apart from that thought it best to leave well enough alone and avoid contact with either God or the devil until one had to.

The social fabric of the community was kept intact by a system of greetings. *Bail ó Dhia ar an obair* (God bless the work) you said when you came upon someone working in his or her field, or driving the cattle or milking the cow or goat, or fishing or mending a net. The answer was *mBa hé dhuit* (same to you). When you entered a house you said *Bail ó Dhia anseo* (God bless here) and the answer was 'same to you'. If you were surly or did not answer, it was regarded as rude or lacking in manners. It is interesting that the word for 'good manners' in Irish is *múinte* and bad manners is *mí-mhúinte* or *droch-mhúinte* which literally translates as properly 'trained', 'taught' or 'badly trained'. My parents must have made a conscious decision early on in their marriage not to swear or take God's name in vain in front of their children. From the little I know of their families, I suspect they were not in the habit of swearing anyway. I never heard either of them swear. As a result we grew up without the habit of swearing. We would not use bad language in front of them, not because they'd be upset but because we considered it *mí-mhúinte* and offensive. Like shouting at people, it was something *daoine múinte* (people with manners) just did not do.

One of my earliest memories is after supper, the whole family kneeling down to say the rosary. Usually my mother led the prayer and each person said a decade. When the rosary was over, my mother did 'the trimmings': a list of people, some dead, some alive, that the family wished God to treat kindly. If a visitor entered the house while we were praying, they just quietly knelt down and sometimes joined in with the responses.

2

CHILDHOOD ON ARAN

Our kitchen was large. The centre-piece was the table and of course the fireplace. There were no soft chairs, just a few wooden stools or benches by the walls and one big chair (*cathaoir mhór*) by the fire. Grandfather used this 'big chair' in his later years. Towards evening a big pot of potatoes was hung on the fire to boil. When boiled, they were strained into a *ciseog* which was a wicker basket specially woven for the purpose. The *ciseog* was then covered with a cloth until it was placed in the middle of the table for supper. Before the pot was taken off the fire the dried fish was left to steam on top of the boiling potatoes. There was home-made butter and buttermilk and salt. We had plenty. But we were often reminded that this was not always the case and that we should be grateful to God.

In the 'old days' before modern fertilisers, crop yield was smaller and families often ran out of potatoes in early spring. That was before the new potatoes were available and if the stored dried fish ran out at the same time, which sometimes happened, there was near famine. The family then ate what was referred to as *scadán caoch* literally translated as 'blind herring'. You dipped the potato in the salt and pretended to yourself you were eating salted herring. My father barely remembered such a hardship, but our old neighbour, Pítirín, remembered spending all day fishing, subsisting on a boiled potato in his pocket and a bottle of buttermilk. Most nights, especially in winter, neighbours visited after supper.

Pítirín's generation was the first generation of Aran people to have had the opportunity of having universal free primary education. But few availed of the opportunity. My father was an exception. He badgered his own father, who eventually relented and let him attend school. Pítirín was a bachelor because he could not have afforded to get married. He was a fisherman all his life but he could turn his hand to almost anything, whether it was building a house or making a chair, a basket or a currach. I marvelled at his native intelligence. He was self-trained in everything but he could not write his name.

Pítirín had two sacrosanct dates on his less than busy calendar: St Stephen's Day (26th December) and St Peter & Paul's Day (29th June). Until he got the old age pension, Pítirín had little money, so he saved up. But on those two special days he walked to Kilronan to drink. We all knew then that we wouldn't see Pítirín again for several days. My mother described his bogus excuses for these absences as 'hangover'.

When eventually he recovered he regaled us about the fights he watched inside and outside the pubs. We learnt that when someone said "hold my jacket", it meant that person had no intention of fighting. I concluded that these fights were more contests of strength than real fights. The use of any sort of weapon, particularly knives was anathema and viewed as cowardice. Over the years there were some acknowledged champion fighters and this tempted various young up-starts to challenge them. Apart from the occasional black eye, we never heard of any serious injury. The fights were the talk of the island for weeks.

After supper, the table cleared and dishes washed, the visiting neighbours pulled the stools towards the fire and chatted. The women-folk usually knitted as they conversed. In my younger days, conversation usually turned into story-telling. 'True' stories were told about the Sídhe, the headless coachman and the mermaid who was related to the Conneelys. The latter relationship was the reason why you must never kill a mermaid or a seal; the belief was that you might be murdering a human being. Pítirín had a wealth of stories from the Fenian Cycle, heroic stories of love and single combat, of eight legged dogs and sea monsters. We believed them all and never tired of hearing them repeated. Occasionally when Pítirín did not turn up we asked another visiting neighbour, Mairtínín or Josie, to tell a story. Sometimes they told one of Pítirín's stories but changed it, or imitated Pítirín's style, making fun of him. They might add an extra eight-legged dog or insert a seven-legged dog. We did not like these innovations because they gave the impression that the stories were not true. The themes underlying these *heroic* cycle of stories were all alike and based on a simple code of honour

Glaine 'nár gcroíthe, Neart ár lámh, agus Beart de réir ár mbriathar!

(The purity in our hearts, the strength of our hands and being faithful to one's word!). We liked this simple code.

One night the story-telling turned to how the married couples in our village first met. Pítirín told of how my grandfather gave him and another man a bottle of whiskey. He asked them to go to my mother's father and ask for my mother's hand in marriage. Neither my father nor indeed my mother had any foreknowledge of this. My mother agreed to marry my father, a dowry was arranged, and so started the beginning of a very happy alliance. Not all match-making turned out that well. He told of another time when the match-makers went to ask for a girl's hand in marriage, only to have her refuse and volunteer to marry one of the match-makers instead! It was months before the first prospective groom heard of what had happened and he never spoke again to the match-maker nor to his wife. Another neighbour, a fishing colleague of Pítirín's, was playing cards in a neighbour's house. He was poor like Pítirín and not able to afford a dowry. The other card players started to tease him about not getting married. He was a fine-looking man.

"Ah", he lamented, "who would marry me?"

"I would", piped up the young girl of the house, "if you asked me!"

He did, and they were married within the month and produced a very large and happy family, all of whom did well in life afterwards.

In time, my mother bought a bicycle and this was great fun. We all learnt to ride. My father had a bicycle when he got married but had to sell it because there were no tyres to be had during the war. Then my mother bought a radio that worked with a big wet battery which had to be charged every two weeks. Generally it was my task to bring the battery the eight miles to Kilronan on the bike. The local policeman had a little generator and he charged batteries for all the people on the island. There were not many batteries as there were not many radios. Now instead of the story-telling the visiting neighbours listened to the news in Irish. It did not kill the story-telling, but it brought more options into our kitchen. To the annoyance of some, I spent many hours fiddling with those dials on the radio, generating more crackle than sense. I loved listening to news from far-off lands though, as yet, my limited grasp of English affected my comprehension.

Another distraction was a gramophone my father had brought from America. He had a big stack of records. There were jigs and reels and sad exile songs, the ones favoured by the Irish diaspora in Boston during his time there. On very rare occasions – I don't know what triggered it – the gramophone was brought out from the parlour. Nobody was allowed to touch the gramophone but my mother. People would ask for a particular song or dance tune. Before one knew it, the stools were put back by the wall, the table pushed into a corner and a dance had started; sets, and the *Walls of Limerick* were popular. My mother could step-dance and if Mary Bhríd Rua—an old school friend of my mother's—happened to be visiting, the pair of them would take the floor. I once saw my mother take the floor in the parish hall and Marcus, a young fellow of my own age from the village, join her.

My father did not dance but occasionally—though usually quiet and subdued—was coaxed into giving us a song. Each song told a story, sometimes in as many as fourteen verses. The older men smoked their pipes and listened. From time to time, someone got a mug of buttermilk from the churn. Then my mother would make tea and everyone had a slice of bread and butter and sometimes jam, if we were in luck. Tea was the sign that the session was coming to an end. On those very rare occasions we were disappointed to see our neighbours filter out into the night and we were rushed off to bed. As we grew up, such occasions got even rarer. The world, perhaps, was changing.

I do not remember having any toys when I was very young. Occasionally my father hammered together something with nails and a wheel he found somewhere. Pítirín might make what we called a 'top' which we first spun with a whip on the kitchen floor and then along the road. We had little competitions to see whose top spun best. I played with round stones from the shore which I imagined to be cows, donkeys and horses, sheep and goats. I walled off little nooks on the *creig* (enclosure of flat rock) for them among the rocks and kept changing them around from nook to nook, as I saw my parents do with real cattle. I brought them hay and water and built tiny walls to hem them in.

We learnt how to use a scythe (*speal*) and sickle (*corrán*) to cut oats and bring sheaves to the cattle or the horse. The poor donkey was left to his own devices. Everyone assumed a donkey was well able to look after himself. Sometimes one had several sheaves (*dornán*) of freshly cut oats to carry over several walls to feed the animals. It was a heavy load for small children and we returned home exhausted. Hens, ducks and geese were the province of my mother and my sisters, though if you had a pet seagull, you went to the shore to get barnacles and periwinkles to feed it. Sometimes you spiced this menu up with *plubógaí*, small fish you caught in the crevice in the rock pools left by the receding tide. For this you needed to make a hook out of a safety pin and put a periwinkle on it as bait. Also, on a weekly basis we had to move the animals around from field to field and then fill their drinking vessel with water from the nearest well.

For me the biggest thrill was moving the horse, which I rode bareback and galloped at full speed along the narrow roads (*bóithríní*). That was until I was reprimanded by my father for galloping the horse too fast, so that it lost two shoes kicked over the walls. We found the shoes and re-shoed the horse ourselves, as was the custom. I helped my father do it. Sometimes, especially in spring we saddled the horse (not a riding saddle – we used none) to carry seaweed to fertilise the fields for planting the potatoes. So, by the time we reached school-age we all had our individual accepted chores which, we believed, was what life was all about.

An item native to most Aran households at the time was *an túirne* or spinning wheel. I don't know why my mother did not inherit one. Her mother, Nainín Thomáis, or *An Cailín Bán* as she was referred to locally, *maimeó* to us, had one. I remember the delight on my mother's face when her new *túirne* arrived. At that time there was nobody on Inis Mór who made spinning wheels, so she had it made by a handyman in Inis Oír, one of the two inhabited neighbouring islands. By then people were not spinning their own wool any more but after shearing their sheep they sent the wool to the mill on the mainland. The thread that came back was very thin and could not be easily knitted. My mother used the spinning wheel to twist two strands (two-ply) together and this is what was used to knit the Aran *geansaí*, socks and *caipín bobailín*. The *caipín bobailín* is native to Aran, though the islanders no longer wore it. But it sold well to the tourists. It is warm and more or less waterproof. Most of us still wore the *geansaí*. But it was not the white *geansaí bán* variety, favoured by the tourists. The Aran people dyed their *geansaí* black or brown or, like my father, they preferred the *geansaí glas* knitted from the wool of a black sheep. For this reason we kept the wool of our black sheep separate.

Soon after the arrival of our spinning wheel, my maternal granny, Nainín Thomáis walked over from Onacht bringing her *cárdaí* with her. She did not often visit our house because the hill was too steep for her though we frequently visited hers. I remember her as being very kind and gentle. The *cárdaí* were a pair of wire brushes used to roll the wool into fluffy little balls which were then attached to the spinner on the spinning wheel (*fearsad*) and spun into thread. Since the arrival of the spinning mills on the mainland this particular skill had become obsolete on Inis Mór and I suspect my granny only practised it as a curiosity item. All the other village women gathered in our kitchen and participated in the exercise. My granny was one of the last people who still owned a *cárdaí* and I think she only wanted to show off how it was done 'properly' in the 'good old days'. Anyhow, I never saw a repeat of this performance.

My father liked to wear flannel trousers. But people complained that one couldn't get a proper pair of trousers made any more since the last of the tailors on the island had either died or gone out of business. Older people kept up their trousers by wearing a 'crios', a colourful woven belt that we all learned to make. Apart from a few older men, nobody on Aran wore a *crios* anymore. But, like the *caipín bobailín*, it was much sought after by the tourists.

On Aran, men and women, boys and girls had their allocated places in the system of island life. Men were expected to do certain things and women others. Built into our nurturing was a certain amount of stereotyping. For instance, men toiled the land, women cooked. Men rowed currachs, fished, repaired roofs and went into pubs. Women knitted. Men smoked pipes. Women not at all! Much of that is now changed, of course.

My mother, who was no great respecter of tradition, did what needed to be done regardless of expectation. I saw her climb up on the roof to fix a loose slate when she thought my father was not responding fast enough to her urgings. Likewise she mixed the cement and altered the shape of our fire-place so as to avoid any discussion of the matter when my father returned home in the evening. He pretended not to notice. I pestered my mother about learning how to knit and she taught me how to knit a sock, which no self-respecting boy would admit to doing.

When I was fourteen I accompanied her bringing a cow to the bull because she did not have the patience to wait for my father to return home in the evening. Or perhaps the cow couldn't wait. For me, it was very embarrassing watching what the bull got up to. But my mother did not bat an eyelid. She handled it the same way as I saw her delivering a calf.

Bean a' feadaíl, cearc a' glaoch, / Sin dhá ní nár ordaigh Críost.

(A whistling woman, a crowing hen/two things Christ did not ordain.)

Add to that a boy knitting.

Our people collected seaweed throughout the year, dried it on the shore and stacked it in large heaps called *cocaí* (cocks). They then waited for the time to burn it as kelp in the spring. We children gave a hand in doing all of this. Some of the larger families had several cocks of seaweed to burn. Kelp-burning was a village event. Once the fire was started, it had to be kept going and everyone in the village took part and helped to keep the kelp fire burning over several days and nights. There was a festival atmosphere about the event. The menfolk were all blackened from the smoke and the women-folk and the children constantly travelled back and forth between the village and the shore carrying tea, buttermilk, buttered bread and jam – a delicacy then. We children tagged along, played among the cocks of seaweed and felt very important, indeed, carrying out the various tasks given to us by the adults. For weeks one could see columns of thick smoke rising from the island as each village burnt its kelp. When all the seaweed was burnt, the residue was put in bags and sold to a mainland merchant.

Another community and family-centred activity was picking *carraigín*, a type of seaweed that grows on shore-line rocks and can be picked during the spring tides when the sea recedes out very far. We went as a family and I remember it more as an enjoyable outing, a fun activity, than as work. It was exciting getting wet and slithering about in the warm pools that the receding tide left behind. In these pools we also happened on crabs and little fish which we spent a lot of time chasing and catching for the benefit of our cat and pet seagulls. When the tide was on the turn we had to pick our way gradually to the shore making sure we were not cut off by the oncoming tide. I remember being exhausted but content. We then spread out our bag of *carraigín* on the rocks to dry in the sun. We were each allowed our own space so we could compare how much work we had done. The *carraigín* was later sold to buyers from the mainland and we felt good for having contributed to the family income. Also, as a result, our pets enjoyed gourmet meals.

One other sort of festive occasion I remember occurred in during spring tide when the sea receded very far out. The wind too had to be on shore. The people of the village came together to cut seaweed, *ag baint fheamainne*. First we all went to the shore and the menfolk divided the shoreline into sections. They then cast lots to assign each section to a particular family. I remember them sharpening their knives. For us children it was great fun for we all had an excuse to splash about in the pools. We stayed with our own family, avoiding the few cranks in the village who considered children as surplus to requirement.

I remember the men working furiously keeping an eye on the receding or incoming tide. They'd cut the seaweed with broad sweeps of the knife, tossing it out of their way with their left hands as they progressed. I don't remember my mother participating in this but I remember my uncle Ned who did everything differently from everyone else. I remember him holding the knife in his mouth and using his two hands to clear away the cut seaweed. For some reason he also preferred to hold the reins of the donkey or horse in his mouth, which intrigued me. When the tide came in, it carried the cut seaweed with it. Each family gathered whatever landed on their piece of shore-line and carried it in baskets up the rocks (*duirling*) to dry. There was always someone who complained about drawing a useless piece of shoreline.

CHILDREN'S GAMES (*AG BUALADH BÁILL AIRD*)

There was no football or football-field on the island. One day a neighbour, John Sheáin Neilín, found an oddly shaped football blown ashore. I now know that it was a rugby ball but nobody could fathom the odd shape. Josie Phítir, the local expert, tried to make it round but only succeeded in spoiling it. The opinion was that the same Josie spoiled most things he touched. In spite of that we managed to kick it about for a while.

Instead of football, we played a game called *báill ard*: a variant of Rounders but played on a straight stretch of road. Boys and girls took part. As there were about thirty teenagers in the village, it was not difficult to find two teams. Generally we played outside our house, much to the annoyance of my mother who feared her flowers would be trampled on. The game was simple to set up and play: all you needed was a ball and a stick (a broom handle was excellent). Two teams were selected and two stones (*caille*) were placed on the road a stone's throw from one another. One team took turns to hit the ball while the other team spread around the surrounding fields to 'defend'. When you hit the ball you ran between the two stones. If a defender caught the ball in the air, the two teams changed sides. Also, if someone hit you with the ball while you tried to complete a run, your team was 'out'. There was no score kept. There were frequent breaks while the defenders searched for a ball when it fell among nettles or down a *scailp* (fissure), or when someone fell over a wall, or if a cow or a donkey had to be let pass, or when Michaelín Dainín went by. Michaelín was the local misanthrope, or pretended to be so. He disliked children, or affected such a dislike, which we reciprocated. Invariably, as he tried to pass, a ball hit him. This gave him the opportunity to harangue us. Once when I owned up to having thrown the ball, he turned the sharp edge of his tongue on me, listing all my failures and those of my forebears. The next time, I let someone else 'accidentally' hit him. Later, as an adult, when I got to know him better, he was not at all like I had imagined him as a child.

Girls had a more lady-like game called *screaga*. It consisted of throwing a number of stones up in the air and catching them on the front or back of your hand, first one, then two and so on. They sat under the shelter of a wall and played their game for hours. Only girls were allowed to play. If a boy approached he was called a *fiteóg* which was not regarded as a compliment to one's manhood.

Adjacent to our house was a sunken area among the crags. When it rained it filled with water forming a sizeable temporary lake that was over ten feet deep in places. We referred to it as *An Loch*. When this lake dried, its bed was dark and mossy, and good for nothing except growing *sailí* (sally or willow rods). Since time immemorial it was used for that purpose. For that reason it was called the Sally Garden. My father tended it well, pruning the sally bushes and managing their growth so as to get a good crop each autumn. Sometimes he spread seaweed to fertilise the soil. Each year this garden produced a dozen or so bundles (*beartanna*) of 100 rods each which my father sold for five shillings per bundle.

He also harvested another dozen bundles of smaller saplings (*barrógaí*) for making smaller baskets and *ciseógaí* for straining the potatoes from the pots. As the need arose he made some creels and baskets for our own use but he did not pretend to be expert at this type of wickerwork. However he taught me whatever he knew and I learnt the rest from watching Pítirín, who was the acknowledged expert in this field. At that time most households had perhaps one horse and a few donkeys. They were saddled regularly with creels. These were used for carrying all sorts of loads from bringing potatoes home from the fields or carrying turf or seaweed. Pítirín made these creels and people came to him, even from the far end of the islands, to have creels made. He also made lobster pots; for these he did not use sally but the more durable hazel rods that were available only in Gort na gCapall.

Our sally garden was surrounded by a high wall to keep out goats that could have destroyed a whole season's crop in a matter of minutes if they got access to the place. One evening when I was quite small I was playing alone at this lough, sailing 'boats' I had made from shells. I tripped and fell in. The water was very deep, away out of my depth. I sank to the bottom. When I surfaced I managed to get hold of some ivy trailing from the wall. It took me a long time to pull myself back onto the lakeside rock. I knew it was useless to shout or cry in that dark lake surrounded by high ivy-clad walls because nobody would be able hear me or see me. I hid in the ivy and could hear my mother yodelling and calling me in for supper. I ignored her calls and waited until it was dark, hoping nobody would notice my wet clothes or my chattering teeth. I was afraid I'd get a scolding. But of course, as soon as I entered the kitchen, my condition was immediately noticed. I was stripped of my garments, wrapped in a blanket and placed by the fire. My mother made jelly for me – my favourite sweet. I pretended I had just fallen into a shallow place, keeping my dark secret to myself. I was well aware that I had narrowly escaped drowning.

SCHOOL

When the time came for me to attend school, we were already well socialised. After the education we got at home, school was an add-on. Though, for me anyway, it was a welcome one.

I don't remember exactly my first day in school. It must have been in early spring after my birthday, April 16th, because I remember walking barefoot the one mile or so to the schoolhouse. I remember my toes bleeding from striking against the rocks. The road was surfaced with jagged stones and gravel. Up to the time they went to school most boys wore flannel petticoats. But my mother, who considered herself modern, got me out of the petticoat early. All the children of Bungabhla walked barefoot during spring and summer. In winter we wore knitted grey woollen socks and pampooties. I was probably the last of the generation that went barefoot to school. None of my siblings did so.

The pampootie (*bróg úrleathair*) is described by Wikipedia as being peculiar to the Aran Islands; it is, perhaps, a more legitimate Aran symbol than the currach or the *geansaí bán*. The closest type of footwear resembling it may be the moccasin of the American Indian, except that the pampootie is made out of raw cowhide, not deerskin. Pampooties are ideal for manning a currach or running over the rocks because one can use the toes to obtain a grip. In summer the cowhide hardens but after an over-night soaking, it is as good as new. In my young days most adults on the island wore pampooties, pulling their boots on only to attend Mass on Sunday. On Saturday nights, my father soaked his pampooties in a basin of water. Every so often his foot wore through his pampooties and I watched him cut long strips from raw cow-hide and make himself new ones.

When autumn came I got my first pair of *bróga móra* or boots. I was very proud of them. I wore them the first day of term and it was exciting to be now able to kick the stones without having my toes bleed. My mother soon put a stop to this, telling me that the shoes had to last me all winter.

On my first day, anyone willing to look was invited to examine my shoes. This included Mary Dainín, a neighbour a year or two older than myself and therefore in the upper school and part of *na gasúir mhóra* (the big children). To me she was an important person and in charge of sharing out the cocoa at lunch-time. We of the Infants class all lined up in the yard to have our mugs filled. I proudly stuck out my foot showing her my new footwear. She playfully made a swipe at my boot, accidentally hitting the clay jug against one of the many rocks in the school-yard. Unfortunately the jug cracked. We all referred to Mrs. Flannagan, the teacher in the infants as *An tSean-Mhissus (the old Missus)*. I was summoned into her presence and scolded for kicking the jug and cracking it. I knew I did not kick the jug, but nobody asked for my opinion. I was given a letter of complaint to bring home to my mother. I felt lucky that my mother did not make a swipe at me too. Nor did my mother ask me what happened. She just assumed the teacher was right. Next day she put a few shillings in an envelope and a note telling the teacher to beat me if I was bold. She read out the note for me. The teacher sent the money back. The episode took the gloss off my new boots and I never showed them off after that. I thought the way I was treated was very unfair but I would not dream of saying so. One look at my little boots should have convinced anyone that a kick from them could not have cracked the jug. But obviously the old Missus was no Sherlock Holmes.

The 'old Missus' was a gentle soul and never harmed anyone. She got the job when her husband, the school master, was drowned. He went on a pilgrimage to Croagh Patrick with two locals. But their currach was swamped by a wave as they crossed over to the island from Connemara on their return. By all accounts, Mr. Flannagan was a severe headmaster, who slapped his pupils needlessly. At the time, parents appreciated no other method of teaching and they encouraged corporal punishment in school. When Flanagan was drowned, the people of Onacht lamented the loss of a brilliant schoolmaster and compared other teachers, who did not use the stick, unfavourably with him. There was always a stick hanging on our dresser at home but I never once saw it used except to beat the top of the table, which act made a frightening noise. My parents did not believe in, or indeed ever needed to use any corporal punishment. I never even heard them shout at any of us.

I loved school and everything about it. As we got older, before we marched off to school like my father before us, we each had our own tasks tending real animals. In the mornings we had a goat to milk. At dusk you had to catch the kid goat and lock him off in what we called a *púirín*, (a nook in the rocks that could be blocked up to keep the kid imprisoned all night). Sometimes when the kid got too big for the *púirín*, we placed a *gobán* , a piece of wood, in its mouth so it couldn't suckle. The *gobán* was tied to the horns to keep it in place. If the kid had any sense he suckled enough milk during the day. Sometimes it took two people to catch a kid. The task might be to milk the goat, bring oats to the horse or carry water to the cow. We had to be much older before we were expected to milk the cow. From the moment we started off in the morning, each with his satchel and a sod of turf under the arm, I found school to be a great adventure. I took to learning easily and do not remember ever being beaten by the teacher until I was in grade seven. But that's another story.

By the time I reached grade seven, there were about forty pupils, divided almost equally into seven grades, in the school. There were two teachers, Mrs. Flannagan, for the Infants and grades one and two and her son, known to all as Dónaí Flannagan, for the Upper School. In the upper school, each class sitting on the benches alternated between sitting on the benches for writing, drawing or 'doing sums' and standing up for reading and testing tables. Tasks completed, all the pupils marched round the desks, some to stand at the back of the class to be tested for reading or arithmetical tables, while the rest of us sat. Because I started attending school at an early age, I was below the average age when I reached grade seven and had to spend two years there. There being no secondary school on the island, there was nowhere else for me to go after grade seven except hang around until, when old enough, I caught the emigrant ship. Most children left school after grade six to help their parents.

By the time I reached grade seven I knew my standard reading books off by heart. I can still recite the first couple of chapters of, *m'Asal Beag Dubh* (My Little Black Donkey), word perfect. One day Dónaí noticed I was not turning any pages and crept up behind me to watch. He said nothing but went back to his desk by the fire. I was reciting the text, not reading it. Just like our parents, Dónaí believed that a bit of stick helped pupils to learn. He kept a sally rod always on his desk and used it liberally. I don't think he enjoyed using it but it was the accepted method of teaching at that time. A wrong answer and you got a slap on the hand. By the time I reached grade seven, a few of us boys had become good friends. We were not mischievous, but more bored than bold, so to speak. Indeed we were quite docile compared to children I taught years later in London. During my last months at school, Dónaí seemed to be using his stick more frequently as a teaching tool. I escaped it but some of my friends didn't.

One day, as our group walked around the desks in preparation for our next task, one boy Patsy Dainín from Bungabhla grabbed the door-latch and ran out of the classroom. Dónaí took after him but failed to catch him. We all climbed on our chairs to watch through the window, which also rattled Dónaí. Patsy ran home and never returned. Next day it was my friend Dara's turn. He had got a beating for not knowing his tables and as he passed the door, he grabbed the latch and took off. Dónaí did not even try to follow. On the following day Dara returned accompanied by his angry father. Dara's father was a small man but he had a loud voice. We all heard the exchange. Now that the spell was broken, Dónaí must have begun to wonder who was next to take off. He had lost control of his pupils, a frightening thing for a teacher. All it needed was one incident and his whole class might stampede like cows through a gap, leaving him to swing his cane in an empty classroom. The situation had become tense.

We all took lunch in the yard, those who had finished their assignments going out first. Each morning my mother carefully and individually wrapped our lunches: two slices of bread each with butter and, perhaps, jam and a bottle of milk. As I was opening the wrapping paper, the bread intended for my brother Thomas fell out on to the sand, face downwards. Thomas grabbed the bread and ran off to show it to Dónaí. This was a surprise as Thomas was not a snitch. He must have been particularly hungry on that day.

Who did this? snarled Dónaí.

"Patsy" came the answer.

I was sent for.

"Do lámh," (your) hand, said Dónaí.

I did not respond.

"Your hand", he shouted once more.

When a few punches did not soften me up, Dónaí got more furious.

I stuck both my hands in my pockets and as Dónaí tried to extract them, a small crowd gathered. The Old Missus in the next classroom heard the commotion and came to plead with me. I liked her because I knew she liked me.

"It is only one slap", she pleaded.

I allowed her take my hands out of my pockets. Dónaí slapped my right hand really hard.

"An lámh eile", the other hand he demanded.

"'nois," he said expecting me to move off.

But I stood there still holding out both hands. He continued slapping until eventually his mother persuaded him to stop.

When I emerged into the playground, I got a hero's welcome. Everyone wanted to examine my swollen hands. I, who was never beaten, had got my respectability back in the eyes of my peers. I could not use my hands for the rest of the week. Quietly and surreptitiously, Thomas did all my allotted chores until the swelling went down. Anything rather than have my parents find out what had happened! We'd both be in hot water then. I never blamed Thomas and we never referred again to the incident.

I only met Dónaí once in adult life. I suspect he remembered the occasion and still regretted it. Just as when I myself meet past pupils of mine, I remember things I'd rather have forgotten! It is one of the hazards of teaching.

Around this time I became an altar boy. It seemed every boy in the school became one after they made their First Communion. If there was a barrier, it was clumsiness. I was handy enough around the altar and did not knock over any candles or spill any cruets.

The one drawback as far as I was concerned was the extra scrubbing I had to undergo every Sunday morning. In those days the district nurse regularly visited the school and I remember the occasional warnings of head-lice epidemics. My mother was adamant that none of her offspring would ever harbour a nit in their hair, even if it meant scrubbing their heads off. So, every Saturday night, or Sunday morning if it was a late Mass, a big basin was placed in the middle of the floor, filled with warm water and everyone's head was washed with soap. Not for us the costly shampoos of modern times. There was much splashing and spilling and wailing, what with soap going into eyes and water into ears. But the real torture was the *cíoradh* or combing with a fine-tooth comb. That was when the wailing really started and it varied in pitch from the oldest down to the youngest.

Because I was serving Mass I was tortured first. It was a great relief to be released and sent east the two miles to the school-house where Mass was said. I walked alone and, as the wailing in the house got more distant, I became more bored. One day I hit upon an interesting plan: I'd walk all the way to the school-house along the top of the stone walls. On two Sundays I made good progress and this encouraged me. On my third Sunday, I was doing very well until about two thirds of the way I reached a sturdier wall and giving in to impatience, I started to run. As misfortune would have it, the next *creig* was inhabited by a huge fearsome billy-goat, the same billy-goat that two years previously had chased me. At that time also, I fell and had a spike of stone penetrate my forehead giving me a nasty cut, the evidence of which I bear to this day. In my nervousness at seeing this particular billy-goat, I lost my balance and fell off the wall, almost at the feet of the disapproving billy-goat. My face and hands were cut and my "Sunday best" was bloodied and in tatters.

Under the reproachful eyes of the billy-goat, I crouched at the foot of the wall watching through the holes as the people of Bungabhla went east to Mass. The ponderous eyes of the billy-goat followed my every move but he did not move his position, made no sound or betray my presence in any way – for which I felt grateful. At last, having calculated that all the people of Bungabhla had gone to Mass, I climbed back over the wall and slowly made my way home to await the scolding that was surely to be mine first for missing Mass. But also for spoiling my 'Sunday best'!

My people were puzzled at not seeing me serving Mass and hurried home to investigate. There was no mention of my torn shirt or even of my missing Mass. I was bandaged and molly-coddled for the rest of the day and no mention was made ever again of what had happened. The wall on top of which I was running, soon passed along the edge of a cliff and had I made it a few hundred yards further on, I could very easily have fallen to my death instead of at the feet of the billy-goat. Sixty years later when TG4, an Irish Television channel, was doing a programme about my work in Africa, they interviewed my mother, who was quite old by then. She recalled this episode and referred to me as a *gasúirín aerach*. I don't know exactly what she meant by this but I am sure it does not translate as a 'sensible child'.

Perhaps it was because I was at my most impressionable at this time or because, as an altar boy, I came into close contact with organised religion. In any case, I remember my inner feelings during this period most vividly. Our parish priest, Fr. Kileen, was a small man and as if to make up for his lack of stature, he tended to shout when he preached. On Sundays, he always seemed to have worked himself into a lather about some real or imaginary sin. He ranted and raved, which was the style of preaching before the advent of microphones. I was not accustomed to hearing adults shout and Fr. Kileen frightened me. Mercifully, he did not say Mass every Sunday. The curate who alternated with him was a gentle soul who had a smile for everyone and he rode a motorbike. On the altar he did not shout. He occasionally gave me a lift on the road from Kilronan. It puzzled me that two such different people worked for the same God.

My last year at primary school was idyllic. But as soon as summer came, I rushed home from school, grabbed my fishing line and bait and set off over to the rocks to fish. It was often dark when I returned home, sometimes with half a dozen fish which my mother cleaned and salted. Sometimes we ate one for supper. The surplus fish was put in brine for two weeks, then dried in the sun. Someone had to watch the drying fish to prevent the seagulls snatching them. When dry, the fish were stacked between layers of dried fern (bracken). The salted fish was sold in the autumn. My parents showed great confidence in me. I think they were very trusting to let me off fishing like that. Sometimes I fished from slippery rocks and sometimes from the tall cliffs and occasionally I climbed down to narrow ledges in the cliff face where I could have easily come a cropper. The utter sheerness of the cliffs I used to climb frightens me now when I look at them.

At that time in Ireland, areas designated as *Gaeltachtaí* (Irish-speaking districts) were particularly backward and undeveloped. By way of helping them, the government of the day allocated a number of scholarships that allowed some of the brighter primary school children access to teacher training colleges. Gaining one of those scholarships was the only passport a child like myself had to avoid the emigrant ship. Parents evaluated schoolmasters according to the number of their pupils who obtained one of these scholarships. At the end of grade seven, pupils were tested in Irish, English, arithmetic, history, geography and music. I could not sing, nor could my teacher, so music in any form was not taught in the school.

Even so, Dónaí decided to enter me for this exam. Because of my age, I had two shots at it. Dónaí tried his best to coach me but he could not do anything about my singing ability – or lack of it. He even had me over to his house at evening time to coach me. I got to know him better and came to like him. He was not at all the angry person that my earlier encounter with him suggested. He was the first person to give me books to read and introduced me to reading as a hobby. At my first attempt at the preparatory school test I passed all subjects except music. I was not disappointed because I accepted the fact that I could not sing. I had come to terms with the handicap.

For us from Bungabhla, the Gaelic-speaking west end of the island, the people of Kilronan were very foreign. They spoke their own brand of the English language—quaint colonial British army-type English—and they made no secret of looking down on us and our Gaelic. They referred to us as 'The Westards', or less complimentarily, *aisle an Chinn Thiar* (the donkeys of the West End), no matter that *asail*, not *aisle* is the plural of *asal* (they loved getting Irish words wrong, which proved to them that it was not their language). They also used English phonetics whenever possible, like G *gwitch* instead of *Dia Dhuit*. The people of Kilronan generally ignored us as if we were invisible beings. We smiled indulgently, as did my mother who had many friends among the Kilronan people. She'd just remark: *"cuid de'n mhuic an driobal"* (part of the pig is the tail). Today, however, Kilronan is one of the few success stories of the Irish language revival movement. The attitude among the locals has changed and Irish is the spoken language, not only among those born on Aran but among those who have moved there from the mainland. People are once more proud of their Irish heritage and language and are actively involved in their preservation.

Most Saturdays I rode our communal family bicycle the 8 miles to Kilronan to meet the ferry, do some shopping for my mother and bring the radio battery to be charged. There are a number of steep hills down into Kilronan and it was an exhilarating feeling freewheeling down these hills at top speed. Coming back was different especially as I often had a heavy load of shopping and I had to push my bicycle up-hill. At the top of one hill there was a big house inhabited by the O'Hehirs, a schoolmaster and his wife. Mrs. Hehir was from the island, a sister of Tom and Liam O'Flaherty, the writers from Aran. Mrs. Hehir was in the habit of tending the flowers in her garden and talked to anyone passing by. She always engaged me in conversation about her flowers and invited me into her garden and house. She became very interested in how I was doing at school and asked if anyone was helping me with music. Sometimes she invited me in for tea and allowed me to browse through all the shelves stacked with books. I had never seen so many books in my life and I loved even looking at them. She encouraged me to borrow and read. She started with Dickens which at first and for a long time was too difficult for me. But she taught me how to use a dictionary for the first half a dozen pages and told me to try and make sense of the next ten without a dictionary. The following week she questioned me on how well I'd got on. She questioned me about what singing we did at school and tested me to see if I could sing a song. She found out that I couldn't.

"You cannot pass that exam if you cannot sing" she warned me. "They may let you off not being able to read music, but not if you cannot sing."

She was pleased to hear that I had one more attempt at the test and came up with a solution.

She arranged that every Saturday on my way to Kilronan, I stop off at her house and she would coach me in music. I enjoyed the visits and learnt how to read music though hardly to sing. Mrs. Hehir cautioned me never to tell a soul about these secret meetings.

"Because, if Mr. Flanagan finds out, he will be very upset with Mrs. Hehir."

I kept the secret. Easter came and the preparatory school examination with it. I failed music.

That winter went by very fast. Between borrowings from Mrs. Hehir and my own teacher, I had so many books to read that I hardly had time to listen to Pítirín's stories anymore. My father started to buy the local paper, *The Connacht Tribune* and translated as much of the goings-on on the mainland as he thought fit. At school we subscribed to a missionary magazine called The *Far East* which I avidly read. It was in English but by then I was able to get the gist of it – just about. The magazine described the adventures of Irish Missionaries in China and Japan and I was captivated. By this time also, I had started to read some classic love stories borrowed from my teacher Dónaí.

I decided I would like to be one of those missionaries and, in my childish English, I wrote to the *Far East* asking if I could become a missionary. I was very embarrassed when I received an acknowledgement in the post saying that I could join once I finished my secondary education. My mother was not meant to know but I could not avoid showing her the letter. I did not bring up the subject with my mother again and she did not ask any questions. I now viewed the prospect of becoming a missionary as an impossible dream.

Later, my religious mentors labelled this episode, a 'vocation' or a call from God. Perhaps it was! But I never felt anything or saw it as anything other than a process of self-selection where I volunteered myself for an exciting adventure. I was attracted by the idealism of others and by the adventure such idealism entailed.

That was when I fell in love with an ideal. For the next thirty years this ideal dominated my life – for the better, I think. It fell into line with all the heroic stories I had been listening to since childhood. I did feel a call to "do good" but I did not consider this in any way unique. I found out later that helping others is addictive, but the call to do so was a product of my upbringing and environment. I don't know whether it was environment or nurture that determined my consciousness but I doubt if an Ideal such as the one that grabbed my attention would have done so in this age of the iPod and the iPhone. Yet, I strongly believe that God works in strange ways and, as the Portuguese proverb says, "writes straight with crooked lines". He certainly did that for me.

THE ARAN CURRACH

The Aran currach has become as much of a symbol of Aran as the Aran *Geansaí* and is probably more authentically so. When I was a youngster about twenty currachs lined the road by the Bungabhla shore. As very small children we played hide-and-go-seek around them and underneath them. We all longed for the day when we'd be allowed to row them. The currach is not remotely related to the coracle, which is always at the mercy of the sea, whereas the sleek oblong-shaped currach is designed to manoeuvre the waves and use their power. The name comes from the Gaelic word *corrach* which means 'unsteady' and in the wrong hands the currach is indeed anything but steady. The currach is built on a basic timber frame of 7m by 1m The bottom is semi-circular. The frame is covered with canvas and tarred to make it completely waterproof. Unlike regular rowing boats, it is not designed to cut through the sea but to glide over the waves and use wave-power to best effect. As it says in the song *Óró Mo Bháidín*:

Nach éachtach a léimreach thar tonntracha árda. (How magnificently she leaps over the high waves).

The currach has no keel and if not handled carefully it can easily overturn. It sits lightly on top of the waves, sliding gracefully from one to another, propelled along by long oars that have no blades. It seldom sits level on the water but at a slant, with the windward side several inches higher than the other side. The oars cross inside the currach with one hand above the other. This enables the rower to lock the oars to steady the currach in an emergency. The disadvantage of this design is that, as a child learning to row, you knock the skin off your knuckles. But a currach is not meant for child's play. It needs to be light enough to be carried up over the rocks away from the waves and to safety and to be carried down to sea by two men and shoved into the waves in a hurry. A seven metre currach has six oars (for three men) while a *curach mór* has eight oars (for four men) and is about eight metres long. Most families owned a currach – it was their means of livelihood. My grandfather owned one but my father did not, preferring to own nets instead. I was disappointed that we did not own a currach. I would have wanted to be out on the deep in it all the time.

That last summer at primary school came and went. Every day I fished from morning till well after dusk and had my first opportunity to go out in Pítirín's currach. Since I was a small child I had fished from the rocks but fishing in the currach with Pítirín was my idea of nirvana. I was barely strong enough to help him carry the currach down to the sea, but once in it I felt very much at home. Pítirín taught me a lot – how to respect and fear the sea at the same time, how to read the currents and watch out for the breakers. The sea is unpredictable and anything can happen there. Anyone depending on the sea must always be well prepared and ready for the unexpected. When dealing with the sea, one must always have a 'Plan B'.

Some days Pítirín put me ashore on Branach Island while he rowed around all day dragging a line and fishing for mackerel and pollack. After a day's fishing from the rocks, at evening, he had me jump from the rocks into the currach as he steadied it in the high waves. I now know that it was a dangerous, perhaps even foolhardy, thing to do. It showed what confidence he had in me.

Some days Pítirín went fishing from the rocks and I rowed the currach trailing the fishing-line. I came home with my knuckles skinned and bleeding but I was deeply contented. I have very long arms, and I often wondered if it is as a result of those days spent rowing. My wife delights in telling me how hard it is to find me a jacket that fits; my arms are too long, she says. In school in Africa, I often turned round suddenly to surprise a couple of students in line behind me imitating my walk – elbows bent as if I had only lately come down from the trees.

Some days instead of going to Branach Island we spent the day fishing off the rocks on Eeragh Island, where the lighthouse was. The lighthouse and its keepers fascinated me. The keepers were always welcoming and sometimes invited us in for tea. Later, as a teenager I had the opportunity to work during the whole summer holidays on the lighthouse. Two of us, Michaelín Tom Mhóir and myself, were hired to help a builder who was repairing the damage done to the cliff by a winter storm. The storm had hurled huge rocks at the cliff face and punched away the concrete stairs going up the face of the cliff. The builder would have been a good teacher. He asked me to measure the length of plank needed to contain the diagonal concrete casing up the side of the cliff. He would not allow me to use a tape or a measuring rod. "Just measure the height of the cliff and the horizontal along the beach at the bottom", he said.

"Use your head, man. You have been doing it in school", he challenged.

Eventually he led me to solve my problem by use of Pythagoras' Theorem, one of the early lessons in our geometry class. He traced it out on the smooth sand on the beach. It was a Eureka moment for me. Up till then I saw little practical use in what I was learning at school. I never forgot the lesson on that beach underneath the cliff in Eeragh.

The following summer, I worked for nine weeks on the lighthouse as substitute for a keeper who was ill. I was only supposed to be there two weeks or at most a month but weather conditions intervened. There were two other professional keepers, Dick Spencer and Paddy Kane. Life on a lighthouse is divided into three 8-hour shifts or watches. I being the temporary keeper got the least popular watch 10 pm till 6 am. Normally a relief boat brought provisions and mail every two weeks but on this occasion the weather prevented the currach from landing. I was waiting for my Leaving Certificate results. My uncle was the shore contractor for the lighthouse and every two weeks he semaphored from the main island to take our orders for food and any other messages.

Over the years, I had mastered semaphore and sometimes communicated with the lighthouse keepers in the place of my uncle. We never had anything of importance to communicate but this time I got my Leaving Certificate results by semaphore. Dick Spencer decided that we should celebrate. He suggested we slaughter one of the three goats on the island. I was ordered to kill the goat. I had never done this before but I had watched Pítirín do it several times. I felt I was being put through some form of 'rite of passage' and dared not refuse. Dick helped me skin the animal. I passed the test and we had a good supper but I never again wanted to kill an animal. The memory of that poor goat remained with me for a long time.

During my last years at primary school, I was expected to take part in more adult work, such as digging with a spade and helping my father make land. For three months, every winter and spring Galway County Council ran skills-training night-courses for the local unemployed youth. Though I wanted to attend, I was too young and still at primary school and therefore technically ineligible. My parents encouraged me to apply. The courses were poorly attended which was probably why I was accepted in order to fill some quota or other. The first of the courses was net mending (deasú líonta). It was not nearly as interesting as I had hoped. There is not much to mending a net once you learn the basic technique.

However, next year I was accepted for a course on carpentry which was much more interesting. We made chairs, tables, ladders and book cases. Once we had paid for the timber we were allowed to take the items home. We learnt technical drawing – everything we made we had to draw beforehand. I proved fairly handy at both the drawing and the carpentry. I learnt skills that came in very useful in later life. In fact it was the start of my flirtation with technical drawing, a subject I was to teach much later on at a Muslim secondary school in Africa. The skills I picked up were transferrable skills that enhanced my work for ever afterwards. The night courses in Éamonn Concannon's old store in Onacht were the inspiration of a course for a master's degree in Design Technology I took at Reading University in the UK half a century later. But more importantly, these courses bolstered my already well-developed sense of self-confidence. Much as I loved this work, when summer arrived all I could think about was fishing and the sea.

Each afternoon after school, we walked home, boys usually six abreast and briskly with girls meandering behind. At that time I subscribed to *An Club Leabhar* (book club) that sent me one booklet each month. I remembered the main character was called Rex Carlo, a detective. I believed every word of the stories and read them out loud at home. On a few occasions I was prevailed upon to tell one of the stories as we walked home from school. I don't remember holding the attention of the others for too long. They became bored and took up throwing stones and walking along the top of the walls.

There was a little man called Peaitín Sheáin who lived in a small thatched cottage on top of the hill. The road passed by his door and the temptation to knock on it was overwhelming. He used to get very angry and, waving his stick at us, he chased us away. We considered him odd because he wore a hat at a slight angle.

Further up the road there was an old woman called Júda Tom Mhóir. She too lived in a thatched cottage. She wore a red petticoat and a black shawl. We thought her very cross and when summer came she was always airing what we were told was her shroud. She hung it over the stone wall and she always screeched at us to "get down" whenever we wanted to walk along that wall. To us, the shroud looked a lot more interesting than the clothes she was wearing. We also thought it odd for her to have a shroud because she did not look in any danger of dying. But die she did and I accompanied the rest of the village to say a prayer by her bed-side. When I mentioned that she looked much better dressed in the shroud I was told, it was not a proper thing to say.

Sometimes, on the way home, I visited a relative of ours called Tom Pháidín, a younger brother of my dead paternal grandmother, Ceata Pháidín. I was trained to enquire if he needed anything. Tom was a kindly old pensioner who lived alone in a small thatched house by the side of the road in the village of Creig a' Chéirin. Most of his family had died of TB; several families in the locality suffered a similar fate. The few of Tom's family who survived emigrated to California, never to return. They prospered in America. In winter Tom sat by his fire poking at it with his stick. But in summer he sat by his door exchanging greetings with everyone that passed. Tom had a dog called Friday to whom he constantly chatted in Irish. Like his master, the dog had only a few words of English – words like "stop" and "come here", which were also the first words of English I learnt as a child. For some strange reason, people thought dogs understood English better than they understood Irish. We used to listen in as Tom engaged passing tourists (strainséirí) in conversation. We knew he was fibbing.

Often the conversation came round to the fact that everyone on the island was Roman Catholic; even the animals were Catholic, according to Tom. To prove it he'd go to his old dresser, fetch a piece of bacon that I am sure he kept there on purpose and throw it on the floor. The dog would jump up and grab it. Tom would point his finger at the dog and mutter "Friday" and the dog would look up, drop the piece of bacon and slink off to sit guiltily in the corner. Old Tom's first experiment may well have been contemporaneous with those of the famous Russian psychologist, Pavlov (1849-1936).

Other times on our way home, a donkey might stray into our path and one or two might ride it the rest of the journey with the others chasing behind and shouting.

But my heart pined for summer to arrive and with it fishing in the currach. On summer days when the sea was flat as glass, our currach looked like a floating beetle on its surface. Later when I was at secondary school or at university, my cousin Stiofán Phaddy joined Pítirín and me in the currach. I found Stiofán a congenial soul. Sometimes, in those later years, he accompanied me on my motorbike. I remember once we were driving to Limerick and had a narrow escape when we hit a flock of sheep and Stiofán lost his cap. Later he complained that I was driving too fast. I liked driving fast. By myself one day, I hit a hen that crossed the road in front of me. The old woman, who came out of the house ready to do battle, cheered up when I paid her a few shillings for the dead hen.

Some days in the currach we'd anchor off a headland to fish or to set a trammel and then we'd row about, dragging fishing lines after the currach. There might be as many as six basking sharks (liamhán) swimming nearby. They never bothered us. They did not take bait even when, unbeknown to Pítirín, one of us, I forget which one, dangled a mackerel in front of the sharks' open mouths. The only time I remember Pítirín getting upset with me is when he discovered us doing this. We never did it again. The shark was longer than the currach, which meant 18 to 20 feet in length. One flip of the tail could have tossed our flimsy boat into the sky and us with it. The sharks looked friendly and behaved that way, but when they came towards the currach with their mouths wide open they looked fearsome as if going to swallow us. Pítirín said that this was how they ate, sucking in the sea water. Later on, I discovered that the basking shark is the second largest living fish after the whale shark. Before the arrival of kerosene, Aran people killed basking sharks for their shark liver oil to light their homes.

Another diversion was the muca mara (sea pigs) or dolphins. Unlike the basking shark, they played with us and with the currach. They too were friendly. Sometimes a school of them consisting of possibly several hundred gathered in one of the enclosed bays for what looked like a sort of a dolphin 'Sports Day'. They chased one another, jumped over one another and raced about. Curious as we were, we did not dare approach them for fear they might accidentally hit us and capsize us. Pítirín tutored me well in the ways of the sea and, in time, I became a competent oarsman, if I am to believe comments from currach men whose judgments I came to respect. I was very athletic and perhaps foolishly fearless, asal breá scafánta (a fine agile donkey), as Páraic O'Conaire remarked about his donkey. My father crewed a currach that 'relieved' the lighthouse every two weeks. Whenever, because of the roughness of the sea, it was necessary to take a curach mór (8 oar currach) to brave the high waves, the crew were pleased with my company as the fourth oarsman. That was later on in my youth.

How I loved these forays in the face of the uncertain elements. I was called upon one Sunday morning to man the curach mór to go to the lighthouse; Páraic Tom Mhóir was in the prow, Michaelín Patch Bheaitlín next, then me, with my father in the stern. The sea was rising and with the change of tide it might have improved or got worse. They were not sure if they should try it – certainly not in the *curach beag* (six oars). They needed to earn the meagre fee that a completed 'relief' of the lighthouse provided. In a potentially treacherous sea like that, the judgment of the man in the prow is pivotal. Páraic, now quite old, had spent his life in currachs and knew every rock, nook and likely breaker in this area like the back of his hand. He was a man of few words but when he gave orders to the oarsmen, you listened because you knew that your life might depend on it. A slight mistake in the angle of the prow as you climbed an impending breaker could mean the difference between being capsized or climbing over the top. I never had occasion to be out in a currach in such sea before. In my ignorance, I revelled in it. Though I never forgot Pítirín's warning that the man who did not fear the sea was dangerous.

It took us a long time to row around Branach Island. Sometimes I wondered if we might be smashed against the rocks. I often thought of Pítirín's 'Plan B'. I was the only person who could swim, not that that skill would be of much use to me in this situation. There was a sigh of relief when we started to row the passage between Eeragh Island and Branach. It seemed that the worst was over. Between the two islands, there sometimes rose a breaker that stretched almost the whole width of the passage. That particular day the sea looked calm but one never knew with the sea.

Then half way through the passage, Páraic quietly gave orders to change the hand that was uppermost and face westward into a huge oncoming wave that suddenly had materialised out of nowhere. All four of us dug our oars deep and in unison flipped them at the end of our pull. Páraic gave a bearing to the man in the stern (in this case, my father). His job was as crucial as Páraic's own – to keep the stern from swaying so that Páraic could pinpoint the angle of the prow at the oncoming wave. Páraic was economic with words and only used one when a grunt might be ambiguous. There was not a sound as each of us bent our backs and pulled as I certainly never had done before. The currach was now at an angle of 60 degrees or more and gathering speed. Then suddenly, as we skimmed over the top, the breaker broke with a deafening roar as the stern hung in the air. The white foam stretched all the way to the far shore. We would not have stood a chance. Not a word was spoken until Páraic gave the next instruction and we knew the danger was over.

"That was a near one", he murmured, as if describing a hit from a seagull flying overhead.

We never made the 'relief' that morning. The breakers under the cliff where we were supposed to land were too erratic and threatening. Anyway, we were spent. Wet and tired, we headed for home. Mercifully, this time, the breaker in the middle of the passage remained quiet. Had it been chasing our stern, we'd have been swamped, as it would have taken too long to turn the currach around to face it.

But the above episode happened several years later, when I was in my late teens. After that, I don't remember an occasion when my rowing skills were called upon. Nowadays the lighthouse is automated and serviced from the mainland by helicopter.

There are two other occasions when I remember being out in rough seas. Once, as a young man, home on leave from Africa, I was on the pier in Kilronan watching a boat being loaded with lobster to take them to the buyer across the bay in Connemara. There was a Force 9 gale forecast for later in the day. Cancelling the trip was out of the question because any delay meant that many of the lobsters would die. Force 9 is fairly fearsome in a small overloaded lobster-boat at sea. I had just promised the parish priest that I would do the Sunday Mass for him in Onacht village. One of the fishermen, Michaelín, my next door neighbour of whom I was very fond approached me. He reminded me of the day long ago when I accompanied them in the *currach mór* to the lighthouse and the breaker between the two islands nearly swallowed us up.

"Patsy," he said, "could you come with us to Connemara this evening? I don't like this gale that is forecast and I don't have much confidence in some of the others on board either."

I read his mind. I knew that he and my brother Thomas were lobster-fishing partners and that they had in the past some differences of opinion with Tomás Joyce, one of the other fishermen on board. Also I suspected that Michaelín, thought I had an inner track to *Dia Mór* or perhaps at least was a lucky omen as turned out on the day of the *currach mór* going to the lighthouse when the breaker almost swamped us. Fishermen tend to be superstitious. I cannot claim to be completely free from such superstition myself when faced with the unknown.

"Sorry, Michaelín," I said, "I can't. I have promised the parish priest to say the Mass in the morning in Onacht church."

Michaelín seemed very disappointed and replied:

"I'll talk to Bertie. (the skipper) and get him to return to Aran immediately the lobsters are off-loaded."

Bertie agreed not to delay in Rosaveal but return to Aran immediately, so I jumped on board. I was not happy about the weather forecast but I did not want to disappoint Michaelín or show any sign of my inner reluctance. Unlike Michaelín I was not at all confident that *Dia Mór* would show me any favouritism whatsoever in a storm.

Half way out the bay, the gale started to blow and pinned us down between the waves which were coming broadside. In the cross-currents, white-crested breakers were hitting us from all sides. I felt grateful that I did not get sea-sick thus casting doubt on my sea-faring credentials. It took us longer than usual to make the crossing but we landed without mishap and by the time the lobsters were offloaded, the storm was at its height with spray lashing over the pier-head. Attempting a return to Aran was out of the question. The fishermen—some with obvious relief—repaired to the local pub to sit out the storm. By closing time, there was no sign of the storm abating, not that anyone seemed to care much by then, and the small unsteady party of fishermen made their way back to their boat tied up at the pier. The cabin below deck was cramped and stuffy and as the night wore on, the conversation got louder, punctuated only by the creaking of the fenders against the pier and by the sound of the storm in the rigging.

I had given up on returning to Aran that night or even next morning. However, by dawn Bertie decided to venture out into the bay. In the meantime a brawl had erupted. In the confined space of the cabin, it was difficult not to become involved. I was never in a brawl before, not even in school. For my companions though, I felt that the brawl was more like a game.

My natural instinct was to intervene and try and make peace, which was not considered playing the game. For my efforts I achieved little except perhaps attracting some of the punches meant, no doubt for others. Sitting beside me was one John 'Johnny' Bhrienín, a giant of a man whom I always considered sympathetic to my way of life. He did his best to shield me. I know it all sounded good in the re-telling over a long drawn out pint of Guinness in the pub afterwards, but I did not enjoy it at the time and wished I was somewhere else, anywhere else. However, I marvelled at the strength of these men, muscles developed as a result of years of pulling ropes and lifting nets. It was dawn by the time Bertie pointed the boat towards Aran. The wind was from the south west and did its best to blow us back into the shelter of the harbour.

After we escaped into the bay, it took us several hours more than usual to make our way back to Aran and by the time we arrived we were well past Mass time in Onacht and the congregation had all gone home. Some told me later that they sat on the wall watching the small boat battling with the waves as it struggled to cross the bay. I did not mention what had happened. I knew that they would hear it all later with embellishments. By the time we arrived back in Kilronan most of the fishermen had sobered up and were on nodding terms, if not yet talking. As the un-welcome peace-maker, I had the opportunity to get to know some fishermen for the first time. Some, like Tomás Joyce, I had never spoken to before but, in the months that followed, I spoke to Tomás several times. I am sure it was one of his punches that grazed my cheek and he probably knew it.

On another occasion I was again on the pier in Kilronan when the Aran Lifeboat was heading across the bay on a mercy mission to bring someone to hospital. The coxswain, Coley Hernon, knew that I longed to accompany them and he used the excuse of being one member of crew short to invite me on board. On this occasion I felt safe and in competent company, each man proud of his seafaring skill. On that particular occasion the sea was spectacular to behold and the voyage was not an excursion for the faint-hearted.

One thing I remember about those summer days as a youngster with Pítirín on Aran was the lack of urgency about anything. We could investigate things leisurely and as we wished. Sometimes we pulled our currach up on the beach and chased after seagull chicks to take home as pets for the younger children. It was this time also that I taught myself to swim. At that time, very few on the islands swam. A local seanchaí, Dara Neide Phaidi, was talked about with wonder because he was reputed to be able to swim across Kilmurvey harbour.

In my final year at primary school, the last big school event was Confirmation. For this the bishop came to the island in the lifeboat. If the event coincided with stormy weather, as it sometimes did, there could be as many as 50 Spanish trawlers sheltering on the 'road' in Kilronan harbour and they gave the bishop a colourful and noisy welcome with their sirens blaring and flags flying. The bishop arrived with a retinue of priest attendants who took turns examining us in the catechism. For weeks before the event we learnt the catechism by rote, all the questions and answers whether or not they made sense. For example there was a difficult answer there on adultery and fornication. Nobody ever knew what these words meant. Also we had to make an effort to understand the Irish of the examining priests. After all, their first language was English and they pronounced, for example, the word *Dia* like G in the alphabet. There is a story about one twelve-year old from Gort na gCapall, Ronan Dan.

"*Cé mhéid Dia ann?*" (How many Gods are there?)

The youngster thinking the priest was referring to the alphabet letter, proudly answered:

"*Tá dhá G ann, G mór agus g beag!*" (There are two Gs, capital G and small g.). Correct and more profound than the youngster realised!

Generally we kept a safe distance between ourselves and our priests, whether *g beag* or *G mór*. Over the centuries, Aran people built many monuments that still stand today. Some may be to ancient unknown gods but others bear witnesses to a people's Christian past. However, there are only three monuments built by the modern Aran man: one is to two British soldiers who in 1966, landed in Aran after rowing a small boat across the Atlantic. This is the type of courage that the fisher-folk of Aran admire. Courage (*misneach*) is the Aran man's most treasured virtue. Another monument is to commemorate the tsunami that struck early morning, August 15th 1852. Fifteen people were swept out to sea and perished - almost the entire male population of the villages of Cill Éinne and Oir Áirne. The monument also commemorates about forty other Aran men drowned at sea. The third monument is in the form of a stone cross set up in memory of the islands' beloved parish priest Fr. O'Donoghue who died in 1893. He was the visionary pastor who is reputed to have sent a bitter letter to the British administration in Dublin asking for help. It said:

"Send us boats or send us coffins."

By kick-starting the fishing industry in Inis Mór, he laid the foundation for the island's present-day prosperity.

MAKING LAND (STÓCÁIL)

By June 1951, I had completed my last year at primary school. By September there was no more school to look forward to. Like my classmates I helped my parents while waiting for the time when the emigrant boat would take me to England. In spring and summer, most men fished, in a currach if they owned one. Or, off the rocks if they didn't! In winter they worked their piece of land, building walls and making new land or *ag stócáil*, as it was called.

All the land on Aran, no matter how barren-looking, is owned by someone and every patch of it is walled off from its neighbour. There is no common land that I know off. A *creig* is a walled off patch of rock. A *buaile* (field) is a *creig* where someone has put clay or sand to entice grass to grow there. A *creagán* is a *creig* on the way towards becoming a field. It seemed that over the centuries Aran men spent their lives turning every *creig* into a *creagán* and *creagán* into a field. This process was called *stócáil*.

When I was a child I used to accompany my father when he was making land. This entailed removing all the loose rocks, filling in all the fissures (*scailpeanna*) and covering the area with clay and soil gathered from wherever it could be found. Finding soil was the main problem and I remember the delighted look on my father's face whenever he happened on a deep fissure full of clay. He scraped it out, filling the cavity with stones. This clay, mixed with sand made good top soil and with seaweed added in, it produced an excellent crop of potatoes. When at boarding school on the mainland I often thought of how delighted my father would have been if he had access to the heaps of clay in the fields all around me. He was probably the last of the generation of Aran people that did *stócáil*. One could view it as a struggle with the land but I don't think they ever saw it as a struggle. It was more a labour of love. I too grew up dreaming of all the *creigeannaí* I would convert into fertile fields when I got older. But, just when reclaiming the land became easier to do, the need for such work ceased. The population on Aran had decreased and hunger both for food and for more fields disappeared.

Like all the older people, my father was a bit superstitious. If a crow landed beside him, he would down tools and go home annoyed. It was believed that the crow was bad news. It only came when a close relative or perhaps even oneself, was about to die. Hence the phrase *"ar an liosta ag an bpréachán"* or to be "on the crow's list" was not a good omen. I used to shoo the crow away, so Dada could continue his work. As I write this, I am reminded of the crows my dad dreaded. This morning, two came and sat on the wall outside my window. I am sure they had no list or piece of paper with them. For old time's sake, I shoo'd them off and they flew away. It would be just my bad luck if they returned with an iPad or Kindle with my name writ large upon it.

NA FAOISDÍNÍ (THE STATIONS)

Each family in Bungabhla took it in turn to have Mass in the house once a year. It was an established custom and a big occasion for both the household concerned and, indeed, for the whole locality. Everyone in the village came to the Mass; the two priests based in Kilronan came and sometimes, weather permitting, they were accompanied by the priest based on Inis Meáin. The priests first heard the confession of the assembled villagers. Then they said Mass on a table arranged as an altar. That was where the expertise of us altar servers came in useful. We regarded ourselves as kings for the day. But what we looked forward to most was the feast afterwards – cakes and biscuits and jam. We had never seen the likes of it.

After the Mass the household provided breakfast for the clergy and this in itself was an event worthy of note. Tea and cakes were served all day while people came and went. People who hadn't spoken to one another for months made it up for the occasion; family, friends and neighbours visited. With eleven houses in the village it took almost as many years for our turn to arrive. We all looked forward to it, counting the years till our turn came. My mother dreaded the idea because of all the preparations. The house was scrubbed and cleaned both inside and outside, walls white-washed, furniture repaired or replaced, doors and gutters painted. The street was tidied up, flowers planted, footpaths covered in fresh sand and stones brought from the shore. While the fever lasted, even the outhouses were tidied and made to look smart. It was a mammoth spring cleaning of our surroundings. People said that if it were not for the threat of 'Na Faoisdíní' the place would be a wreck. Other houses too did some tidying so as not to appear derelict by comparison. It was a time of reconciliation. Everyone buried their sulks and knelt for prayer together in the kitchen. Occasionally a household was allowed to miss its turn but this was frowned upon. If someone was old or feeble, the neighbours offered a helping hand in the clean-up and saw to it that nothing was wanting on the day – like a white tablecloth, presentable teapot or china cups for the priest. Chipped plates like blackened saucepans were put out of sight.

As a child I regarded these events as a form of play but as an adult I now see them as the glue that kept the community sane and healthy.

One day in early September 1951, instead of cycling to Kilronan as usual, I went fishing in the currach with Pítirín. My mother cycled to Kilronan instead. That night, I eaves-dropped as my parents discussed a suggestion made by Mrs. Hehir. It entailed my attending secondary school in Galway. I would lodge in town and attend a day-school called St. Joseph's. The fortnightly ferry to Galway sailed next day and without any consultation with me, I found myself dressed in my best Sunday clothes and accompanying my mother into Galway. Nobody had more than two sets of clothes: one's ordinary working clothes and one's Sunday best. One did not mix and match like today. Though my father had better English, my mother was the organising force in our house. My dream was coming true.

3

TO THE MAINLAND

THE ADVENTURES OF SLIBFA

My mother and I lodged with Mrs. Coleman near the docks. She could not put me up for the term but suggested a Mrs. Lawlor in Market Street who might be able to do just that. We visited her and my mother and herself came to some understanding. To my child's eyes she was a cross old woman dressed in black (*sean-chailleach chantalach*). I did not look forward to staying with her but I had no say in the matter.

When we went to see Brother Leonard at The Bish (colloquial name for St Josephs, a Day School run by the Patrician Brothers), however, he suggested a Mrs. Duggan in the Claddagh who might provide me with cheaper lodgings. She had three children at The Bish. Bro. Leonard arranged for my mother and me to have tea with her and her family at 4 pm. My mother wanted her boy to grow up speaking proper English and as we walked back to Market Street, I knew she did not like the conversation at Mrs. Duggan's table. Though my mother understood very little English, she knew enough to realise that every second word did not start with the letter "F". And that was how I ended up staying with Mrs. Lawlor. The old crone cost more but she swore less.

Mrs. Lawlor's was a lodging house with three upstairs bedrooms. At first I could not speak or understand English and this was a source of annoyance to Mrs. Lawlor. She made no secret of her dislike of people from Aran and, indeed, of all people who spoke Irish. According to her, they were pampered by the state at the expense of the real people of Ireland. She never used my name, always referring to me as the Stupid Little Boy From Aran, which soon was to become Slibfa in the word games I played with my classmates at school. Fortunately the nickname did not stick but I continued to use it in my diary in case Mrs. Lawlor ever happened upon it.

Mrs. Lawler's married son Eddie occupied the downstairs front room which he also used for his work. He was a shoemaker. His wife had left him but he had a daughter called Mary, a tall thin creature. She never spoke to me, but glowered at me, having obviously taken on board her grandmother's theory about Slibfa. Her father, Eddie, was always very nice to me. I don't think he held the same theories as his mother. Or, if he did, he never expressed them. Lodgers were mainly commercial travellers and seldom stayed more than one night. My bed was smaller than the other beds, but comfortable. The narrow metal frame was easy to wheel about. I could be sleeping in any room, depending on where the other lodgers wished to sleep. Some wanted a room to themselves, others had no choice.

My worldly possessions, which consisted of a few items of clothes, some books and a chess set, were stored in a battered oversized suitcase under my bed. I had always wanted to play chess; my heroes played that game in the stories of the *Cúchulain* Cycle told by Pítirín. My pocket money was nil or next to it but I could not resist buying the second hand chess set, though I had yet to learn to play. Occasionally Eddie sent me out to the hardware store next door to buy some item or other. He never wrote his message down and often I returned with the wrong item. Eddie never showed he minded but sent me out again. It annoyed me when Mrs. Lawlor made great capital of the story, telling it to any locals who came to visit her. Proof indeed of her Slibfa theory. I never bought into her theory. When, as term progressed school reports started to arrive, Mrs. Lawlor demanded to see them. When my marks turned out to be consistently high, she pointed out to the visiting neighbours that this confirmed her theory that the Christian Brothers too were guilty of favouring me because I spoke Irish. She persisted, even after I presented her with my improved marks in English. All very puzzling for a little boy!

I was aware that the old woman was not making much profit from me, so I was not upset when I was no longer allowed to use the parlour to study. Waste of electricity, she complained. So I had to do my homework in the kitchen with the radio blaring and Mrs. Lawlor recounting the latest adventures of Slibfa to visiting neighbours. As regards food, I was always a finicky child. A hair on the plate would put me off my entire meal. I am sure that the food at Mrs. Lawlor's was good and it was also plentiful. But I had a small appetite and when I could not finish the food on my plate, it was taken from me and handed to the dog on the floor. Next day when I got dinner on the same plate, I could picture the dog licking it; this did not improve my appetite one bit.

I loved The Bish and the Patrician Brothers who ran it were a fine body of dedicated teachers. I was the only pupil there from Aran. My classmates were curious about where I was staying or if I came in from Aran in a currach every morning. I shared with them some of the adventures of Slibfa and obviously they brought stories home as children do.

Before term ended one of the parents, a Mrs Ryan, came to me at the school gate and asked me if I would like to shift lodgings after Christmas. She had three children at The Bish. I was thrilled. For the rest of the year and for many years afterwards, Mrs Ryan became almost a second mother to me. Mrs. Lawlor expected me back after Christmas and often asked me if I was writing to my mother telling her how much I was enjoying my stay at her place. I lied to her unashamedly. A couple of days before I was due to go home for Christmas, Mrs. Lawlor had me pose with her lanky granddaughter, Mary, in the yard. She gave me the picture to take to my mother to prove how much I was part of her family life in Galway.

I did not like the picture of little me standing beside her sulking granddaughter, towering over me like a stick insect. I stuck the picture in my pocket. I had no intention of ever showing it to anyone, least of all my mother. When I went up to my bed, I took the picture out and crunched the faces. Next morning, after a hasty breakfast, I dragged my oversized suitcase downstairs and was ready to take off for the docks to catch the 8 o'clock ferry to Aran. It was still dark when Mrs. Lawlor came to the door to see me off.

"Have you the photo?"

"Yes, Mrs Lawlor."

"Show me."

"It's in my suitcase", I lied.

"Open it".

She stood over me on the doorstep as I unlocked the suitcase and searched inside it.

I must have looked every inch, the lying eejit that I was.

"Where did you put it? Is it in your pocket?".

"Yes Mrs. Lawlor." and I handed her the crumpled photograph.

"Why did you do this?

"I didn't. It crumpled in my pocket", I lied

"You stupid little boy"

I knew that for the first time, she had hit the nail on the head.

After moving in with the Ryans, my stay in Galway was idyllic. I felt completely at home in the atmosphere of that family. It was ten minutes' walk to school each morning and if we had a spare halfpenny we bought an apple each in a little shop by the canal. By then I had made more friends at school, notably with the Cook family with whom I kept in contact into my late teens. On summer evenings, or weekends, we cycled for a few miles outside town to some woods to play cowboys and Indians. Other times, to put together a few shillings, we pooled our resources and hired one or two rowing boats to row the half a mile up river to the ruin of Menlo Castle on the banks of the river Corrib. This ruin was ideal for engaging in war games. On the way there we staged battles between the boats, playing hide-and-go-seek among the tall reeds. As an adult in later life I sometimes hired the same boats in an effort to recapture the pleasures of those school days.

From early on, I was befriended by the Cook family, particularly Francie and Junie. There were four of them at The Bish. Francie spent a week with me on Aran. I often stayed with the Cooks into my early teens. I have never forgotten their kindness to me.

For a while in the second term I shared a desk with a bulky boy from the Claddagh. His name was McGuire and he barely left room to open my book on the desk. My grasp of English was still rudimentary. McGuire was easily distracted and against most things, particularly the young English teacher who tried to interest us in poetry. I don't remember any of the poetry but I still remember McGuire's mutterings whenever that teacher entered the classroom:

Oh, me belly
Oh, me bum
Cow's malaki
And horse's dung.

It is one of the mantras that I still use to mark time in order to extricate myself from a tricky situation.

Time at The Bish passed quickly. Sometimes in my last term a frail sun-burnt missionary came to talk to the students. His name was Fr. Cummins and he wore a long white cassock. He looked the picture of ill-health. He described working in Africa as a missionary. It revived my memories of reading *The Far East* and when, at the end of his talk, he enquired if anyone would like to be a missionary I put my hand up along with four others in my class. That's how I ended up in a boarding school run by the Society of African Missions, a small secondary school of 40 pupils who wanted to be missionaries.

BOARDING SCHOOL ON THE MAINLAND

The Society of African Missions (SMA) had its Irish headquarters in Cork and it sent missionaries to Africa, particularly Nigeria. The 1950s and 1960s was the heyday of the modern missionary era in the Irish Church and by the time I joined, the SMA had several hundred missionaries in Nigeria. The Society had started its missionary activity in West Africa towards the end of the nineteenth century. At that time the area was referred to as "The White-Man's Grave" because of the inhospitable climate. For the early missionaries it was indeed a 'call to martyrdom', many of them dying after only two years at their station.

When I joined up, the teaching staff at Balinafad College were all former missionaries full of wonderful stories of excitement and adventure. I took easily to boarding school, perhaps helped by my experience of lodging with Mrs. Lawlor. I spent four years in Balinafad. I cannot describe those years as being other than 'deeply satisfying'. It was an ordinary secondary school with an extraordinary staff. I did my Leaving Certificate there and I was sad when the time came for me to leave the place. I retain only one negative memory.

For a term or two after my arrival, we were taught English by a Fr. Phillips, a returned missionary on sick leave as all our teachers were. I was just beginning to acquire a handle on the language, still thinking in my native Irish. Phillips gave the class an essay to write each week and in my first week, the topic was entitled, "Sunset". Still grappling with my English, the content of my essay was a translation of the thoughts in my head, which were in Gaelic. I imagined myself fishing from a currach at sunset as I often did. We were anchored off Eeragh; the red orb of the sun was slowly sinking into the waves to the west with Eeragh's tall lighthouse framing the picture and the cormorants and seagulls diving for their evening meals and me waiting to catch mine. I described the noises I heard in my head.

Fr. Phillips was a small man in every way. He entered the classroom with the bundle of exercise books under his arm. He plonked them down on the desk and picked out one which I recognised to be mine. Standing by the blackboard he surveyed us all imperiously and exclaimed:

"This is the best essay I've read in a long while."

I felt great pride as he looked across at me sitting in the corner at the back. I smiled as he read my essay for the class. Then he paused.

"Tell me," he said, "where did you copy this from?"

I was flabbergasted. My balloon was burst.

"Father," I explained, "I did not copy it!"

He refused to believe me and I am sure the rest of my classmates followed suit.

I felt very hurt. It was many years before I ever again tried to be original in what I wrote and certainly not while at Balinafad. But the experience, I hope, was not altogether wasted. When I became a teacher myself, I always made it a point to respect whatever explanation my students gave, even when it went against my better judgment.

In Balinafad we had alternate afternoons for sports and manual work. I bought a hurley-stick. And new football boots. Time passed quickly. Through the grounds of our secondary school at Balinafad, there ran a river. In the summer we dammed it and swam every day after class. That was where I perfected my swimming strokes. It was during those glorious summer months that I really got to love and admire the returned missionaries of the Society of African Missions. I believed them to be good people worthy of emulation.

THE NOVITIATE – INITIATION INTO MISSIONARYHOOD

Once I passed my Leaving Certificate, I applied to join the Society and become a missionary. I was one of a band of about twenty young men from all over Ireland to gather at a place called Kilcolgan, near Galway City, a place known as The Novitiate, to be initiated into the Society. The year-long period was referred to as a 'Spiritual Year'. The aim of this year-long isolation was to prepare and help us decide if we were cut out for missionary life. In reality it was a formation period where we were systematically indoctrinated. I had no problem with that. There was a strong emphasis on saving one's own soul and by the end of the year one was aware

My first year at college.

that this was not an easy task. In fact it looked an impossible task unless you followed God's call and became a missionary which, in any case, was the object of the exercise.

At any age, but especially for young idealistic people, the desire to help others—the wish to do good—is a powerful and addictive drug. Under the influence of this drug, one is willing to sublimate all one's other urges, such as starting a family and accumulating wealth. In the novitiate we prayed a lot and studied. The subjects were Church History, which I liked, and the Lives of the Saints about which I was somewhat sceptical. Much was made of the importance of blind obedience, whereby one suspended the working of reason in order to carry out the commands of religious superiors, no matter how deranged they might seem to be. Supposedly holy abbots tested prospective monks by ordering them to plant cabbages up-side-down. Carrying out such orders was considered the height of virtue and worthy of emulation. I think most of us thought this silly but we were smart enough not to argue in case we might find ourselves with one-way tickets home. The prevailing model of the institutional Church was the authoritarian, monarchical model, a model of a church dominated by clerical control where any sign of individualism, intellectual creativity and theological reasoning were viewed with suspicion. Submissiveness to established authority and obedience to religious superiors were promoted as the primary virtues, away ahead of Faith, Hope and Charity. In our youth and innocence we did not dare question any of this.

Study always appealed to me but prayer and meditation I found difficult. Again, as in boarding school, two afternoons a week we had outdoor games, Gaelic football and hurling. Sometimes soccer, but I only remember one game of rugby. Our Director, Fr. Gantley, was a noted Galway inter-county hurler and he came to join us on the field occasionally. He played hurling under an assumed name because for some obscure reason, the bishops of Ireland had forbidden priests to play football or hurling in public competitions. Two other afternoons were devoted to manual labour, a meaningless type of work that did not make much sense except to keep students occupied and in the fresh air.

During one of those two-hour meaningless work periods I was assigned to the orchard and told to shift a pile of rubble from meaningless A to meaningless B. Fr. Beausang, the Assistant Director, an amiable enough fellow, was in charge of 'manual work'. He was a returned missionary. It was a particularly dreary day as I started in the drizzle to shift the rubble from A to B. My wheelbarrow sank into the soft soil, digging a deep rut between A and B but it was easier that way and I saw no logical reason for changing the path. When Fr. Beausang came along, he thought otherwise and commented : "You'd think you'd change the route!" . He then went away. As I saw no point in the exercise anyway, I did not think anything about the route except that it was easier than ploughing a new one. I continued as I was. Before the end of manual work, Beausang came around again to inspect. He was less than pleased and barked:

"I told you to change the route."

Then he went away. He returned before the end of work, by which time the rut was quite deep. By now he was very exasperated.

"I told you to change the route", he growled.

My reply was not calculated to mollify him and it didn't. "No, Father. You said "You'd *think* you'd change the route". He was not amused and ordered me to report to the Director's office immediately. Reporting to the Director meant one was in serious trouble, perhaps being asked to leave. Leaving my wheelbarrow with the irate Beausang in the orchard, I spent the next several hours standing uncomfortably outside Fr. Gantley's door, wondering at my stupidity. I was back in Slibfa-land. Gantley was a severe man who gave the impression of not suffering fools gladly. When eventually he opened his door to invite me in, I had worked myself into a state of anxiety. I told him exactly what happened. I thought I detected a faint smile on his face as he told me to "go away" and return to my study. We students suspected that Beausang and Gantley did not always see eye to eye. Perhaps, after all, they were human.

Nowadays, almost 50 years later, when I am being particularly stubborn, all my wife has to do is murmur:

"Wheelbarrows."

Attribute that to Pavlov's theory of 'conditioning' or more likely to Samuel Johnson's view that: "You can do anything with a Scotsman if you catch him young." It is hard to overcome the training of one's youth.

As the year in the novitiate progressed, some students left or were told to leave. Most of us got through to the next stage which led eventually to ordination and being sent abroad as a missionary. The novitiate was an important watershed, a fork in the road. At the end of the novitiate, those prospective candidates who proved acceptable were divided into two groups; one group went straight to the SMA seminary situated in Newry, Northern Ireland. This group studied philosophy for two years and then theology for four. After that they were sent abroad as missionaries. The second group was sent to study philosophy at the National University of Ireland in Cork and then take a secular degree. I suspect that the reason was purely functional: by then many of the independent African states were beginning to find the missionary tag unacceptable and no longer wanted to issue visas for them. A university degree permitted us to enter these countries as teachers. I found myself among the second group.

Within this group, some, like me, who did honours, attended all the philosophy lectures, sitting for the philosophy degree examination in June and for our honours degree in September. As long as we could show on paper that we had passed the degree exam in philosophy at university, we were excused from spending another two years studying the subject in the seminary before starting our four-years of theology course.

UNIVERSITY

I relished every minute of my three years at University. We were all housed in a hostel run by our Society and we cycled to college each morning. For someone like me, who was doing an honours degree and attending all the pass Philosophy lectures, it was a heavy burden of class-work. But I took it all in my stride. I made some friends then that I still cherish to this day. In my last two years, I specialised in history and Irish. As part of my course in Old Irish, I studied International Phonetics. I treasure this particularly because in my second year I was awarded a studentship to study the phonetics of the Connemara Gaeltacht, a work I carried out with enthusiasm during my summer holidays. I based myself near Rosmuc and cycled hundreds of miles criss-crossing the countryside between there and Roundstone mapping out the area where Irish was still spoken. I turned up on my bike, seemingly out of nowhere, to surprise people cutting turf on a bog or sitting outside their houses. I drank a lot of strong tea and was offered much stronger stuff if I would take it. People tried to guess from my accent where I was from. Eventually I learned to use words like *carcair* for 'hill' which to many people identified me immediately as coming from Aran, which made me even more welcome. I made friends, true friends. Among those who became very special to me then were the extended Mannion family in Rosmuc. I got to know them by accident and we have kept in touch ever since.

For me, my days at university were halcyon days. Among the

subjects I studied in my first year was Logic followed by two years of philosophy. I attended lectures in Irish history given by the young John A Murphy but the person who inspired me most was Professor Hogan who taught Honours History. He made a lasting impression on my young life. For him, *Thought* (call it ideology or philosophy) was what mattered. Though he did not couch it in those terms, ideology was the rocket that propelled humanity forward. Subsequent action, be it historical battles or political activity, was only the debris left by the after burner. We studied Plato, Aristotle and Augustine, the rise of Christianity and of Islam, the Enlightenment, the French Revolution, Marx and Engels and the rise of Communism.

In our final year we were given a list of topics for our essays. I chose Dialectical Materialism, a subject that intrigued me greatly. In order to improve my understanding of the subject I signed up for a correspondence course on the subject with Radio Moscow. I gave them my Aran address and every week a bundle of lectures arrived in the mail. I studied the material carefully. Suddenly when the packages

ceased coming, I enquired why. When Radio Moscow confirmed that they were still sending them, I immediately suspected my mother of not forwarding them to me. On enquiry, I discovered that, having found out what the packages contained, she had decided to burn them. At first, I was annoyed but I forgave her. She was only practising at being a *Dia Beag*, like her sister, my aunt Mary Bhilla. In spite of my mother's effort at sabotage, I got an "A" in Dialectical Materialism – no thanks to my mother or to Radio Moscow. I never felt any leanings towards Communism.

University, 1958.

After sitting my philosophy examination in June, I sat my Honours BA examination in September 1960. At that time, final university examination results were published in the national newspapers and it was appropriate that the first (and only) person to congratulate me on my results was my old friend, Mrs. Hehir. I had not disappointed her this time.

THE SEMINARY

After finishing university, I did not go home to Aran but set out immediately for the seminary situated in Newry, Northern Ireland. I looked forward to studying Theology. Like many a layman, I hoped it would answer all my remaining questions about the meaning of life, but it didn't. Systematic Theology, disappointed me. But I did like reading theology as it worked itself out in the lives of men like Thomas Merton, Teilhard de Chardin, and the great missionaries of the past. Canon Law I disliked. Church History and Biblical Studies enthused me.

Up till now I kept reasonably quiet at home in Aran about wanting to be a priest. I did not want to be laughed at by my peers. All my contemporaries in Aran were by now working on building sites in England. But I could no longer hide the fact that I was on a different path. At home, nobody spoke about what I was up to, but they knew.

My father's world view was coloured by his experience while living in Boston in the late 1920s. For him, some people were good but others were bad and could not be trusted. Top of his bad list were the Italians. Next, *An Fear Gorm* and after them, the Poles. The Connemara man was not far behind. Oddly enough, the Polish race went up in his estimation when his favourite niece married one. He did not understand why I wanted to go and spend my life working with *An Fear Gorm*, someone he viewed as being most unreliable.

"They will let you down," he warned.

My father's views on Connemara people surprised me because I thought Aran and Connemara were extended family. However, when I enquired further, I found that the dislike was mutual. Connemara people in Boston had songs describing marrying an Aran person as the worst thing that could happen to one. During the famine of the mid 19th century, Aran people set up vigilante groups to patrol their shore to prevent raiders from Connemara coming and digging up their seed potatoes in the spring. The poor starving people arrived in their *báid iomartha* (row boats, not the *púcán* used for ferrying turf to Aran) at night. So, folk memory ran deep. My father's view about my becoming a priest was expressed much later when he heard me tell of my misadventures in Africa. If I wanted to be a priest that badly, he remarked, why not become a proper one like our parish priest, Fr. Moran, who drove a big car. My father knew I liked cars and motor bikes. He did not labour the subject further but I understood what he meant. The matter was never brought up again. I knew that all he ever wanted for me was to be happy and he saw me achieve that. My wishing to become a priest was not something I ever talked about with my mother. I don't think my parents ever discussed it among themselves. Normally on Aran, the first child would grow up, emigrate, get work so as to send money home to help the rest of the family. My going to the seminary was a great financial burden for my family but they never referred to it as such.

During my second year at the seminary I decided to go and work in England during the summer holidays. The previous summer I had tried my hand at lobster fishing with Dan Beag Dainín from our village. We had wanted to make some money but our venture was a flop, either because the lobsters had escaped the pots before we got to them in the morning or because someone else emptied our pots for us. An observant neighbour suggested the latter. I had another motive for wanting to work in England. All my pals at primary school now worked in England and I felt I had got out of touch with an important part of my heritage. The fact that the seminary forbade students to work during holidays weighed little in my thinking. Anyway, I was tired of enforced idleness on Aran during the long summer holidays and I wanted to earn my keep. Perhaps most seminary students were farmers' sons who could work quietly on their family farms. I had no such luxury. Also, I felt the restriction on working during holidays was silly. My decision was contrary to what our seminary mentors taught us. However, I felt I could argue my case if I had to. I was still innocent enough to imagine that, if right and reason were on your side, you always won. So, I took off for London the day after the Sports on Aran. I had won enough prizes in these competitions to pay my fares. I was determined to make my own way and my own friends, so I contacted none of my buddies working in London.

I got a job working on construction, starting on the concrete gang which was very tough on my soft student hands. I stayed in digs in the East End of London, well away from the popular haunts of the Irish. My co-workers were British, a few from the Caribbean and one man from Connemara, Pat Conneely. Pat was a kind and gentle soul who immediately took me under his wing. He introduced me to his family and I often had lunch and supper with them. I later visited his father, who was then in his 90s. He lived in An Rinn, near Rosaveal, a little harbour in Connemara where the Aran fishermen landed their catch. Pat warned me not to speak to him in Irish in front of the other labourers because he did not want us pigeonholed and mocked.

"It will only isolate you," he warned. I hope that nowadays he'd be proud to speak Irish.

Pat had a young family who were involved with Irish music and culture, a credit to the Irish Diaspora. I kept in touch with Pat and his family for many years and knowing them made my stay in London so much more pleasant. Being with them was like being back home on Aran. I lodged in the Isle of Dogs with a British family and on my second week there they offered me the use of a spare bicycle. This saved me endless hours standing at bus stops but also enabled me to explore much of the East End of London as I cycled to and from work. My foreman on the building site was from Ireland. I was the only student on the job. He had had bad experiences with students in the past but he seemed satisfied enough with me. He gave me little jobs that came up, which was a much appreciated relief from the back-breaking work of wheeling and pouring concrete. One day he came to me and asked if I knew anything about scaffolding. He had just sacked a scaffolder and needed a replacement urgently. I had never done scaffolding but I had experience climbing cliffs and liked heights.

I had figured out how scaffolding worked and I told him I could do it. For the next couple of weeks of a beautiful summer, I worked high up on the scaffolding. I don't think I got much extra money but I certainly got a better view. It was a job that could not be easily supervised. So, some of my companions spent much of their time looking out over London and whistling at women passing in the street below. At first I was so thrilled with the job that, at the least excuse, I ran up and down the scaffolding not always availing of the ladder. The scaffolder in charge called me aside and told me to stop being an *eejit* and slow down.

"You're up and down there like a whore's knickers. You'll fall off."

I was so innocent then that I did not know that whores even wore knickers. But I took his word for it. My colleagues seemed experts on the subject; it was the constant topic of their conversations.

As a student in London at the time, you either catered for yourself or lodged with a family. Or, in student terminology, you either "Ate yourself or had your whole board". Well I "ate myself" and, as a result, I often went hungry.

It was not the best time for an Irish person to be in England. The IRA were threatening to bring their bombing campaign to mainland Britain, injuring innocent people and thus fuelling latent anti-Irish sentiment. Yet, I did not experience anything other than friendship from the British.

As a seminarian, I felt I should be doing something 'religious'. So, one evening a week, I tagged along with a Legion of Mary group that worked in the Red Light district. I also visited the lodgings of my Caribbean co-workers to help them with their income tax forms. I suspect that some of the locations I visited were not all that safe but, in my innocence, I was unaware of this at the time.

One day while wandering around the East End of London, visiting places of interest and generally gawking, I came upon a Catholic church still open. I popped in to say a prayer. The priest was in the confession box, so I decided to go to confession. It was just closing time. I knelt down and the priest tore strips of me for coming so late. I said nothing but quietly walked out. He must have thought about it and how he had missed an opportunity to save my soul. Anyhow, he came running down the street after me, apologising and begging me to come back into the confessional. Perhaps he thought I had murdered someone. I could not go back in because I had only a few peccadilloes to confess and then he'd have known that I had really wasted his time. I hope he got over his scruples.

In the seminary, as in our other training institutions, the model of the Church was the hierarchical one: an undemocratic, top-down institution totally absorbed with the importance of preserving the status quo. The emphasis was not on love or even faith but on blind obedience, submission to authority and conformity to established rules.

Our Missionary society would not be known for its attachment to tradition; it would have followed more in the steps of innovators like Matteo Ricci, the 16th Century Italian Jesuit missionary who pioneered the introduction of Christianity to India and China. In fact our founder was rapped on the knuckles by Rome and recalled home for having the temerity to suggest ordaining natives as priests. He was later allowed to found a new missionary organisation for Africa if only to get him away from Rome, where his pestering had become a thorn in the side of the establishment. He sailed to West Africa with the first group of his missionaries and died within six weeks. The rest all died within two years.

It is the nature of missionaries to break new ground. But we were part of a larger Church, many of whose key functionaries resembled the Pharisees of old, who loved their phylacteries and their rules more than their God — people for whom the width of plastic around a priest's neck took precedence over the breadth of any vision within his head. Some, especially those of us who had studied history, were well aware that there were alternative and more acceptable models of the church. But we were also aware that, as mere students in a hierarchical institution, we were best seen and not heard. However, I was fortunate that the churchmen I had so far encountered in my life were people of integrity, imbued with the same enthusiasm as myself. We sublimated all our desires to the needs of the cause we served. Indeed I never met any other type of churchman, either then or later, who surpassed them in dedication.

After returning to the seminary in September, I made no secret of having worked on construction in London over the holidays – mainly because I thought it was a logical thing to have done in spite of the prohibition on working during holidays. I was not therefore surprised or upset when one day I was summoned to the office of the Superior, whom we all referred to as John Joe. Trained in Rome, where conformity and submission to authority is rated highly as a priestly virtue, it was naïve of me to expect a sympathetic hearing. I had broken the rule and that was it. No discussion! I was quickly made aware of a big black mark against my name. At the time it did not upset me; I was conceited enough to imagine I was right, even if I did rebel against a stupid rule.

Sometime during term, I received a cheque from Revenue, a PAYE tax refund, the largest sum of money I had ever so far laid my hands on. I had never asked for anything for myself, so my mother asked me to spend it as I wished. I had taken a fancy to a second-hand 250 cc motorbike that another priest in the seminary was selling, the first toy that I could ever call my own. That same bike got me into more trouble in the seminary than my whole two months working in London. I did not know how to drive it. But I had got my first driving licence without a test as, at that time, testing in Ireland for motor cyclists had yet to be introduced. I got a local farmer to store the bike for me and planned to ride it home to Aran during the Christmas holidays. Every Sunday, the students of the seminary went for a long walk in the country-side, strolling along two by two or in threes. On a couple of occasions, I slipped into the farmhouse for a lesson on how to operate the bike. It was mainly a matter of using the manual to familiarise myself with the bike's various parts. I could not ask the priest I purchased the bike from, as 'God forbid', he would be breaking the rule.

The day before the holidays, a notice, signed by John Joe, went up on the seminary message board. It stated: "All students must leave the seminary on the means provided", which in this case was a bus to the railway station. I knew the notice referred to me and that some pious soul, anxious to ingratiate himself with authority, had reported me. Much as I disliked Canon Law, it had its uses in a Church obsessed by rules. There was a particular Canon which read: "If there is a loophole in the law, you are entitled to go through it". I liked that! I studied it and could quote it in its original Latin.

I left the seminary on the bus provided, but hopped off it as it reached the farmer's house. I did the next several hundred miles home on my bike without any mishap. Except when once, at a sharp corner in the middle of a shower of hailstones, I skidded and found myself turned round in the opposite direction. It gave me a fright but there was no time to worry about it. Night was falling and I still had not worked out how the lights worked. By the time I reached Galway it was dark – and no fun at all trying to figure out the lights for the first time. However, by the time I reached my destination, I felt that I was a reasonably well-practised rider. I gave no further thought to the seminary rules that I had broken. They seemed irrelevant. The rules of the road took all my attention.

I was a final-year theology student and it was taken for granted that I'd be ordained a sub-deacon the following June, a deacon in September and priest in December. Normally anyone for the chop was ditched well before this stage. In June, a list of those called to be sub-deacons was posted on the notice-board. The 'chosen ones' then did a fortnight's retreat before the local bishop ordained them sub-deacons. After that they went home wearing their white plastic collars for the first time in public. It was a big, joyful day in the seminary. The same happened in September when they were ordained deacons. And of, course, the really major celebration was in December for ordination to the priesthood.

That particular year the list of the 'chosen ones' was late in going up. As the day dragged on, I had a horrible premonition that my accumulated rule-breakages had finally caught up with me. This was confirmed when, after lunch, John Joe sent for me. He listed for me the rules I had broken, the worst being ignoring his notice that 'students were to leave the seminary on the means provided'. I compounded my mistake by quoting the relevant (perhaps, in the circumstances, irrelevant) canon Law code in Latin, which I was asked to translate. John Joe was not impressed. In fact he was irritated. I could see a 'thought bubble' inside his brain and it said "Smart-ass. I'll show you." My confidence was not bolstered by the fact that, after my three years in the seminary, he still kept calling me "Peter", which is not my name. He told me that he had concluded that I was not a fit person to be ordained and that I should leave next morning. The bursar would drop me off at the train station. I told him I was prepared to leave, as I did not have much choice if that was what he wanted. But, I insisted that he would have to officially expel me and give me the reasons in writing. This he refused to do.

"It would be better, Peter," he said, "if you left quietly of your own will. There is no guarantee, Peter, that you will ever be ordained here."

"I will finish my theology here and then I will seek ordination elsewhere," was my response.

"As you wish Peter! But remember what I have said!"

I did remember what he had said, but particularly that my name was not Peter. As I left his office, my legs were buckling under me. I did not see it then but, on reflection, it was obvious that anyone who broke the rules, silly as they were, as I had done, was not a fit subject to become a priest of the hierarchical church that John Joe Conlon represented. He should have had the courage of his conviction and kicked me out. But he didn't and I went on to finish my theology. Eventually the seminary concluded I'd done my penance satisfactorily and had me ordained, along with the rest of my class, in December 1964. In the meantime, I had to be broken on the wheel — tested in the furnace and humiliated as much as possible. During the next couple of months I discovered much about myself that was good and some things that were bad. Before then I had never doubted myself; but during those following months it took all my will power to keep positive. I often thought of old Pítirín and his 'Plan B' when one is facing the unpredictably high waves.

Each week, The *Sunday Times* was left in the student common-room, so we could keep up with what was happening in the world (though this too was considered "worldly-minded" and frowned upon). Rome saw its seminaries as fish-bowls full of tamed fish, fed centrally and all going round in similarly sized circles. We did not have access to radio or TV. For the first time in my life, I looked up the job adverts, giving a bow of recognition towards my Plan B. The only advertisement I responded to was for pilots in the Royal Air Force. The RAF sent me details and application forms which I duly completed and mailed. It was consoling to know that with my Double First at university, my good physical health and fitness, I'd have no problem qualifying. The thought of becoming an RAF pilot excited me for a while; but Plan B had to wait. In the meantime in the artificial atmosphere of the seminary, I was encouraged by the reaction of the other students, and indeed by the rest of the staff, who quietly gave me the thumbs up as they passed me on the stairs. I knew that they would have been forbidden to talk to me; but one elderly professor, Fr. Gerry McGahan, the professor of Moral Theology, felt confident enough to flout the injunction. He stopped me in the corridor.

"Pat," he said," persevere. It was one vote against the rest of us. But that man had the casting vote and final say."

Our history professor Fr. Andy O'Rourke, whom I liked, beckoned me into his room one day.

"Pat", he said "I don't want to be seen talking to you in the corridor. I don't agree with what has happened. I spoke up for you at the meeting."

"Why? What did you say?"

"I told them how I once gave your class an essay on The Inquisition and asked for 30 pages of an answer. You gave me 15. When I reprimanded you, you did not complain but the following week quietly handed me 30 pages, remarking that 15 of them were padding. It was just your way of doing things."

These and other similar incidents gave me the hope I needed in order to persevere.

During the remainder of that Summer Term in the seminary, as my classmates glided about the lawns saying their prayers and immersed in spiritual exercises in preparation for their ordination, I donned my manual labour clothes and worked on the seminary farm. I dug holes and trenches, mindless tasks, as I had done six years earlier in the noviciate. When ordination day arrived for my classmates, I was appointed altar-boy (there wasn't a lower position available) and carried the candles in the procession. Back in Aran during the summer, I told my parish priest (in case he was ever quizzed on how I was coping with my punishment) what had happened but nobody else – except one English friend who knew I had got flak for working on the buildings in London.

If anyone, usually visitors, asked me when I was to be ordained, I answered that I did not know. This puzzled them. I did not elaborate. I had resolved that I was not going to complain, or moan or show disappointment. I did not imitate the saints who, in such a predicament, might have suffered gladly and gained merit for it in heaven. I consciously practised stoicism, not necessarily a meritorious activity. I participated with apparent enthusiasm in all seminary activities – manual work, games, debates, and, of course, class activities. No more teaching myself to draw during Canon Law class, while hiding behind class-mate Tim Cullinane's broad back! I kept every rule in the book, no matter how silly, keeping my regrets and disappointments to myself. My English friend sent me a one-line quotation that helped me:

"Obstacles are but stepping stones. It depends how one approaches them."

When I returned to the seminary in September, after three months of relative idleness on Aran, I put on a brave face. I hid my real feelings, even from my closest friends. I made a point of not going near a spiritual director to seek any sort of counselling or consoling. I knew my own mind and needed no advice. I put my whole heart into playing football and hurling and I, who hitherto had whittled away my time on the playing-field hiding somewhere on the wings, now found myself playing centre-field with gusto. People told me they were amazed at how I improved my game, but none was more surprised than I was myself. For the first time in my life, I was indeed playing a game.

At that time the Vatican Council II was in session in Rome. Occasionally, if I met him in the corridor, the Director of Students would ask me how I was doing and I'd answer:

"Fine, Father." Period.

I deliberately avoided approaching him or anyone for advice. I kept my own counsel and anyone who wanted to know had to guess how I felt. I behaved as if my situation was normal, which it was far from being so. I had reconciled myself to the fact that I would not be ordained as a priest in this particular seminary. During my last year, John Joe Conlon's term as "Superior" expired. He was replaced by Fr. Mick Grace, a straight-talking missionary on leave, who was untainted by any Roman training. He called me to his office and told me he had inherited my problem and would allow my case to run its normal course. I understood what he meant. At least he addressed me by my correct name.

One day in early December 1964 as my classmates were finishing their final retreat prior to ordination to the priesthood, I was summoned to the Director's office.

"Have you been practising to say Mass?

"No Father. Should I have been?

"Well, the seminary council has decided that since you have handled your situation so well that you will be ordained with the rest of your class on December 14th (less than two weeks away). But there is a problem!

I was flabbergasted, but tried not to show it.

"You have missed the retreat and have not been practising how to say Mass. But we can surmount this. The main problem is that we cannot find a bishop to ordain you. They are all in Rome at the Council. "

Cautiously, I replied:

"As regards saying Mass Father, I am confident I can catch up." I felt it was not rocket science.

I was warned to keep all this new development quiet until the seminary had found a bishop and the ordination was definitely on. And so it happened that, on the following Monday, I was ordained sub-deacon in the seminary chapel by the bishop of the Solomon Islands, who was home early from the Council. On Tuesday, some other missionary bishop ordained me deacon. On Wednesday I joined the rest of my class to be ordained priest by our own local bishop. I just had enough time to invite my own family. who came to the ceremony in a minibus from Galway.

I arrived back in Aran on a trawler from Connemara. It was night-time and people had lit bonfires the length of the island. The whole thing had burst upon me so suddenly, and so unexpectedly, that I was lost for words. Nobody on Aran knew what a near-miss it all had been. A cavalcade of cars accompanied me from the trawler to my home in Bungabhla. What surprised me most was that this was organised by PJ Mullin. PJ had a fishing boat and used to fish over our side of the island when I was a youngster. He used to anchor in the shelter of the cliffs while waiting to draw his lobster pots. Old Pítirín and I often approached him when we ran out of bait and he was always generous. We'd talk about tides and the best place to fish and about sea currents. For some reason, perhaps by local reputation, I had always assumed him to be an avowed atheist and completely out of sympathy with my beliefs and what I stood for.

FINISHING UP IN THE SEMINARY

Back in the seminary the first two terms of 1965 passed quickly and pleasantly. Like all the newly ordained, I was now exempt from afternoon manual work and strolled about the grounds, dressed in my new cassock and reading my breviary. I still had my motorbike. But I made sure to keep it at home on Aran, far away from the seminary and the memories it evoked. At Easter I got my first lesson on how to drive a car. After the pub closed one night, a kind neighbour, Stiofán Twenty, allowed me to drive his car the six miles from Kilronan to Bungabhla. It was late and we had just enough time to go through all the gears except the reverse.

The following week I needed to go from Galway to Limerick, a distance of perhaps 50 miles. My sister Máire was with me. I showed my licence, hired a car and we threw our bags into the back. I started the engine. The car was facing the wall. Then I remembered I'd never learnt to reverse. We sat in the car for a good while discussing the situation before taking our bags and returning to the office.

"My sister does not like this car", I lied.

It took us a while before we found a car facing outwards. It was a dull and wintry day and, to complicate matters, it rained and nobody had shown me how to use the wipers. I drove slowly and pulled in a few times in order to practise how to reverse and to find out how lights, wipers and such minor things worked. By the time we reached Limerick, I had become reasonably well practised as a driver.--- though other road users might, with reason, have considered me a nuisance.

4

TO AFRICA

The modern missionary movement flourished in the waning days of Empire. It was based on the Gospel injunction:

Go therefore, make disciples of all nations; baptise them in the name of the Father and of the Son and of the Holy Spirit.

In other words: "Go out and convert the peoples of the world to Christianity."

This movement was referred to as Evangelisation and countless Christian missionaries dedicated their lives to promoting the idea. It was considered a very worthwhile cause. Over the years, Church structures were put in place to facilitate the endeavour and the scaffolding supporting these structures stayed in place long after the idea itself began to wane. With Vatican II new models of the Church gained prominence, the concept of evangelisation also changed, much to the annoyance of old-time missionaries who did not keep step with changes in theology. Those still viewed evangelisation as "the harvesting of souls for God" whereas the new thinking saw Evangelisation as a labour of love. This was based on what Christ referred to as "The Greatest Commandment": *Love God above all things and your neighbour as yourself.* Christianity is about love not power. "How many divisions has the Pope got?" enquired Stalin.

Baptism was no longer seen as necessary for salvation. All people of good-will could attain heaven, no matter what their religion. This made the old missionary imperative obsolete. We were forewarned in the seminary that since the missionary structure on the ground was still in the hands of the older missionaries who might view our beliefs with suspicion, we younger missionaries would need much patience and perseverance to survive. We were advised:

"Keep your mouths shut and eyes, ears and bowels open."

As a result of my own predicament with my motorbike etc., I had some practice at this in the seminary but it is not easy to overcome old habits and I fear I did not learn as much from my seminary experience as I should have done.

Shortly before setting out for Africa, I met this wonderful woman Imelda Smith who lived (still lives, Allah be praised) near our village of Bungabhla on Aran. Some years before I met her she had been working with the World Health Organisation in the Congo. One day, she wanted to go to confession and she found a young white man, probably a Belgian missionary and about my age. She did not speak any of his languages nor he hers. He handed her a list of possible sins in several languages. All she had to do was to tick off the ones she had committed. She told me she always regretted having to hand back the list because it contained many wonderful new sins she would not have imagined in a million years. I think she told me the story as a lesson of how ridiculous evangelization had become. I did not forget the story.

Since the 1880s or thereabouts when the Irish SMA missionaries first started going to West Africa, the Society's HQ in Cork held a special Farewell Mass to mark the annual departure of new missionaries. In the early days many missionaries never returned. The sicknesses they encountered were new to the white-man and deadly. In September 1965 it was the turn of my class - the Society's latest 1964 crop of young missionaries. There were twelve of us, all eager and excited. Afterwards we took the mail boat to Liverpool where we were kitted out with tropical gear before boarding the Elder Demster liner *Aureol* for the two week sea voyage to Lagos. We got our first taste of Africa when we stopped briefly at the port of Tema, Ghana: the intense muggy heat, the sounds at dusk, chattering cicadas, buzzing mosquitoes, strange animal noises - and the people in their multi-coloured garb, the babble and the bargaining. Then we sailed on to Lagos, our final destination. We were shepherded through the chaotic customs by a missionary based locally. It was a slow process that had to be constantly renegotiated. No one could avoid noticing the systemic corruption everywhere. It took most of the day to clear customs and bargain our way out of Lagos. We were heading for Ibadan, recognised to be the largest shanty-town in Africa. It was one hundred miles inland and it was here we were to spend the next six months immersing ourselves in the Yoruba language and culture. On the day we arrived, a simmering protest against corrupt politicians escalated into a fulltime uprising against the elected government and led to the assassination of Akintola, the premier of Yoruba-land and later the assassination of Tafawa Balewa, the Federal Prime Minister of Nigeria itself. Ibadan was in flames as we approached it and along the way, locals, carrying sticks and pangas, reported all sort of rumours, until eventually our progress was brought to a halt on the outskirts by armed thugs shouting and waving guns. Houses were ablaze all along the route and there was sporadic gunfire everywhere. It was the first time I saw the ancient muzzle-loading *dane gun* that was, we were told, as dangerous to those behind it as to those in front. We had no choice but to sit by the roadside while our driver (another missionary) tried to reach our people in the city to let them know our predicament. Eventually a safe passage was negotiated. I don't know whether or not money passed hands but for us newcomers the situation was exciting. People were being killed and I knew from history and from my psychology lessons that mobs are unpredictable and that the situation could turn ugly for us too at any time. Eventually we reached our destination shortly after dawn and were pleased to see our house still intact. We could see other houses in the distance still burning. Our house was called Tyro, short for the Latin word *Tyrocinium* or novitiate. It was the headquarters of our missionary society in the south of Nigeria.

After a couple of days getting ourselves acclimatised, we started our immersion Yoruba language course. There were several strands to the training, only one of which was language.

As the only house belonging to the Society in the south of the country, the Tyro was the focus of all members travelling to Lagos or to the administrative centre of Ibadan. Therefore we had a constant stream of interesting guests. Some we knew by reputation but had never met. Now we learnt more about them and their thought patterns. Few had much time for us or for our new-fangled ideas and they resented our questioning their methods of evangelisation. One thing became clear very quickly: all these men, wonderful though they might have been as missionaries, had, we suspected, not read a theology book since they were in the seminary. They were all believers in the hierarchical church and they were all proud of the numbers they had baptised - the souls they had harvested for the great number-crunching mathematically-minded God in the sky. It hurt them that we were unimpressed and uninterested in following in their footsteps. Of course we never doubted their good faith, but I suspect that they had grave doubts about ours.

Missionaries are open to the charge of cultural imperialism and though the Africans themselves wanted and badly needed the benefits of Western medicine and clamoured for Western education, introducing such was not necessarily the function of evangelization. Given their own history of anti-colonialism, Irish missionaries in particular were touchy about any accusation of imperialism, religious or political, so it was not difficult to stir up feelings of hurt among our older confreres. Fr. Kevin Carroll had done much to revive interest in the dying art of Yoruba wood carving which hitherto had been very much associated with pagan worship and culture and it was no surprise to us younger missionaries to find Carroll and people like him under suspicion among the older generation of missionaries. After all didn't the old missionaries spend their lives trying to eradicate all traces of paganism? But what Carroll was doing fitted in perfectly with the new 'missiology' that favoured local languages over Latin in the liturgy and insisted we respected indigenous cultures and incorporate them into our religious structures and liturgies.

In the past, some missionaries acted as if Christianising a people meant replacing their pagan culture with the missionary's own. I felt very sensitive to this, knowing how on Aran our own Gaelic way of life and language had been supplanted, sometimes by our priests, in order to serve political expediency. To my generation the Church consisted of the sum of believers, not a token Rome-appointed list of office-holders. So, it was not difficult to stir up a vigorous debate around the table. Furthermore, the belief was then rampant that Africa never had any worth-while culture or civilization of its own. It would have come as a big surprise to earlier missionaries - and to the white man generally - to learn that over periods of history, parts of

Africa had highly developed civilizations, equal if not superior to our own.

Living in the Tyro was probably the most important part of our education and was an introduction not just to Nigeria but to the missionary culture of the era. Along with this experience, we had lectures from such acknowledged authorities on Yoruba culture and art as the already mentioned, Fr. Kevin Carroll, the author of several books on the subject. Later, I had the honour of Carroll's company for brief periods when he came to stay with me at Osi-Ilorin, the centre of Yoruba wood-carving. The Number-Cruncher School of Evangelism would have destroyed such carvings as smacking of paganism.

Just as important was the second strand in our training. Every weekend we worked with the local churches referred to as "missions". Each mission had numerous outstations which were in fact embryo parishes. These missions presented different and varied models of how the church in Africa worked. We could study their methodology and copy the best practices in our own missions later. There was Fr. Jim O'Connell in the Political Science Department at the University and Fr Jim Foley in the Science Dept. Between them they ran the University church. There was Fr. Tom Galvin, an old-style "fire and brimstone" preacher whose style was no longer in fashion. I accompanied Fr. Tom on many a week-end trip into the bush and I learnt what a good and dedicated person he was. The fact that he was not given a mission of his own indicated his status. There were Frs. Des Clifford, Frank O'Mahony and others who ran thriving self-supporting city parishes, where the members had full control. There was Fr. O'Donnell who liked to live "in the bush" opening new missions, building numerous churches and schools and clinics with money from overseas. Fr. John Travers was an architect who built innovative churches and schools.

The third strand in our training was the language. We rose at six and finished at dusk. For the week-end we had sermons to prepare, translated into Yoruba, taped and imitated as best we could. Each weekend we spent in the bush, often sleeping on camp beds in un-plastered mud-walled classrooms. The parishioners brought food. One watched out for snakes and scorpions and did one's best to minimise the mosquito bites. It was a great feeling after trying out your 'learnt-off-by-heart' sermon to have parishioners come up claiming to have understood what you said and praising your grasp of the language when you knew in your heart that your knowledge was minimal but, we hoped, improving each week. Unlike English, Yoruba is tonal and therefore very difficult. Then you drove home Sunday afternoon, looking forward to the familiar food in the Tyro and the comfortable bed.

The six months in the Tyro were very rewarding. Fr. Bart McCarthy, an intelligent and caring missionary kept up-to-date with missionary ideology and sympathised with both the old and the new. Fr. McCarthy who was in charge of the Tyro was adept at guiding discussions around to points of conflict – all for our benefit, I am sure. Because the Tyro belonged to the Society, most missionaries in the south of Nigeria stayed there on their way to and from the airport. It is now difficult to imagine what a monumental change Vatican II brought to the Catholic Church. Until then the Roman Curia, old men steeped in rigid tradition, ruled the church but at the start of the council, the assembled bishops rejected the Curia's suggestions for limited reform and drew up their own agenda. This surprised everyone, including the Pope. It was no wonder that older missionaries steeped in the reverence of Roman ways, were slow to reform. Bart McCarthy availed of the situation in the Tyro to introduce the new missionaries to the older ones and vice versa. Over supper he invariably started a discussion, often over something controversial. After a while we realised that he was just drawing us out and likewise the older missionaries. Once, Fr. Richard Tobin from Ilorin was staying at the Tyro. I should have been more circumspect about my statements. Whatever my contribution to the discussion, it must not have been to Fr. Tobin's liking. He cut in sharply with the remark:

"You are one of those youngsters who, as George Bernard Shaw said, 'knows the price of everything and the value of nothing'."

Because I was taken unawares by the reprimand and, somewhat stung by it, I thoughtlessly responded:

"With all due respect Father, the quote is from Oscar Wilde, not Shaw."

How was I to know that Tobin regarded himself as something of a literary buff! McCarthy had a field-day afterwards warning me that Tobin as my new boss in Ilorin would not forget. A pyrrhic victory one might call it and so it turned out to be.

At the end of the period in the Tyro we received our appointments. Mine was to the newly created Prefecture of Ilorin, a vast undeveloped area, almost the size of Ireland, in the centre of Nigeria. I was considered lucky. In missionary terminology, a Prefecture is the prelude to a diocese and the person in charge is called a Prefect Apostolic. Later on, a bishop is appointed. Ilorin was vast with only a dozen missionaries, almost all of them youngish and thought to be very enterprising and adventurous. The man in charge was Richard Tobin, already referred to, a somewhat pompous individual. He made no secret of his ambition to be a bishop but he overplayed his hand and alienated all the young missionaries. He was typical of the type Rome liked as a bishop – he believed in the hierarchical church, in conformity to rules and automatic obedience. He subscribed to the Number-Crunching Theory of Evangelisation. In a territory where mission stations were several hundred miles apart, it would have taken a more diplomatic man than Richard Tobin to impose his stamp on the young missionaries. For once, Rome listened to wiser counsel and passed him over to appoint William Mahony as the new Prefect Apostolic and later bishop of Ilorin. The missionaries did not conceal their delight.

I was appointed as assistant priest to the mission station in the small town of Osi-Ilorin, a backward place on the way to nowhere, which was what I wanted. We had ten outstations, some of which we could only reach on foot by wading through fast-flowing rivers. In most outstations we were building churches and schools and medical clinics, which were fast becoming the most visible signs of Christianity in an area. My boss was Fr. Gerry Murray, a few years older than myself and one of the most likeable of companions one could hope for. We were constantly short of money. Once returning home with a week's provisions, we had to sell a crate of coke at a petrol station to buy enough petrol to bring us home. What we lacked in money we made up for in enthusiasm. It is amazing how one can sublimate all one's needs if the cause is worthy enough. I knew Fr. Gerry from the seminary and we worked very well together. I spent a few of the most pleasant years of my life with Fr. Gerry at Osi. We were expected to live off the money the parishioners brought and it was not easy. The only thing I did not like about living in Osi was the food, which was usually goat meat and yam and the occasional bowl of rice. This was augmented with some green leaves, a local variant of nettles that, I am sure, was very healthy, if not appetizing – to my palate at any rate. Some previous missionary had planted a mango tree in the Mission compound and it was in full bloom laden with mangoes when I first arrived. I made the mistake of telling the cook that I liked his mango dish. As a result I got mangoes day in and day out. For years afterwards I couldn't bear the sight of mangoes. Indeed, the hardest thing I found with missionary life was the food, but that problem was peculiar to me and my tastes. Other missionaries seemed to have had no such difficulties.

As the resident *Fada*, people expected me to be on call all day and night to run mercy missions to hospital or console the dying. My first memorable task was of a man bitten by a snake. He was bitten above the ankle as he walked to his farm in the bush to get there before dawn and before the oppressive heat of the day slowed down all activity and made people want to seek the shade of a tree and lie down. In order to prevent the poison reaching his heart he had cut his leg arteries, but he was too late and when I reached him at his compound, he was as good as dead. The youngest of his four wives was a catechumen and she had sent for me. We buried him under the floor of their mud hut as was the custom. My next mercy errand was again in the small hours of the night to take a woman in labour to a government hospital about 80 miles distant. Osi had no hospital then and I had to speed over a corrugated laterite road, occasionally sliding off the track and braking hard. We did not make it to hospital before the pounding in the back of the truck warned me to pull in. Eventually the villagers who accompanied us, stretched the woman out on the hard margin and we all gathered around as they delivered a still-born baby. I found it doubly distressing because when dawn broke, I recognised the mother was someone I knew and liked.

In my early days in Osi I spent many of my supposedly obligatory *siestas* sitting in the workshop of Bandele, the famous Yoruba carver. He was a Catholic and I became quite friendly with himself and his wives. I got to know him first through Fr. Kevin Carroll while writing about Yoruba carvings. Bandele later presented me with a number of his carvings, which, if I could lay my hands on them, would now be quite valuable. I took them home to Aran and left them with my mother who used them as door-stops and gave them away to the first visitor that showed any interest. My mother who cared not a straw whether your pagan god had ten heads, or none, took immediate offence at the large bare breasts that Bandele bestowed on the women in his carvings. We now have in our possession only one carving.

At Osi, it was all work and no play, and never an interesting visitor, so it was a pleasant surprise when one afternoon I answered a knock on the door to a vision from the past. Automatically I exclaimed "Anita Murphy" and was surprised to find that she also recognised me. Though I had never before spoken to her I remembered her from my history class at University several years previously. As seminarians we were not supposed to notice such matters but one did. I also remembered her name from the roll call. I invited her in and over a cold drink I discovered that she had been stranded for two days in the bush when her transport from the airport broke down and her driver disappeared (to summon help, I presume). Over a cold beer (neither Gerry nor I drank alcohol at the time but we always kept a few beers in the fridge for occasions such as this) our visitor sheepishly admitted that she was one of those educated Catholics who, over the years the office-holders in the Church had alienated. She had decided that she would never have any further truck with the Church or its institutions but after a night in the African bush, the mosquitoes had weakened her resolve, and, come morning, she swallowed her pride and enquired of a passing motorist about the location of the nearest Catholic Mission. That's how she came upon us.

She had accepted a teaching post at Government Teachers' College, Kabba, about a day's journey from Osi. Gerry Murray and I were without transport at the time but if she could delay a couple of days, we offered to take her to Kabba when we were mobile again. We outlined the options and gave her a choice. We could have put her on a lorry to Kabba but instead we offered her a bed, and killed the fatted chicken. She must have concluded that though we were missionaries, we were sufficiently normal, so she accepted our offer. Having an articulate female like Anita among us was a bonus. In a couple of days when we got our transport back, I drove her to Kabba, entering the cost of transporting her in our ledger under the heading of "evangelization", which would have amused Anita and saved the bishop any scruples. Though I was not to know it at the time, I was to meet Anita at Teacher Training College seminars on several occasions in the next couple of years. Last time I met her, she stayed with me at

Bacita on her way to the airport to take up a new teaching post in Singapore.

TEACHER TRAINING COLLEGE – SUMMONED TO TEACH

I had got very friendly with the people of Osi and the surrounding towns and my grasp of Yoruba rapidly improved. I expected to be there for a long time. Therefore, it was a shock to drive into the mission station late one Friday evening to find an envelope with a piece of chalk in it and a note saying:

"Report Monday to the Teacher Training College in Ilorin to start teaching 'Agricultural Science' 'Teaching Methodology' and 'History'.

The chalk was Murray's sense of humour. He had predicted this would happen. Ilorin was 60 miles away, half the distance on red laterite (gravel) roads. There was no time for 'goodbyes', never mind reading up on the subjects I was to teach. There was nowhere to do the reading up anyway, so I hoped the Teacher Training College had a library. Nigeria was at last at war with itself and Ibo teachers had fled to the supposed safety of Biafra. I had no qualification in Agricultural Science, had never studied it, let alone taught it. So, for the first few weeks I burnt the midnight oil (literally) and managed to keep a lesson or two ahead of my students who were as old as myself and in their second and final year of Teacher Training. It was made no easier for me when we found that my predecessor had taught the wrong syllabus for the whole of the first year. In Africa one quickly develops a 'Can-Do' philosophy. I am proud to report that all my 30 students passed their final Grade Two Teachers' Examination. They said I was a good teacher. I certainly tried.

The two years I spent at Mount Carmel Teachers' College were full of adventure and discovery. I loved the teaching and I am convinced that I learnt as much if not more than my students. The massacres of Ibos that led up to the Biafra war caused more teachers to flee. It was a difficult time for everyone. Once I was awakened at 1 a.m. by Fr. Higgins, a staff member, knocking on my bedroom window:

"There's a rumour that it is planned to attack the Ibos in town tonight and that the College too may be attacked."

There was nothing we could do but wait. Higgins liked dramatic gestures and mystery. The attack on the college never materialised but some Ibos were killed in town.

Food at the College was better than at Osi and I was able to put on some of the weight I had lost. One day during the Dry Season, the students surrounded a patch of long grass and burnt it. As the rats escaped the heat, the students killed them with sticks and then went on to fry them and eat them. They told me that much of the meat in the market was roasted rats. That did not help my appetite when I returned to Osi for the weekends. Our cook bought our meat in the market and who was to say what type of meat it was? The students said it was rat.

DEATH ROW

The priests in the Training College, attended to the spiritual needs of those Catholics among the sixty or so prisoners on Death Row in the local prison. The prisoners were housed in concrete blocks, about a dozen to a cell – as many as the number of timber planks (10'x 1'x 1") that fitted on the mud cell floors allowed. The mahogany boards were the prisoners' beds, the only item other than their prison uniforms that each prisoner possessed. The boards were shiny from constant use and, I was told by one of the guards, were the main cause of disputes between prisoners. The number of Catholics attending Mass changed from week to week. Executions seemed to be dictated by the need to make room in the cells for newcomers. Nobody knew who was next for execution. Like the executions themselves, it was not a subject ever discussed. Only a few had their execution postponed beyond a week or two. The exception was Patrick, a former policeman and an Ibo. He was always waiting near the gate to greet me. He would take my Mass box, marshal the Catholics together and prepare the altar – a couple of sleeping boards stretched across two empty rubbish bins.

While Patrick was preparing the altar, I sat on a concrete block nearby and my small congregation queued up for confession. Patrick served the Mass and sometimes read one of the readings. He read and spoke English well and often responded to the prayers in Latin though I always said the Mass in Yoruba to make sure the illiterate guards did not suspect anything underhand was happening.

Like most of the others, Patrick told me his story. He never complained and thought his death sentence was just and proper. His colleagues told me that the reason why he was not already executed was that the prison authorities liked him and that, anyway, he was too valuable to the illiterate prison guards by helping them fill their tax forms and write their letters. I normally said Mass in the shade of a tree but when it rained Patrick negotiated with other prisoners for the use of one of the prison cells. This was easy if a majority in the cell was Christian but sometimes Muslim prisoners objected and on these occasions it took all Patrick's negotiating skills to arrange for the use of a prison cell.

Having listened to their stories, I felt as if I had got to know each prisoner. Once a person was sentenced, there were no visitors. It seemed families too cut off all communications. Prisoners did not talk about families. I felt sad for them and thought them very brave. Each Sunday, as I drove along the potholed road towards the prison, I could not help wondering how many of my new-found friends had been executed in the previous week. I always hoped Patrick would still be there. Executions happened without warning. If you weren't selected for the manacled "work party" that left the prison yard at dawn each day, there was a good chance that you were scheduled for execution that morning. Family was something one did not mention, nor was execution talked about. A guard told me that when execution time came, a prisoner was stripped to his loin-cloth, tied to a stake and unceremoniously shot. The work-party helped bury the body. In prison, Sunday was a day of rest for everyone, guards included. No executions, no work-party. Just Mass for the Catholics. I never met another Christian minister there, or for that matter, a Muslim. For me my visit to the prison was a humbling and sobering experience and it took me some time to shake the memory of it out of my head.

THE TOBIN EXPERIENCE

Just as I had come to grips with my teaching load, I was approached by Bishop Mahony. He told me he had made new appointments in the diocese and had assigned Fr. Tobin to Osi.

"The work is too much for him and I would like you to help him out on the weekends. You know the people there."

I was delighted. This meant that after class on Fridays, I drove all the way to Osi. Fortunately, I liked driving and the rougher the road the better. Some of my students were from Osi and I generally took one or two with me for company or even safety. Sometimes in the rainy season a bridge was down and on one occasion, driving back in the dark, a scream from the student sitting in the passenger seat saved me from going over a precipice. The bridge had been washed away overnight. It took a long wait and half a dozen men to pull the vehicle back on to the gravel road.

Working with Tobin was not easy. He had no sympathy with my eating habits or with my philosophy, not that we ever bothered debating it. Nor did we ever discuss Shaw or Wilde either. The period with Tobin is memorable for only one thing. When I was leaving to come to take up my appointment at Lafiagi, Tobin decided to throw a farewell party for me. It was mainly in order to make peace with the two Dutch nurses in charge of the hospital. Matters had become strained and Tobin wanted to patch things up before I left. They were the only two guests.

Tobin who professed to know everything about cooking (and everything else) bought a turkey and, over a couple of weeks, he had the cook Hegg fatten it. The cook was named after the peculiar way he pronounced the word "egg". The previous cook that Murray and I liked had been sacked by Tobin who insisted on putting his own stamp on everything. The day prior to the big day, Tobin sent me to Ado Ekitti to fetch a load of eroko timber to make benches for the church. I had strict orders not to return without Paxo which I understood to be some sort of stuffing for the turkey. I asked for Paxo in the shop, not realising that there was also Paxo for fish. I handed the lot over to Hegg. As the big day dawned I watched Hegg chase the turkey around the yard. Tobin had given the cook a glass of gin which he was supposed to feed to the turkey before the marathon in the yard commenced. From Hegg's gait, I suspected that there was more of the gin inside the cook than inside the turkey, but I kept my suspicion to myself. The dead turkey looked good inside the half drum on the fire in the yard. It even looked better as Hegg put it on the table for Tobin to carve. Tobin made a big ceremony of sharpening the knife before he sliced through the bird only to reveal the unfamiliar stuffing. It was brilliant red. Hegg ran on the double and fetched the package from the bin and it clearly said in large red letters: FOR FISH ONLY. I was never good at reading instructions. After that, nobody felt like eating.

I had failed my last missionary test in Osi. The goats nibbled at the market stalls and the kerosene lamps flickered dimly as I walked the two Dutch girls across the town to the Mission hospital but we noticed none of it because we laughed all the way.

In my last six months at Mount Carmel, I found myself Acting Principal, standing in for the Principal, Fr. Vincent Brennan who had a slipped disc. I still continued with my week-ends at Osi. Somehow with all the multi-tasking, I managed to mislay the key of the tabernacle in the Mt. Carmel church. This was a serious offence if one had been proved careless. Canon Law suggested excommunication. I did not worry because I knew I was not careless. I got a Christian blacksmith from the town of Oro to come and make a new key. It was fascinating to watch him work. Using the smoke from a candle, a file and a hacksaw, he spent a whole week on the operation. I did not report the matter to the bishop but it was obvious to anyone using the tabernacle that the new key was not the original.

5

BACITA: PARISH-WORK WITH A DIFFERENCE

When I was appointed to teach at Mt. Carmel Teachers' College, the bishop promised that, once the teaching crises eased, he would release me from school and post me out bush again. After two years or so, he appointed me to assist Fr. Beausang at Bacita Mission

Bacita was a small mosquito-infested village on the Niger flood plain before the Government established a sugar plantation there. After that it became a small shanty town flooded not just with water from the river Niger but with thousands of migrant workers from all over Nigeria. Originally the inhabitants were Nupe with some Yoruba traders. The nearest big town was Ilorin about 120 miles away. Catholic mission had built a church, a priest's house and a school in the village. Later on, the sugar company built a reservation for its senior management, mostly expat, three miles outside town – far enough away to escape the pollution of the shanty town.

There were many Catholics among the migrant workers but many also among the senior management living on the reservation, which I often visited. Courtesy of the Sugar Company, Bacita was the only bush station that had electricity and running water. The senior management at the reservation were very kind to the mission and to me personally.

HAVING A DOG'S LIFE IN BACITA

It happened during one of my occasional visits to the Government reservation at the Sugar Plantation. In Beausang's absence , I was the priest in charge of Bacita parish. Mrs Bawn, the petite wife of one of the Sugar Company executives, approached me with a smile.

"Our Chi-Chi likes you", she said.

Somewhat flattered, I hastened to acknowledge my gratitude. I was careful not to dwell for too long on the subject, since I gathered from her tone of voice that I must surely know Chi-Chi. In fact I did not know Chi-Chi. And was glad when my ignorance passed unnoticed, hoping that sooner or later the identity of my admirer would make itself known.

Later , in conversation, Mrs. Bawn mentioned that the family was going on overseas annual leave shortly. We discussed their itinerary and the places of interest best visited during that time of year. But Mrs. Bawn soon returned to the subject of Chi-Chi.

"I'd like you to look after him while we are on leave," she confided. "He needs good care and I feel I could entrust him to you."

Of course one cannot reject off hand such admiring confidence, no matter how ill-founded. One needs a good excuse and I could not think of one off hand.

So I promised to keep an eye on this Chi-Chi while she was on leave. I assured her that it was no bother at all: it would be a pleasure.

Afterwards, as I drove back to the mission station, I scratched my head and contemplated my impulsive undertaking. I was not so sure now that it would be no bother at all or that it would be any pleasure whatsoever.

Though I was based at the Mission house, the nature of my work left me seldom at home and I now realised how foolish it was of me to promise to look after anybody. What if this Chi-Chi was a bit of a rascal! I could not carry him about in the mission truck all day nor could I let him wander alone in the house. And if anything should happen to him – the Lord forbid – I'd be in trouble. Supervising one's own cook was one thing but taking care of somebody else's responsibility was different. I felt I had undertaken a job akin to minding mice at a cross-roads.

So, I decided that my best bet in the next few weeks was to lie low, - make myself scarce, play hard to get and stay out of Mrs. Bawn's sight. This required very little effort as I tend to be somewhat restless by nature and travelled a lot.

In the busy weeks that followed, I forgot Chi-Chi as I ploughed along through the tall grass that covers the African bush towards the end of the rainy season. My job was organising various tribal villages, building bridges and initiating community development projects. Each week I covered many miles of rough road and ate whatever my old man cook could find in the local markets – rice and onions and yams and beans and the various local leaves called "efo" that you could cook to resemble cabbage but in fact always to me tasted like the hot nettles my mother on Aran gave to our pig. The meat too was always leathery in spite of the battering it got from the cook. My hours of work were as irregular as my meals were unappetizing and unscheduled – or the menu indeed predictable.

Community developers like myself had to rely on the Catholic bishop and on various overseas donations for money. That necessitated strict book-keeping, an odious chore by any account, and an evening in his office trying to balance the books was not exactly what a missionary might have termed 'recreation'. It was a burdensome bore.

One such penitential evening, as I sat at my desk putting the finishing touches to a monthly account sheet, who should drive up to the house but Mrs. Bawn. Her pleasant appearance was a diversion from the conflicting mundane figures before me. A native-style handbag slung from her shoulder and from a leash in her hand swung a tiny dog viewing my newly-planted shrubs with the practised eye of an irrigation expert. There followed a competent-looking boy carrying a heavy basin on his head.

This beaming youth boldly marched into my house and 'without your leave sir' proceeded to deposit the contents of his basin in my refrigerator. I thought it a bit cheeky. I was about to say something when the thought of Chi-Chi bade me hold my peace.

Could this fellow be the Chi-Chi that liked me? I sincerely hoped not. And as I racked my brain for viable excuses to release me from my one-time hasty undertaking, Mrs. Bawn diligently searched her handbag and produced a substantial cheque. The sight of the cheque put a new construction on the whole Chi-Chi affair. Immediately I saw possibilities and thought of the yawning gaps in my monthly returns. I was just about to open my mouth – and most surely put my foot in it - when suddenly it hit me. Chi-Chi was the dog.

I was speechless. The changed situation took me completely off guard and the excuses for reneging on my original promise had to be thought out anew.

So this was the Chi-Chi that had taken a fancy to me! Nice of him indeed! Well, I decided to reserve my judgment about Chi-Chi for the present. In my hand was a £10 cheque and my refrigerator was full of good dog food to last at least a month.

To tell the truth, I'm not a good "dog man." Somehow I feel out of it in the presence of dogs. I love dogs (in the abstract) but dogs classify me as slightly snobbish. I can't small-talk to a dog, for instance. Most dogs ignore me as I ignore them – a sort of mutual arrangement arrived at long ago but that has suited both parties perfectly.

Mrs. Bawn gave a brief history of the dog. She recited a lengthy list of his habits, of his likes and of his dislikes. The latter, in spite of his brief life, seemed fairly well-developed. This dog, I discovered, had in a few years of existence, developed more bad habits than myself. And he was getting away with it – which was more than I always managed to do. Some of the habits, I judged, were downright silly if not absolutely outrageous in a dog of its size. But I kept my thoughts to myself as I fingered the glossy cheque in the palm of my hand.

I always sympathise with people who are finicky about food. I am finicky myself, though out of sheer necessity or common politeness, I often have to eat what I dislike. This dog had a special menu – more than I could afford for my very self. What's more, he seemed to be a trained gourmet, capable of passing unfavourable judgment on all sorts of food and turning up its doggy nose on many a dish I was often glad to have.

I could see from the start that life with Chi-Chi was not going to be easy. One of us was going to lead a dog's life.

Mrs Bawn went her way and here was I, the busy missionary, with a dog and a cheque and a fridge full of frozen meats bought in the fashionable supermarkets of Ibadan 200 miles away. I seldom saw such choice meats and I kind of envied the dog from the start. I handed the animal over to the old cook to care for it and in the confusion of balancing my accounts for the Bishop, I thought no more of the dog *palaver* for that day. I did, of course, enter the cheque into the accounts under the heading "donation" (omitting the "for dog" label). Nobody would believe me.

Come lunch the following day I thought I suspected an improvement in the quality of my meal. The cook explained that this was the food that "madam brought". I told him that this food was for the dog and not for me but the old man shook his head and muttered something like "fool dog" as he went out.

After the meal, I got anxious about the dog and my commitment to it. You could call it 'qualms of conscience'. I went in search of the dog. The cook swore by the Gods of his ancestors that he gave the dog my own food, *the chop the masta do chop every day*, but that the little dog refused it. This I took as a kind of slur on my accustomed way of eating if not on my habitual manner of living. It annoyed me.

Though at first I felt a slight guilt about eating the food meant for the dog, I gradually began to rationalise the whole man-dog situation. I ate the dog's food; the dog ate mine. What could be more comradely? A fair exchange was no robbery, or so I reasoned. It was a true spirit of share and share alike. And while I chewed the juicy meat, I philosophised in my own favour and concluded that a little dog does not know what is good for it.

Now, £10 was a month's wages for an instructor working in the bush and I spent a little less on my own personal food bought in the local village market. The £10 cheque for the dog and the cost of the frozen food added up to a sizeable sum of money. So I figured that it was in my financial interest that the dog and I should live peaceably together.

At first the dog refused to eat. I feared a hunger-strike. I brooded about this whole affair as I munched my defrosted meat at supper-time. I remembered my mother's saying to us as youngsters – that hunger was the sweetest of sauces – and I tried it on Chi-Chi. It worked marvellously.

As time passed Chi-Chi and I became very good friends. We didn't mix socially, of course, but we ate one another's food. The old cook claimed that Chi-Chi even got fat on my simple food while I did not add a single ounce to my weight. This made me feel that, perhaps the dog had got the better part of the bargain after all.

Chi-Chi slept on the mat in the cook's house and the cook kept me fully informed of his progress. The last time I saw the dog he looked fat and contented and while I gloomily eyed the gaps in my monthly account sheet, I also looked forward longingly to the grateful comments of Mrs. Bawn on her return from leave.

There was however, one point that worried me. You could call it a scruple. I feared the dog had got to like the humble market food. The old cook advised me to retrain the animal on frozen foods before Madam returned. This I was reluctant to do – not because I wanted all the processed food for myself – but I hated to have Chi-Chi leave Catholic Mission with a dog-size chip on its shoulder. It would have been cheating.

The northern part of Ilorin diocese consists of several hundred square miles, much of it uninhabited. In this whole area we had only one missionary, Fr. Paddy Beausang, a tireless worker who lived on next to nothing in the bush. To my great delight the bishop appointed me to work as Fr. Paddy's assistant. Beausang's main work was with the Nupe tribe, so, all my effort learning Yoruba seemed time wasted. I offered to start learning Nupe if the bishop guaranteed to leave me with the Nupe, but he could not promise that. I found later that most Nupe were bilingual, speaking both Nupe and Yoruba.

Beausang's mission was located in the old Bacita village. He had several bush outstations among the Nupe and a new mission among the Kamberi, at Ujiji, 250 miles further north. The Nupe were mainly Muslim and animist but the Kamberi were primitive and pagan. Both areas were administered by Muslim Emerites and any community that showed an interest in Christianity soon found their community tax increased and their local government services reduced or cancelled.

The Catholic Mission maintained a number of schools and medical clinics in the villages and advised the people on digging wells and on how to keep healthy by boiling and filtering their drinking water. By the time I was appointed to Bacita, Beausang was spending much of his time among the Kamberi in the far north leaving me to administer to the Nupe. When Beausang went on leave, I had both areas to look after. It kept me very busy but I enjoyed the novelty and the variety. I was constantly on the move.

In Bacita there was a large transient population working on the sugar plantation. A high proportion of these were Catholics, especially on the administrative side. My congregation was a mixture of different tribes and we had to have three interpreters on a Sunday, Tiv, Yoruba and Nupe. I had started a catechumen class and to my surprise it grew very large. They were all Tiv, mostly women, all very attractive and lively. They volunteered for all sorts of odd jobs, putting flowers on the altar, sweeping the church, tending the flower-beds – you name it. They sang as they worked. I was very pleased with them and said so from the altar. Afterwards one of the Yoruba elders came to me to complain. All these women, he said were *ko f'orun* or 'women who did not like the sun'. I looked up *ko fe orun* in my Yoruba dictionary and found it meant prostitutes. I argued against what the man said but he had plenty of witnesses.

"If *Fada* goes to the market at night, he will find these women working "five-shilling-five-shilling", which was the price of one trick. Prolonged contact cost more. "

I summoned Dennis, the Tiv interpreter, and he confirmed what the Yorubas had said. But I liked them and was very reluctant to turn them away. I understood what a hard life all of them led. Most of the women sent money home to feed their people and I knew for a fact that one of them had a brother in the seminary and I suspected she was paying for him or at least for his books – the very books that condemned her profession as immoral.

During my next class, I explained to the women what the Yoruba had said and that if they wanted to be baptised they'd have to promise to give up the "Five-shilling-five-shilling" job.

Msuu, their leader, a vivacious and likeable woman protested and, with some laughter from the others, jocosely remarked:

"Nobody offer me five-shilling unless *Fada* wants to."

The inference was that she charged much more – should I need to know.

Anyhow, we came to some sort of accommodation that pacified the Yoruba and left me with my jolly catechumens.

I had responsibility for the small Nupe mission stations in the bush and when Fr. Beausang went on leave, I looked after the new mission of Ujiji among the Kamberi several hundred miles to the north. I was constantly travelling in un-mapped territory and I seldom returned home without a patient for the clinic in the back of my car.

Each year the Society sent out more young missionaries from Ireland and they were all posted to the Ujiji area which was very gratifying for Beausang and me.

There were always messengers camped out at the Bacita mission waiting for *Fada* to return. Usually they had a message from their chief asking (begging) *Fada* to come to their village and build a school there or a church or clinic. Many village chiefs believed Catholic Mission brought progress to an area. It was my task to follow up on these matters. I loved doing this: I spent most of my days travelling and long periods stuck in sand or in rivers. It was all one great adventure. It did not entail any direct preaching or converting. We had some successes but often the desire for a school or clinic fizzled out when the Muslim Emir heard of it and as a result levied increased taxes.

There was an army training camp at Jebba on the Niger and the commanding officer was a Catholic who had just completed his training at Sandhurst, the well-known military academy in the UK. He was in need of intelligent conversation, as was I, and he often invited me into the mess for a cold beer and to hear my views on how outsiders like myself saw the Biafra war. Once he invited me to accompany them on an elephant hunt (using sub-machine guns.) Elephant was a rarity in this area and it pained me to think of them being killed. Out of curiosity, and perhaps boredom, I agreed to tag along. After lunch, we set off up river in two army speed- boats. We trekked for a couple of miles inland to where the elephants were last spotted. Happily they were gone. Even I could see that the soldiers could benefit from a few more lessons on how to use their weapons. One did not feel safe in their company. They seemed to have no plan.

The current in the river was very strong and the soldiers did not handle their boats well. In the middle of the river there was an outcrop of rock called Juju Island where pagans offered sacrifice to their gods. The soldiers feared the place but on our return we were almost shipwrecked on the island when the soldiers lost control of their boats. Our two boats separated, and we were sucked into different channels past the island. Suddenly we found ourselves in the midst of a family of hippos. The soldiers panicked and opened fire without much concern for ricocheting bullets, or the location of the other boat. Next day I heard that hungry villagers down river were able to put the meat of the dead hippos to good use. Which was but a small consolation. After that, I declined all invitations to hunt with the army, but never giving them the real reason. Shortly afterwards when visiting the newly-built Kainji Dam, several hours' drive north of Bacita, I was able to discuss my elephant hunt with a real elephant hunter, he warned me of the danger I had been in. He showed me a real elephant gun and compared the size of an elephant bullet with what the soldiers with their automatic machine guns were using.

"You count yourself lucky that the elephants were not there", he said, "You'd only have wounded the elephant and maddened it. A wounded elephant is dangerous," he warned. A maddened elephant can travel at 40 miles an hour in the bush and overtake any land-rover.

The same Kainji Dam was built by Italian workers from Fiat. When the dam was finished a cardinal Montini, later, if I recall correctly, to become pope, came out from Milan to officially bless the project. As Kainji was in Ilorin diocese, our bishop Mahony had to travel the several hundred miles from Ilorin to participate in the ceremony. I was summoned into Ilorin to stay in the bishop's house while he was away. Fr. Paddy Beausang was in charge and Fr. Éamon Kelly was his assistant. The house had three floors. Paddy Beausang slept on the upper floor, I slept on the middle and Éamon Kelly on the ground floor. At about four in the morning, a vehicle drove at speed into the compound with headlights full on and horn blaring. It braked in a cloud of dust at the front door. We were all a bit shaken. Only armed robbers acted like this, so we all jumped out of our beds, probably simultaneously. We were relieved to see that it was only the bishop's driver who had driven through the night from Kainji. He said he had to be back for the ceremonies later in the morning. He handed Éamon a note from the bishop. It was addressed to Beausang as the priest in charge. Written on it were three stark words:

"Send Pluvialium. Urgent."

We were all leaning over our respective verandas. Éamon shouted the message up to Paddy. Paddy shouted down to me:

"Patsy, what the hell is a Pluvialium?"

"I don't know but I'll look it up in the Latin dictionary". I went into my room and checked. I returned to the veranda and shouted up to Paddy:

"Plus, pluvis, Latin for 'rain'. It must be a sprinkler."

Paddy shouted down to Éamon:

"Éamon, give him a f.....ng sprinkler."

Éamon fetched one from the church and the driver drove at top speed back to Kainji, a couple of hundred miles away. Only when Bishop Mahony returned did we discover that a 'pluvialium' was not a sprinkler but what is known as a 'cope', a liturgical cape that dignitaries like bishops wear at liturgical ceremonies. In the bush it makes little difference.

The officer in charge at Jebba had me say Mass for the Catholic soldiers once a week before each batch set out for the front. He also requested that I give them basic English lessons. He had, he said, got tired of finding people lined up at road blocks all with their shoes off – which was not what he expected when soldiers ordered drivers to 'open their boots'. Also, he emphasised:

"Teach them the difference between the word *missionary* and *mercenary.*

The difference I discovered for myself shortly after coming to Bacita – almost to my cost. I had an American Peace Corp volunteer, Barbara Pascotto, come to visit me. I had worked with her on a University of Wisconsin sponsored Teacher Upgrade programme. Since there were few tourist sites in Bacita, I decided to visit Juju Rock and show her the gory evidence of the blood sacrifices made by the pagans. The manager of the sugar company lent me the company speed boat and Barbara and I set off on the five mile voyage. As we approached Juju Rock and were preparing to go under Jebba Bridge, all hell broke loose. The soldiers on the bridge opened fire on us with all their available weapons. It was a wonder we were not hit. I steered the boat across the fast current and into the tall rushes and waited to be arrested. Eventually the soldiers arrived and we were brought before my good friend, their commanding officer. He offered us a beer.

"I suspected it was you *Fada*", he said, with a smile. "The soldiers reported they had sunk some mercenaries. Your English lessons are not getting through."

My stay in Bacita did not last long before another teaching crisis beckoned. I was asked to go to a community college at Omu Aran, near Osi, my old stomping ground. Through mismanagement, the school had run out of cash and my brief was to sort out the finances. I also had to teach maths. By then the Biafra war was in full swing, the Biafrans having broken across the Niger at Asaba, some hundreds of miles down river from Jebba. Several thousand soldiers were massing in our area before going to the front.   There was friction between the young soldiers and my students, mainly over women. Much as I warned the students, there was not much I could do.

One night a group of drunken soldiers raided the student dormitories, capturing a number of students and bringing them the 60 miles to Ilorin as prisoners. It was my job to chase after them to see the military governor and get the students released. Luckily there were no fatalities, but some bruised egos and two students broke their legs when trying to make their escape. The military governor in Ilorin just laughed. He later became my good friend when I was principal of a Muslim Secondary School further north in the land of the Nupe. The soldiers were none too pleased when they discovered I managed to have the prisoners released from custody without even a good beating.

I was not popular in Omu Aran. I tried to avoid road blocks and driving after dark but sometimes I had no choice because Omu Aran was at a road junction between where I lived and the mission hospital at Osi, which is where I was driving one night when I was stopped at an army roadblock near the school. The officer in charge was drunk, staggering about and waving a calabash of palm wine in one hand and an automatic weapon in the other. When he saw me approaching, he staggered to the middle of the road and started shouting:

"Mercenary! Mercenary!"

Wildly waving his automatic, he ordered me out of the car and lined me up against the bonnet. Holding his automatic very close to my face, he was getting ever more agitated. When I heard the click of the safety catch being released, I knew I had reason to worry, but there was nothing much I could do but smile and keep still. The officer swayed unsteadily, spilling his palm wine, which did not improve his temper. I was at his mercy. Seeing what was happening, two of his more sober companions shouted at him to stop, that I was not a mercenary. When he paid no heed, they rushed him, snatched the gun from him and pinned his arms behind his back. Holding him tightly they shouted:

"Run *Fada*, go quickly. Our officer is drunk. We hold him!"

I jumped into the car and sped off expecting a bullet to whizz past at any time. I thought it wiser to stay at the mission in Osi that night and return early next morning, by which time the soldiers would have sobered up from their previous night's drinking and would not yet have started their next day's drinking. I was stopped at the checkpoint, now manned by the pair who effected my escape the previous night. They recognised me and pointing to their officer now sleeping peacefully under the mango tree, they explained:

"Ah, *Fada*, he was too drunk last night."

"But why did he want to kill me? I am your friend?" I pleaded.

"Because *Fada*, he was once expelled from a Catholic school and he gets angry about it when drunk."

"Are you Catholics?"

"Yes *Fada*."

After that, I gave the army check-points an even wider berth. In a couple of weeks these soldiers were all gone to the front to be replaced by a new batch of young soldiers. Few ever came back. I felt sorry for them. I remembered the old maxim:

Old men start wars and young men fight them.

It was very painful to see Nigeria destroying itself. The country had started with such promise. It felt like my work too might be a waste of time and effort.

Another night I was awakened from my sleep in the small hours by men banging on my door. This is always a bit frightening when drunken soldiers are on the prowl. But this was a mercy journey. Six men had carried a pregnant woman on a makeshift stretcher many miles across the thick forest that bordered Kwara State. She had been in labour for several days. As far as I could make out from their Yoruba, all the experts in their village had tried but the young woman seemed to be dying, if not already dead. They begged the *Fada* to take her to the Catholic mission hospital at Osi. It was not the first time I was called out on such a mercy mission. At least Osi was not too far off and much of the journey was on tarred roads. I arrived about two hours before dawn. I knew the doctor and also her husband as he was my deputy at the community school in Omu Aran. They were both from Kerala in India. I drove up to their house and knocked at their bedroom window. The doctor took one look at my patient and shook her head:

"I cannot do much for this woman," she said, "she will not live till dawn when my staff arrive for duty".

Dr. Idicula, whom I knew to be a very caring woman, took pity on the patient and her bearers. She turned to me:

"If you agree to be my assistant, I will try."

I never liked the sight of blood but what could I say? The doctor lit the gas lamp, laid out all the tools of her trade in a line on the operating table, looked at me and said:

"Let's say a prayer, Father. This one has not much chance of surviving".

She laid the patient on her back and with a long fearsome-looking needle, gave her a spinal injection which, from watching it, almost knocked me out as much as it did the patient. The patient's face still looked somewhat alert, so the doctor put a newspaper between her face and the now opened stomach. I handed the doctor the instruments as requested and made a heroic effort not to vomit. She cleaned out a lot of garbage, juju medicine that the local village witchdoctors had inserted. The child, of course was long dead and putrid, which did not help the state of my insides. When the job was done, everything sewed up and my assistance was no longer needed, I asked permission to go outside. Day was breaking as I threw up everything I had eaten for the previous couple of days. It was my first experience of a caesarean. I would not have made a good doctor. I later discovered, to my astonishment, that the patient did live and was soon able to walk the several miles home unaided.

Fast forward three decades; I am now teaching in Nairobi, Kenya. I hear the mother of one of my physics students speaking Yoruba in the school car park. The student's name is Idicula and it immediately brings back memories of Osi-Ilorin. After some further enquiries, I find the girl is the granddaughter of that same Indian, doctor. Furthermore, I had taught her father maths. Small world.

6

RESPITE FROM TEACHING

After completing my allotted period as Principal of the Community College at Omu-Aran, Bishop Mahony, true to his word, appointed me priest in charge of the parish Aye-Ekan. Parish work appealed to me. Also, freed from correcting student homework, it gave me some time to read and think. *Feasta*, a Gaelic language periodical, had asked me to write an article on mission life and, in the flickering light of my kerosene lamp, I wrote a piece which I entitled An *Dia An-ainid* (The Unknown God). In my isolated bush station, I went through a brief period of doubt about my faith and my work. I had difficulty with the food and had trouble finding a suitable cook.

I remember driving the sixty miles to the Mission at Ado where I had heard there was a cook-steward ready for promotion. The young man certainly wanted to become a fully-fledged Mission cook and swore he had all the necessary skills as outlined in his collection of references of which he was very proud but which to me seemed too numerous. I also suspected the Father in the mission of being too eager to be rid of his 'excellent' cook-steward. The fact that the candidate regarded my own mission station in Aye-Ekan as 'bush' compared to Ado did not impress me. We agreed a salary and having at first argued for a small advance, he sulked when it was refused. As we drove north, leaving the dense forests of Ondo behind us and moved into the shrub-land of Kwara State, I noticed my new cook was becoming ever more gloomy by the mile. I missed the laughter that is so native to the African. It was dark when we reached Aye-Ekan mission. He immediately set about inspecting his quarters which I took as a good omen. In the morning I gave him some money to visit the market in the local village. I never saw him again. This experience and other similar ones, produced in me a negative attitude towards cooks in general. As the Mission cook impacted very much on my missionary activity, I thought it only right to give the subject some serious thought .

In Africa, if one is to get any work done, it is necessary to have a cook who goes to the market, cooks your food and looks after the house. Catholic Mission was on a hill at the outskirts of Aye-Ekan village. Originally, before Catholic Mission arrived, the place was a sort of Gihenna where local people abandoned their dead and unwanted babies and where pagans offered sacrifice to their idols. Locals claimed the area was haunted and hoped the presence of the church might exorcise the place. Perhaps it wasn't surprising that none of my cooks stayed long. During my stay in Africa, (but not at Aye-Ekan) I had some brilliant cooks who could conjure a gourmet meal out of goat's tail and I remained friendly with some of them for years after I left Africa and these thoughts do them a grave injustice. I apologise to them.

THE PRIEST'S HOUSEKEEPER – AFRICAN STYLE

In Ireland, the priest's housekeeper has been the subject of many jokes and even a play called "Moll" by John B. Keane.

People often ask about the frustrations of living in Africa and they are surprised, even disappointed, when I don't mention malaria, or mosquitoes, poisonous snakes, wild animals, warring tribes or the politics of Banana Republics. These things, though exciting at first, eventually passed away and left the white man, depending (as always) on that most enigmatic of fraternities, the institution of white man's cook, known locally as *kuku*.

In Africa, the office of cook to a European household is held by a male and is accorded much respect in the community. He is an important 'somebody', a link between the white-man and the native, albeit a go-between more often resembling a gap than a bridge. The white-man is known to the cook as *masta* and between the master and the outside world, the cook is the one who interprets the local situation, translates languages and moods, drives away beggars and advises all and sundry.

The white man in Africa comes to rely on his cook though seldom to trust him. All local agitation, known as *palava* is referred to the cook and his decision is almost always final. Visitors are screened by him and those who would do business with the master bring their gift to the cook and get their briefings by his fireside. He is the authority on the *masta*'s moods, has studied his quirks in detail and knows when and where the master is best approached. The cook is the one who buys food at the market, declares scarcities and plenty in the land and as a consequence puts up prices when he is short of cash. He haggles vehemently whenever the *masta* is within ear-shot. He boasts of great bargains and always manages to make a little profit for himself. The *kuku*, having first cooked the books, then cooks the food.

In order to understand the system of cook, it is necessary to know the various stages through which one has to pass to join the fraternity of cooks. The first stage is that of "boy". Age does not enter into it. A 'boy' does all the menial jobs, gets blamed for anything that is dirty, broken or missing, though everybody knows he is not at fault. He has no rights, only liabilities. The 'boy' runs to the market to fetch forgotten messages, he plucks chickens, drives away goats and stray dogs from the compound and gets himself threatened with the sack on a daily basis. Sometimes he cannot stand it any longer and runs away. Then he is called a thief. But those who stick it out and do not run away, live on to become "stewards"

Now, a steward is a 'boy' who for some unknown reason, had got too smart to remain a boy but not smart enough to be a cook. Nature had let him grow up and his faults had grown up with him. Whatever devious skills he might have acquired, he certainly needs them all if he is to survive for long as steward, for he has two masters, neither of whom he can serve satisfactorily. He is like the proverbial scapegoat that carried the sins of the Fathers into the wilderness and into oblivion. It is a smart steward who can tread for long the crooked pathway that lies between kuku and masta. If he is too efficient, he displeases the cook who suspects him of trying to supplant him and if he is a blunderer, the *masta* blames him for the shortcomings of the whole household. The steward is one too old to be innocent, too young to be wicked and too poor to be honest.

If a smart steward is fortunate, he in time becomes a cook to some newly arrived junior Peace Corps volunteer living cheaply in the bush. More likely than not, he becomes a cook-steward, a somebody who is nothing in particular and always mediocre.

A cook-steward is a steward who got the cook sacked for something for which they were both guilty – usually stealing. Cook-stewards are dangerous forms of life. They enjoy the title of being cooks without the salary or respectability that accompanies that office. They do the work of a steward with the added opportunities of a cook and hence they never do anything well, even cheating and they often come to a bad end like finishing their days in gaol.

A white-man in Africa has to have a cook. It is as essential as breathing. The *masta* who has no cook finds that everybody cheats him, so it is wiser and probably cheaper for him to hire a cook who cheats him officially.

The official office of cook can be filled only after careful scrutiny and research. The vacant post is advertised by word of mouth. This is simple. The *masta* confides his plight to his neighbour's cook and then all hell breaks loose. Usually, the same neighbour's cook has umpteen brothers who are excellent cooks. A wise *masta* never touches any of them. It would have been like building a hornet's nest in one's own kitchen.

Once word of the vacancy is out, streams of applicants beat a path to the *masta*'s door. He can expect a colourful procession of rogues disturbing his peace at all times of day and night until the vacant office is finally filled and the new cook officially installed.

When selecting a cook, the first thing a *masta* must do is to carefully study the applicant's books. These were the treasured references from many former employers (and none) extolling the cook's skills and recommending his services to everybody except themselves. Experienced reference readers are quick to read between the lines. It is where the most useful information is found. They note that what is left unsaid is more important than what is said and that unmentioned qualities are qualities not possessed.

In any case the experienced *masta* does not take the reference too seriously. Most likely the reference proffered doesn't belong to the bearer any more than the name he gave is his proper name. Most likely, the reference probably belonged to a distant 'brother' who has already secured a job with some inexperienced white-man up country.

The ideal cook is something like the Biblical Melkisedech of old, a stranger having neither father or mother. He should have no needy relatives near at hand, no school-going sons in want of school fees, no marriageable daughters needing dowries and no local friends to beg on his behalf when he is eventually let go.

It is also good to recognise the signs that tell the impending end of a cook's term of office. It is generally accepted that only a real dud of a cook betrays any signs of leaving before he finally disappears. A smart cook might try to get hold of his references (now locked securely in the *masta*'s safe) well in advance. He might express fears for their safety in the *masta*'s keeping or he might want to have them framed for posterity. If this approach fails, he might take the bull by the horns and pick a row with the *masta*, usually about market money. Failing this, he could get sudden bouts of sickness at the most inopportune times, especially if there are hungry guests awaiting their supper. A messenger might bring a message that the cook's father has died of a sudden illness and that the cook's presence is required immediately in his home town in far-away-God-knows-where. An experienced master, however would have remembered that the same father had already died two years previously when the cook first came to the house and wanted a month's advance on salary.

Generally cantankerous cooks have, eventually, to be sacked. The format is simple. The *masta* calls the steward and declares him to be temporarily in charge. He gives the cook a month's salary in lieu of notice and grants him an hour to clear out of the compound. The steward, not to be outdone, insists on an inventory of all the *masta*'s belongings. This list is finally signed by the cook before his departure and is used by the steward to clear himself when the *masta* later notices all the things missing in the house.

Occasionally a cook leaves peaceably and honourably. If a *masta* suspects a cook of having such a rare temptation, it is better to nip it in the bud and provide against it by picking a good row.

No matter how the masta and cook part company, there is always the inevitable 'book' to be drawn up – the lengthy reference that adds to the cook's prized collection of personal manuscripts. The graceful master is silent about any hidden qualities that might have caused the cook's downfall but he sadly laments the departure of a noble soul, lists the extent of his term of office, underlines his salient virtues by name, refers to his obvious and very latent potentialities, gives suggestions as to some hidden talents the bearer may have and he does not forget, of course, to end up by declaring that this was indeed a great cook, always eager to serve and definitely fired with enthusiasm.

While working in the parish of Aye-Ekan, one of my outstations was a village called Are. I had got to know the people of Are while I was working at Osi with Gerry Murray. They were a stubborn and poverty-stricken lot. In the 1920s, it seems that, under the influence of a charismatic French old-style missionary called Pére Simon, the village converted to Catholicism en masse. They were Simon's followers only and any religious practices not introduced by him were anathema to them. They even objected to the

**The Aye Ekan Mission
10/05/1969**

introduction of Yoruba instead of Latin in the Mass even though the whole population of the village did not have a single word of Latin between them.

Because the village was so inaccessible, progress had passed it by. The location was very picturesque – mud huts scattered here and there on a hillside interspersed with huge boulders of rock. Unusually there was not a single tin-roofed hut and the people worshipped in a mud-walled church with a straw roof reaching down to the ground. I loved staying in this village but it was a chore to reach it. The congregation was very proud of its Catholic faith but very much resented the fact that Catholic Mission had chosen Osi and not Are as the site for a new parish. It took me six hours to reach Are from Omu Aran but in the dry season it could be reached from Osi in an hour. I thought that it would be easy to persuade the people of Are and their neighbours to clear a path for a road and build a small bridge to connect the two villages. The ministry of Community Development in Ilorin offered me a ton of cement if I could persuade them all to cooperate. I camped in Are several nights and with the elders in tow visited several of their neighbours. Finally I thought we had an agreement on the route. It was decided I would return in a month's time with the cement. In the meantime, the villages were to mobilise their people to clear the path for a road. I concluded that there was only one spot where one could build a bridge with just a ton of cement. I understood that all the villagers were agreed about that spot. I returned after a month, intending to send on the cement later. With great human effort, the villagers had cleared wide paths from their villages to the river. But there was half a mile of a gap between where the two paths met the river. It taught me a valuable lesson – not to be so sure in future that others see things as I see them.

However, I was not very long in Aye-Ekan when Bishop Mahony came to visit me. I knew from his manner that he had something important to discuss. He felt badly, he said, about moving me back and forth like a yoyo. We discussed our newly established missions among the Nupe and he described how many of our Catholic schools that I had helped to set up, had been taxed out of existence and closed down by the Muslim Emirate of Lafiagi. He had a plan to deal with this and I was part of the plan. For a start this approach massaged my ego and aroused my curiosity enormously.

7
A CASTAWAY AMONG THE NUPE PEOPLE

For almost a century, Muslims in Nigeria had shunned education, associating it with Christianity but the Biafra civil war and the advent of democracy had shown them that if they wanted to wield power, they needed an educated Muslim population. At Independence, the Nigerian army was largely under the command of Christian officers, mainly of the Ibo tribe from the south-eastern part of the country. Shortly after my arrival in the country, the Muslims had the Ibo army officers assassinated and this was the signal for pogroms against the Ibos that started throughout the Muslim north of the country. The Ibo heart-land retaliated by declaring itself the independent state of Biafra. This was the start of the Biafra war. After they took control, the Muslims realised that Nigeria lacked a literate Muslim populace. The new Muslim army top brass now urged the Emirs to accelerate the establishment of secondary schools in Muslim areas, just as the Christians had done in their areas. Up till then the Emirs had resisted the spread of education in their jurisdictions but they were particularly averse to the education of women which they considered un-Islamic.

The journey from Ilorin to Omu Aran is long and dusty and it was rare to have an un-announced visit from one's bishop. Bishop Mahony's unannounced arrival took me by surprise. Without any preamble, he came to the point immediately:

"Last week, the Emir of Lafiagi came to see me. He wants Catholic Mission to help him set up a co-educational secondary school in Lafiagi. He was accompanied by his chiefs and by the military commander at Jebba who said he knew you."

The bishop saw an opportunity for reopening those Catholic primary schools that the Emir had so recently forced him to close. The bishop was already helping the Muslim Emir of Borgu to set up a Muslim co-educational secondary school at Kainji. He now wanted me to do the same for the Emir of Lafiagi. The Army commander at Jebba had fore-warned me that Emir Umaru had been planning to approach Bishop Mahony. It was a fantastic challenge but I knew the Lafiagi area and I saw that working with the people there would not be an easy assignment. The Nupe were more advanced and cunning than the more primitive inhabitants of Borgu. The Yoruba regarded them as argumentative and un-trustworthy, though, to be fair, the Nupe did not hold the Yoruba in high esteem either. The bishop, said that he'd let me think about his suggestion and leave it to me to volunteer. From a missionary's point of view, there were benefits. Financially it would cost Catholic Mission nothing. The Muslim community would fund the project, while the government would pay the salaries. I, as Principal, would run the school. The government supported the scheme. I felt honoured that Mahony thought it appropriate to consult me. This is what we liked about Mahony. He treated all his missionaries as if they were adults each with an equal share in our project. He was not too self-important to consult us and make us feel our views mattered and had substance.

Few people of any sense would want to work or live among the notoriously quarrelsome Nupe or in Lafiagi, an inhospitable, mosquito-infested backward place with neither tarred roads, running water or electricity. I asked Bishop Mahony to let me have a few weeks to ponder the situation, though, once I completed my few pet projects at Omu-Aran, I did not view the hardship as an objection.

After I agreed to take on the challenge, I had six months to prepare. My first step was to visit Lafiagi which, on a good day, was about three hours' drive from Omu-Aran, my base at the time. I arrived at the Emir's Palace, sweaty and dusty. A little man whom I later got to know as Baba Doko, led me in and I was offered a chair (after some search because people normally sat on the floor) given a cold drink while awaiting the Emir to appear. He did not keep me waiting long. Soon his various chiefs started to filter into the room and he introduced them all. I sat on a chair with the Emir on another chair, the rest sat on the floor. We discussed the project. The first practical step was to find me suitable accommodation in the town. In the meantime, we discussed briefly the other steps that needed to be taken in order to establish the school. I needed a clear understanding of how they planned to finance the project. They had already given some thought to this. They planned to impose a per capita tax on the adult male population of the Emirate; then open a bank account for my sole use. Catholic Mission had plenty of approved building plans for schools and we would offer them a selection. The Emir would award the building contracts to reputable builders and I would supervise the work and open the new Muslim co-ed Secondary School the following September. All planning permissions and authorisations were already in hand.

Once I agreed to accept the post of Principal, I'd be in full charge. It would be my task then to make things happen. I felt confident I could do this. With the Emir interpreting, I explained my own plans and reservations to the assembled group. In order to select the initial student intake, I would need to set examinations for all primary schools in the Emirate, supervise the exams, correct the papers and select an intake of sixty pupils to start school in September. It was fairly ambitions, knowing how Africa tends to procrastinate. This meant I had to visit a hundred plus primary schools scattered throughout the bush, bring my camp bed and mosquito net and stay overnight in isolated villages. The local chiefs would put me up and feed me. The Emir would give me transport and petrol, the bishop, his blessing. I would visit Lafiagi periodically to keep an eye on how the construction was progressing and I would issue a report to the school's Board of Governors copied to the secretary at the Ministry of Education. Once I had agreed to accept the job, it was then suggested that we all go and look for a house for me to live in. The chiefs had their horses. The Emir enquired if I could ride because, he warned, some of the roads in the town were impassable. The extra horse tethered to the doorpost was for my use. Baba Doko ran alongside me holding the reins. I found out later why they did not trust me to ride on my own yet. Nupe horses were all trained to dance to the beat of drums.

And that was why, on an almost unbearably hot day, I found myself accompanying Emir Omaru and his retinue of chiefs, all of us riding horses and touring the dusty Nupe town of Lafiagi. It was humid and my sweat-soaked white missionary garb felt anything but comfortable. Surrounded by a cloud of flies, and followed by a pied-piper-like procession of children, we visited all sections of the town looking for a suitable residence for the white-man. There was none.

Lafiagi, 1970.

The town was really an overgrown shanty village with neither running water, electricity or a sewage system. There were wells, of course, and a polluted river nearby. Not one house in the town had even the customary "long drop" that served as primitive loo. Simple hygiene demanded this as a minimum. Only the guest-house in the Emir's Palace had a "long drop". Eventually, it became clear that the only habitable place for me was this guest-house. I selected it as much out of curiosity as because it had a 'long drop'. Later, I was told that until my arrival, Christians were barred from entering the Emir's Palace. This strengthened my resolve to live there. Also, the idea of a celibate priest living in a harem fascinated me. The Emir had ten official wives and numerous temporary ones. My bishop, when I later told him, had not anticipated this situation, but he made no comment and was probably as amused as I was. The Emir said nothing either, though I could see it was not his favourite solution.

While preparing to open Lafiagi Secondary School, I lived at the Mission in Omu-Aran, which was in Yoruba-land. There was animosity between the Yoruba and the Nupe. Lafiagi was not connected to the national telephone grid or to any national grid. The postal service was unreliable. It took persistent badgering to make any progress. Everything seemed to work in fits and stops. I had to postpone the official opening of the school for a couple of months when the contractors had fallen behind with the work blaming the fasting at Ramadan. Such delays were built into our expectations. I did not even make the opening day of my own school because of a bridge collapse en route, which I had not built into my expectations. Nor had I built into my expectations that in my absence, the Government Education Officer (EO) would take charge and dismiss a third of my carefully selected intake. At first it puzzled me why some of my brighter students, who seemed so keen when interviewed, had not turned up. The EO explained that they just did not turn up on the day. It took me almost three months to discover the real reason – that the EO had sent them back to their villages because they did not bring him a bribe. He made up the numbers with bribe-paying duds of his own. When the villages later sent a delegation to complain, I took back the rejected students with the result that the school was over-subscribed. It took months to sort out the problems with the Ministry of Education. The episode showed me the extent of the intrigue and corruption I was up against.

The school was amply funded by the tax levy and though much of the money mysteriously evaporated in the process of collecting it, my bank balance was always healthy. The governors awarded the building contracts, often to incompetent friends of the Emir and I paid the bills and was expected to supervise and sign off on the completed work. Though, I was supposed to vet all contractors, I soon had the sense to give up on this idea. If a contractor did not deliver, I had a veto on him being awarded future contracts but I ignored this also. Malam Umaru, the nephew of the Emir, was an important member of the Board of Governors (to which I was secretary). He was also the Education Officer (EO) for the Local Education authority and as such wielded considerable power. He had four wives, the senior one, a daughter of one Malam Shafiyi Audu, referred to by all as Alhaji after he made the pilgrimage to Mecca. Alhaji was a building contractor of sorts though he had never mastered the skill of using the level or hanging doors perpendicularly. My floors always sloped. One learnt to make a stand only on issues of principle and hoped all the buildings would not fall down simultaneously. If you wanted to maintain your sanity, you had to overlook a lot and fight only those battles you were sure to win. You learnt not to take things personally.

In spite of my objections, Alhaji, a most incompetent builder, went on to receive several building contracts in the school. His son-in-law the EO also had airs and liked to meddle in school affairs, throwing his weight around whenever he thought he could get away with it. I had a very good Nupe girl whom I took some trouble to train as typist and secretary but the EO made her pregnant and I had to let her go.

After the departure of my first Nupe secretary, there was a hiatus before I could find and train a new one. Eventually I found a young man. Until he was trained, I had to do my own typing. This is an extract from my early bit of office work. It is a letter of complaint to the Board of Governors and was addressed to the Chairman, i.e. The Emir, and copied to the secretary at the Ministry of Education, Ilorin:

Dear Sirs,

I am disappointed at the progress of our building programme. I have already reported the inferior work done by Alhaji Shafiyi Audu on the first school contract and in spite of my objections, he has been awarded more contracts. As the person charged with supervising the work, I want to put the following complaints on the record:

Alhaji Shafiyi has been awarded the contract for the new double staff house in spite of the mess he made of the Principal's House, the completion of which was 7 months overdue. It had to be reroofed within the year at what will cost the community £1000.00 extra

We are still awaiting the completion of the three classroom block already in its seventh month overdue. Incomplete though it is, we must move our library, clerk, etc. into it. The rains are destroying our equipment in the temporary shed built last December. I hope you realise the inconvenience this moving and shuffling about causes staff and students.

What is completed of the three classroom block is of very inferior quality. I want to register the following complaints:

The walls, including the gable-end are cracked from top to bottom, both inside and outside.

A few window-sills have fallen off.

The Louver window frames are inserted upside-down and inside-out, which means that in the coming rainy season, all the rain falling on them will automatically come inside the classroom.

Some ceilings have already fallen down and I can see woodworm in the timber. This will soon move to the rest of the roof and, like the Principal's house, you will need to re-roof the whole building shortly.

The contractor has departed from plan and used timber doors instead of the double iron doors in the plan. He used the wrong hinges with the result that some doors are already falling off.

Recently when the Military Governor of Kwara State, Major General David Bamiboye, visited the school, he commented on the poor quality of the work. I have his letter in the school file and I'll bring it to the next Board of Governors' meeting.

When I was away on leave the contract for our science block was also given to Alhaji. There too he has hung all the louver windows the wrong way with the result that when it rains all the water will go into the class-room.

Sincerely,

P O'Toole

On purpose, when the military Governor came to inspect the school, I left the water in the class-rooms for him to see. Alhaji Shafiyi was furious with me and after that, he and his son-in-law the EO became my permanent enemies in the community. I was fortunate that neither were popular with the townsfolk or with the students.

I needed staff for the new intake of students in September but, come summer, Alhaji had not yet completed the staff houses – as a way of punishing me, perhaps. I informed the Board and the students that some subjects had to be dropped because without guaranteed accommodation, I could not hire teachers. The students made placards and picketed Alhaji's office in town – having first consulted with me to make sure I would not expel any of them. The EO was furious and rushed into my compound threatening fire and brimstone and asking for the student leaders to be expelled. When I pointed out that it was his father-in-law that was at fault and that the Government had already been in touch with me about it, he backed off. Alhaji made a big show of finishing the staff-houses within a matter of weeks.

When I first took up my post as Principal of the school, I assumed I was offering a welcome service by educating the girls of the locality - that the villagers were eager to educate their women-folk. I was wrong. All these villagers were poor. Some of my brightest candidates had from birth been promised as second or third wives to older men in their communities. These old men had already paid dowries to the girls' parents, who would, by now, have spent the money and could not refund it. Old men did not want to marry girls who had attended school. Unknown to me at the time, there was much pressure on village chiefs to prevent my recruiting girls for Lafiagi Secondary School from the various communities. I was innocently unaware of this even though I knew that the Emir had raised taxes on villages that refused to send any girl I had selected.

Eventually when the school was up and running, one of the first assignments I gave to new students was to write an essay entitled something like: "The Festival I like Best in My Area". In this way we (or rather Catholic Mission) gathered as much information as possible about the catchment area of the school. In some villages in this area we already had clinics or schools or had plans for eventually opening a church. The essays provided me with much useful information and some surprises. For example, one boy, Yakubu, from the village of Patiko, where Catholic Mission already had a thriving Catholic community wrote:

"*Fada* is a white devil."

Being called a devil worried me until I had the opportunity to interrogate Yakubu. I asked him to explain what he meant and this is how he put it it:

"*Fada* came to our village several times. The chief did not want *Fada* to select any of our village girls for Lafiagi Secondary School. Each time the elders put *Fada* up in a hut that was known to be haunted by evil spirits. They wanted to kill *Fada*. They sacrificed chicken and made juju against him. But each time *Fada* got up in the morning more healthy than in the previous day."

"Why would that make me a white devil?" I asked.

"Because *Fada* has 'white power' which is different from 'black power' which is bad. *Fada* proved that powerful Juju cannot harm him. The elders will not try to harm *Fada* any more. His 'Good Spirit' is too powerful."

This made me feel better, even if I was somewhat sceptical of the explanation behind it. The important thing was that the parents of my students believed in it and in Africa word gets around quickly, especially if it is about magic powers.

Because the people of Lafiagi were so proud of their school, it made it easier for me to run it smoothly. An essential part of each pupil's school kit was the bucket, cutlass and a hoe. Every afternoon there were a couple of hours' meaningful manual work and gradually we had a gravel avenue into the school. We levelled playing fields and made a small vegetable plot to enable students to grow a healthy-looking crop of yams. It is amazing what a couple of hundred students with hoes can achieve. At first water was a major problem until I organised the digging of a deep well. Every morning each student fetched a bucket of water from the well and that did them for the day both for drinking and for washing. Things went well for a while and then some careless student forgot to put the lid back on the well and a cow fell in. As I was away in Ilorin at the time the Emir had to mobilise the townspeople in order to help pull the dead cow out. The water was, of course polluted and undrinkable for several days. This convinced me to set about digging an underground storage tank to collect water from my tin roof. The underground tank had a capacity of several thousand gallons of clean safe water. A day or two of rain filled it.

I used my rudimentary knowledge of plumbing to provide gravity-fed hot and cold water for my own house. In town I bought an empty 40-gallon petrol drum, attached it to my gable-end and, almost immediately, the hot sun provided instant hot water throughout the house. When the military governor came to open my science block, he thought it such a good idea that he sent his plumber to study my contraption and copy the system for the new house he was building for himself in Omu-Aran. I warned him to make sure the drum had a safety valve for the steam to escape. It was not rocket science but it suited my immediate needs in Lafiagi. Alhaji, with whom I had a running battle while I was in Lafiagi, also copied my system, but he needed no advice, from the likes of me anyway. Alhaji was one of nature's crooks. He touched nothing that he did not corrupt. When a student told me that Alhaji was copying my hot water system in the house he was building in town for his latest wife, I smiled and said nothing. I was not surprised when I heard later that the drum exploded and blew off half his gable-end. He told people I had put a spell on him. I didn't have to.

Though it was difficult to find non-Nupe willing to live in Lafiagi, I had managed to recruit some excellent teachers. During the first year I had taught physics, maths, technical drawing and Islamic Studies, which included the Qur'an. This latter was only until I found a Muslim qualified to teach the subject in English to West African School Certificate level. I felt it was my duty to give the teaching of Muslim Religion at the school a high profile. I had no problem teaching Muslim Religion but, as a non-Muslim I could not join the students in prayer and for that, I appointed what they officially referred to as an 'Arabist' to lead the Muslim students in prayer. This posed a recurring problem because most preachers, especially during Ramadan, tended towards preaching a mild form of jihad, claiming that a good Muslim should refuse to associate with Christians, pagans or Jews. There was nothing in the texts of the Qur'an in my possession that justified this interpretation, so I had to find a preacher who agreed with my interpretation. I did not want any conflict in school between the token few Christian students and the main body of Muslim students. Luckily the Emir accepted my view of the Qur'an or I would not have stayed.

When starting off anything new, it would be foolish not to expect some problems. At Lafiagi, I wanted flowers and shrubs in what was an otherwise bleak and colourless landscape, but the Emir's goats kept nibbling everything we planted. One day one of the Emir's goats fell into our 'long drop' and the Emir sent me a hefty bill for the goat. I then borrowed a big dog from Fr. Beausang in Bacita. The dog chased all the goats off the school compound. Muslims do not like dogs because they are deemed 'unclean'. In chasing the goats the dog ran one of them in through the glass door of my house and out the other. I sent the Emir a bill for the broken glass which, oddly enough, exactly matched the bill for the goat that fell into the 'long drop'. Eventually we came to an arrangement: I'd return the dog to Beausang and the Emir's goat herder would restrict his goats to the bottom end of the valley far away from my flowers and shrubs.

The Fulani was a different problem. They are known to be a proud and stubborn people and they probably despised my students as a bunch of upstarts. The suspicions and distrust were mutual. A particular nuisance was the roaming Fulani herdsmen. The Fulani are a pastoral people who follow the seasonal rains driving their cattle before them. As well as their cattle they travel with their tents, wives, children, and household goods loaded on the backs of their animals. Theoretically the land on which the school was built belonged to the Emir of Lafiagi but the Fulani grazed it. They resented the Emir giving ten acres of their grazing land to the school, so, at the beginning of each migration season, they refused to deviate from their traditional path, arrogantly marching through our patch of yam, our flower beds, basket-ball courts and playing fields, all so laboriously dug and smoothed by the students with their hoes. We acquiesced in the Fulani's vandalism during our first year because we were trying to be reasonable and were still few in numbers. I had sent several delegations of students to talk and even plead with them, to no avail. I tried to get the Emir to talk to them but he said it was my problem.

By the second year, we had a couple of hundred students and had added a field of maize to our little farm. The maize helped feed the students. One morning as the school lined up in serried ranks for the morning assembly, the Fulani commenced their march as if to taunt us. I sent the prefects to reason with them but they pushed them out of the way, threatening to beat them. The students had been warned not to touch any of the Fulani or their beasts and to keep a safe distance from them. I knew the Fulani did not like the students and would have loved a fight. The Fulani were armed with spears and sticks and I did not want to give them any excuse. When the student peace mission failed and the prefects had returned to the assembly line, the Fulani started to march provocatively through our field of maize. That was it. The students were furious, particularly the girls. They required no encouragement; I just looked at them and said:

"One, two, three: Fulani off the compound."

A few hundred students charging about the place, shouting loudly, ululating and waving their arms in the air soon stampeded the herd. The cattle, many of them saddled with the Fulani tents and utensils, kicked off their loads and galloped headlong down the valley, the Fulani women and children in hot pursuit trying in vain to control them. After the rout, our compound looked like a battlefield though nobody had laid a finger on either man or beast. Normal class continued and we watched through the windows as the Fulani spent the rest of the morning trying to catch their animals and retrieving their chattels. There was no more invasion of our compound, that year or next.

Another weary morning, I had just finished class and was walking towards my house looking forward to a quiet lunch and a rest from the mid-day heat of Lafiagi. Suddenly I was enveloped in a cloud of dust when who should drive past me, as I was shortly to discover, but his temporary lordship, acting Bishop Tobin whom I thought to be several hundred miles away in his mission at Osi-Ilorin. As Mahony was abroad on leave, it was Tobin's first day in power and I was surprised but glad to see him in my isolated outpost. One was glad to see anyone in Lafiagi. Eating alone, with no one for company got boring after months of isolation. Having lived with Tobin the best part of a year of week-ends, I had got used to his rather wicked and mischievous sense of humour. Still I was puzzled as to why he would go so far out of his way, (almost 200 miles from Osi) to visit me, with whom he had no particular bond. Now that Mahony was away for three months, I wondered if Tobin was going to revoke my appointment? But, I need not have worried; the rationale for the visit soon manifested itself.

Over supper, we talked. Then he got up, went to his car and returned with my stained and dusty white cassock. Apparently I had left it hanging behind my bedroom door at Osi. Out of the pocket he pulled the 'lost' tabernacle key of the Mount Carmel church. I had not reported it missing. According to Canon Law, this was a serious offence and if it could be proved as culpable negligence, it might even merit excommunication. Neither I nor, I'm sure, Tobin, thought this was the case. It puzzled me. For one who made me account for every penny I spent on petrol while I was living with him, this 200 mile foray to remote Lafiagi did not make sense. I knew Tobin had an odd sense of humour and that he was not in favour of the Lafiagi project. Now that he was here, he showed his displeasure at the copy of the Qur'an displayed so prominently on my bookshelf, no matter that the Bible was similarly displayed, along with The Thoughts of Mao Zedong,

Machievelli's *Prince*, and several anthropological books on Nupe religion. Guessing how his mind was working, I mentioned how shocked I was after reading a book about medieval Venice at how the Church misused its power of excommunication as a wicked control mechanism. When this hint did not distract him from the issue of the tabernacle key, I poured him another beer and excused myself to go to my bedroom. I presumed the whole visit was Tobin's little joke and thought it was now time for my own little joke. I took a tray, placed on it two lighted candles, a cross, a holy water stoop, a rituale and a purple stole. I placed the lot before Tobin on the table.

"What's this for, Pat?", he asked suspiciously.

"Father. You believe in Excommunication. I don't. Do it, then. It will do me no harm and it may give you some pleasure."

Tobin did not appreciate the irony. Nor would he have appreciated another of Shaw's quips that 'seriousness is a small man's affectation of greatness'.

Further conversation quickly flagged.

Breakfast next morning was equally silent. At dawn my visitor drove out of the compound in another cloud of dust. I never saw Tobin again. Perhaps it was just as well for in his eyes I must have added another sin to my list of crimes: making fun of a sacred cow.

Not long after this I had another Tobin-like visitation from on high. My vice-provincial superior who was based in Ireland but doing an official 'fact-finding' visitation of our missions, spent a night with me, but not at Lafiagi. I drove to Bacita Mission to receive him. Here there was air conditioning and edible food. Fr. Joe Donnelly was a veteran missionary who spent most of his missionary days in the south of Nigeria where competition for the highest number of baptisms was considered fair game among missionaries. Donnelly belonged to this Number-Cruncher-In-the-Sky School of Evangelism. He immediately took issue with my anthropological books on Nupe religion which I foolishly brought along to show him. He had forgotten how St. Patrick converted Ireland or how Irish missionaries converted Europe after the Dark Ages.

When I mentioned that I was in touch with a Professor Messenger of Indiana University in the States who offered me funding if I'd come and do a Masters in Anthropology, he lost his cool and muttered: "such nonsense". In no way would he sanction anything like this for me or for any other member of the Society. We should go out and preach and baptise as he did in his early days in Mid-West Nigeria. He listed the numbers he personally had baptised and they were hundreds – the souls he had harvested for God. Furthermore, he did not agree with Bishop Mahony sending scarce personnel to places like Lafiagi helping the Muslims without ever the prospect of saving a single soul.

I dreamt that night of harvesting souls for heaven and of Nangipe, the Emir's Wife Number 9, totting up the numbers on my calculator, the one I had accused my cook James of stealing.

Joe Donnelly's visit did not boost my enthusiasm nor was it meant to. However his visit had repercussions for me some years later when I found myself editing *The African Missionary* and under his direct thumb when based at our Society's headquarters in Ireland. After falling seriously ill in Lafiagi, I had been invalided home and had the misfortune to be appointed to work in our headquarters in Cork. But more about that later.

AMONG THE WIVES OF THE EMIR

When setting up the school, one of our first priorities after building the classrooms was to build a Principal's house on the school compound but while awaiting Alhaji to finish constructing the house, I had taken up temporary residence in the Emir's Palace, the only place in the town with the necessary "long drop" for a loo. The place was only a short horse-ride from the school; it was adjacent to the mosque and situated at the dead centre of the town. The Emir lived there with his harem of ten wives and numerous servants and relatives.

Being a priest in a harem may seem an odd situation for a celibate missionary but then few missionaries ever have reason to live in harems. It was no missionary imperative or chance happening that had brought me to live in one either, nor was it some ecumenical quirk, a Christian missionary teaching Muslim religion in a Muslim school.

When first I arrived at the palace of the Emir of Lafiagi, the local people did not know what to make of me. Naturally, they were suspicious and the feeling was mutual. I wore my white missionary cassock. The people kept their distance and stared. It was the sensation of the year. Gradually, however, they became accustomed to this white man living in a black man's compound. Initially I was addressed as *sah* (Nupe for 'sir') and later, people followed the Yoruba custom calling me *fada* or just *oybo*, a name derived from the traditional Yoruba for white man (which meant 'skinned' African).

To those who lived in the sea of thatched mud huts surrounding the Emir's palace, I was *Nasara Makanta*, the 'white man of the book', who lived with their king and was building a new co-educational secondary school at the outskirts of town.

The people of Lafiagi were all Muslim and not particularly renowned for their love of Christians and though they secretly suspected that God had given them a monopoly of the world's wisdom, the Government (largely Muslim) did not trust them to run their own secondary school. The involvement of Catholic Mission ensured they got all available government grants.

Which was why their Emir had approached my bishop, the Catholic Bishop of Ilorin a hundred miles to the south and requested the favour of having someone (which happened to be me) come and set up their new secondary school. My assignment was purely educational. I was to concern myself solely with building, organising and teaching. There was much acrimony because everyone of importance wanted to interfere.

Muslim Religion was a compulsory subject on the curriculum and until we were able to recruit a qualified Muslim who could teach the syllabus in English, the onus was on me as Principal to teach the subject myself. This I did with enthusiasm though I left nobody under the impression that I believed it or was anything other than a Roman Catholic.

From the start, the people of Lafiagi were more wary than hostile but gradually their latent hostility towards me abated once they saw me on such friendly terms with their Emir and his wives. Slowly they concluded that my white missionary garb was not, after all, some Trojan Horse, hiding a bagful of devious Christian tricks.

My suite in the palace, if one could call it such, was not very pretentious, nor indeed was the palace itself. My quarters consisted of a bedroom, a cooking room and what was euphemistically called a washroom with a very useful hole in the floor called the 'long drop', which served as a latrine that harboured millions of cockroaches. Water was collected (at 3 kobo a bucket) in a drum beside the door and a watering can slung over the wall served as a shower. In the 120 degree heat of Lafiagi, a cold shower was a god-send.

The front door of my apartment opened on to the outer courtyard of the palace, while the back door – for which I had no key, opened on to the harem, a gang of giggling females of varying shapes and sizes between the ages of 25 and 50. There were ten of them in all and as time went by I got to know them individually as they tried to sell me their bony chickens at inflated prices and jocosely bargained dowries for their small daughters who, they said, would make marvellous 'small wives' (*yawo kekere*) for the white man.

Wife No. 9 (Nangipe). Photo taken in the inner courtyard. Behind is my bedroom.

There were many things that bugged the Muslim about the Catholic Missionary in their midst, not least his celibacy. The wives of the Emir endlessly commented on it. To them I was a 'Pagan', albeit a 'good Pagan' who might or might not reach Paradise, but this caper of having no woman was a mystery to them that not even my paganism explained. And as mysteries are better left unexplained, I just smiled benignly and said I had no money to purchase the 'small wives' (*yawo kekere*) they kept offering me. So they shrugged their shoulders and figured there was a catch somewhere.

The wives in this harem were a happy lot. Each was known by her number. The most senior wife or No. 1 was in charge and out of respect for the Qu'ranic law which says that a good Muslim take no more than four wives, Nos 1-4 had a hierarchy of their own, demanding special respect which, among other things, permitted them to wear the same colour cloth. Even the children referred to the wives by their numbers though the Emir called them by their proper names.

Lafiagi was a thirsty place with the day-time temperature

generally hovering at around the 120 degrees F mark. When I first came to Nigeria I drank only Coke and a horrible orange drink called Fanta. All water had to be boiled and filtered. I was persuaded I had to drink some liquid other than Coke, though I liked Coke. I did not particularly like beer or Guinness though that was what I started drinking, at first 'for medicinal purposes', of course. There was nothing I did in the Emir's palace that wasn't noticed and probably discussed at length among the wives. Whenever I got a crate of Guinness, I noticed that the Emir paid me a visit. The jingling of the bottles in the back of my truck produced a Pavlovian effect that he could not resist.

Emir Omaru of Lafiagei with author. Shoes highly recommended because of scorpions.

Alcohol was forbidden to Muslims but the Emir liked Guinness – for medicinal purposes, of course, like myself. On those occasions the pair of us banished the children from my veranda and retired to the seclusion of my bedroom where he could take his medicines un-noticed. As far as the harem was concerned we were discussing important 'matters of State', though some of the cheekier wives could not resist knocking at my bedroom door with urgent requests to consult the Emir. They were just nosey. They knew well what we were up to. They were not dim. Later, after I moved out of the Emir's Palace to live in the newly-built Principal's House, the four senior wives regularly came to see me. They were chauffeured in the Emir's ancient Mercedes with their husband's flag flying proudly above the bonnet. I treated them and their driver to biscuits and the sour-tasting Fanta. But they were more interested in teasing me and planning how, with their help, I could end my bachelorship. I liked them. They were good-natured people and, I think, genuinely sorry for me for being celibate and a pagan to boot, one who had no chance of ever being admitted to Paradise.

One day when I teased them about associating with the likes of me, a Pagan who'd never make it to heaven, wife No. 1 consoled me:

"*Fada*, don't you worry. You'll get to heaven."

"But how can I, I'm a Pagan?"

"But you're a good Pagan."

In the Emir's palace, each wife had her own room (a 10x10 foot cubicle) with her number clearly marked over the door. Beside her number were scribbled other figures which at first puzzled me, thinking they might be some unusual vital statistics but I later found them to signify the date of her acquisition as wife. Wives were numbered according to seniority and seniority conferred status, though not necessarily preference in the eyes of the Emir who had his favourites. During my stay wife No. 9 or Nangipe was the lucky one. She was my favourite too.

Children were everywhere, scores of them – extremely lovable as all African children are. Each wife tended her own in her room and those wives who had none adopted a baby, usually from one of the other wives. There was a great spirit of brotherliness and kindness. But there were jealousies too and the Emir once told me I made his wives jealous by giving preferential treatment (lumps of sugar or tea-bags) to some children and not to others. Some wives did not speak to me for days if I happened to give a clip in the ear to one of their darlings who pranced around too much on my veranda, spilling my precious beer.

Evening was a joyful time in the Emir's palace, especially when the Emir was away on one of his regular 'tours'. It did not take long for the novelty of the white-man to wear off. The children gathered in front of my door while I sat on the veranda usually drinking a beer or my medicinal bottle of Guinness. They danced in the dust and competed with one another to sing songs into my tape recorder. But bedtime came early and as the night flies burnt their wings against my paraffin lamp, the mosquitoes soon drove everybody indoors and the children said good-bye to my tape recorder, the greatest source of amazement after my hairy legs. It surprised me too that hair does not grow on an African's legs.

Thursdays at dusk, the Emirs official musicians (he had a band of seven) gathered in the courtyard to blow their long brass pipes and beat their drums. They were a motley group of wizened old men. They preceded the Emir whenever he attended important gatherings, which included processing to the Friday mosque. On Thursdays they gathered for a practice in the inner courtyard which was in front of my house. The purpose was to remind the men-folk of the town that the morrow was Friday and that they had to attend mosque – women were exempt. They played in front of my veranda and peered into my room and even into my fridge. At the beginning they were an amusing distraction from the ever-present flies, but as I tired of the noise, the novelty wore off. First they beat their drums, probably to a rhythm unfamiliar to me; followed by a measured pause and then they blew loud piercing wails on their bugle-like brass instruments. Secretly, I recorded them. They had never heard themselves play or understood what a tape recorder was. One day when I tired of playing the cultural ambassador of Christendom, I prepared for their arrival and set up my gear inside my room and pressed the play button when the noise started outside. Except that when the drums beat, I played the wailing pipes and vice versa. They were very confused and searched high and low inside my house looking for my piece of magic. The Emir and his harem were not in on the joke but they enjoyed it. I am not certain that the band did. Neither Missiology or anthropology recommend such hooliganism. Nor would my religious superiors, I suspect.

The Emir had his own house inside the palace and during the day, he sat at his doorstep in the shade. Visitors to the palace removed their shoes at the gate and only special visitors were allowed beyond the inner wall of the harem. Wives came to the king in his own house and it was the job of Wife No. 1 to "mark the sheets" so to speak, and appoint each wife according to her turn. Nupe women have a certain spirit of independence and perhaps it was for that reason that the Emir's wives had a limited measure of freedom one would not associate with harems: they did not wear the purdah and during the daytime they often ventured outside the walls in groups.

All the wives did some trading or sent their daughters or middlemen to trade on their behalf. The Emir gave each some money and with this she had to trade and bargain and make some profit which she used to feed the household when her turn came to cook. Mostly women baked bread and sweet "akara" cakes which sold well in the town.

Cooking for the household was done on a rota basis, each wife taking her turn for a week at a time. The most disparaging taunt one child could make to another was "your mother did not feed us well last week" and serious palace rows erupted from such remarks. No. 1 always played the role of peacemaker and disagreements were seldom allowed to reach the Emir. Sometimes they would complain to me even though they knew that all I'd do was smile. I did not take sides.

MAD ALHASAN

The only time I ever interfered in the ordering of my surroundings was to have mad Alhasan released. He had been almost permanently chained by the leg to a tree in the market-place outside the Emir's palace and it pained me to see him each day as I rode out to school on the Emir's white horse. Naked bar a dirty loin-cloth, he sat on the ground with a vacant stare in his eyes. Baba Doko, a former leper who tended the Emir's horses looked after Alhasan, feeding him a bowl of rice occasionally, releasing him to do his daily ablutions and chaining his up afterwards. Sometimes Baba Doko forgot to feed Alhasan.

I requested the Emir to move Alhasan to a less public place away from the children who tormented him. To humour me, the Emir had Alhasan moved, probably to another tree out of my sight. When Alhasan was unchained he used to follow me around, laughing madly and when I started to grow a beard, rubbing his face to show he noticed what I was doing to myself. I suspect Alhasan belonged to the Emir's household. There was nowhere in Lafiagi to house mad people and most such people, I was told, ended up being killed. I had Awawu, one of the Emir's daughters, tell me about Alhasan and I wrote it into my diary, more or less verbatim as she dictated it. The note is dated 10/02/1971, Emir's Palace, 7 p.m.:

"At times Alhasan is very wicked which is why he is chained to a tree. He runs after people and beats them, sometimes with an empty bottle or just with his hands. He does this because he is hungry, so the people bring him food. He also gets angry when the children throw stones at him and tease him calling him bentegba *which in Nupe means 'you are big for nothing' and is a big insult. Whenever Alhasan becomes angry with the children, he will attack anyone nearby.*

Alhasan is mad because of his mother. Her name is Inasha and she now lives in the small hut beside the market. She was once a beautiful woman and became pregnant by one man but she loved a different man and wanted to become one of his wives. She swore on the holy Qu'ran that the child belonged to the man she loved. But this was a lie. In Lafiagi, if a man makes a woman pregnant and she is not his wife, he pays £50 fine to her family or goes to jail. Inasha wanted to be given as wife to the man she loved and swore the child was his. She swore on the complete Qu'ran of 60 izin, which is not touched unless one does ablution first and puts one's hands to the eyes and prays. She swore that if she told a lie, God would not let her see her child. So the child was born mad and Inasha went blind. She is now old and does not leave her hut any more. People bring her food as they do her son, the mad Alhasan."

JAMES NOBODY, MY IBO COOK

During my time in the Emir's Palace, Northern Muslims were massacring Christian Ibos in areas not too distant from Lafiagi. Our Emir did not approve of this and permitted no pogroms in his Emirate. Late one night, he brought me a young man taken of a long-distance lorry from Kano where many Ibos were killed. The young man called himself James and pretended to be Yoruba. He spoke Yoruba and Hausa and fluent English. Both the Emir and I knew he was an Ibo escaping the pogroms, trying to make his way back to the Ibos' ancestral homeland, now called Biafra. It would have been inviting attack to have an Ibo surname so, while in Lafiagi he became James Nobody, *"Fada's cook"*. The Emir promised to protect him and I appointed him as my cook. I showed him how my gas cooker worked. He was a quick learner – quicker than I was when it came to cooking. In addition to cooking my meals, he was to be my ears and eyes in Lafiagi. I gave him a new copy-book and a biro and each evening he had to present me with three pages of the local gossip and any important news that might affect my situation. An item from the early days of his diary reads thus:

"Until Fada came to Lafiagi, Christians were not allowed to enter the Emir's Palace. People entering the Emir's palace must first remove their shoes and leave them at the entrance. But if I were Fada, I would not leave my shoes at the entrance. They are good shoes and someone will steal them."

In time, everyone, particularly the Emir's daughters, became fond of James. He helped people with their letters- mostly petitions for jobs. He treated them with cold drinks from my fridge. By my bed I kept a big diary labelled "Private. Do Not Open". When something went missing in the house, I wrote about it in my diary, knowing that the first thing James did each morning after I set out for school was to check my private diary.

"My tea-bags keep disappearing. I think James is giving them to the Emir's daughters. I'm drinking no more tea while this goes on."

My tea-bags disappeared much slower after that.

"My calculator has gone missing. Hope James has not given it to Awawu or Nangipe."

The item soon made its way back to my desk.

RAMIDAN, MY CHEERFUL MONKEY

I always wanted a monkey and when I saw one tied to the top of a bus, I took a fancy to it. He was being mercilessly teased by the local urchins. I offered a few shillings to the driver who seemed pleased to let me have it, chain and all. James Nobody was none too pleased and less so when I gave him the job of training the monkey into civilised ways. In my innocence, I thought monkeys had sense and could be trained. It was the season of Ramadan, the time when Muslims fast all day and the monkey too must have been fasting out of necessity if not conviction - judging by the way he pounced on the bunch of bananas in my kitchen, stuffing them into his mouth. He became known as Rami. Each evening when I came home from school, James would let Rami off his chain for a while and if he wandered too far, it was easy to entice him back by waving a banana about. Soon, however, Rami got bored, just as I did myself occasionally. Perhaps neither of us felt we belonged in an Emir's Palace with its chattering harem and noisy children. He would dart around my veranda knocking things about and pulling the children's hair. Suddenly he would grab my book and run up the mango tree with it. Then it was my pen and then my sun-glasses. Retrieving them soon became a nuisance. I had a rosary-beads given to me by a pious old lady on Aran called Máire Chubaird. She made a big issue of bestowing it on me when I was ordained priest and each time I visited her afterwards, I was cross examined as to the whereabouts of the rosary-beads and the use I made of it. I dared not visit her without it. Somehow the monkey found it and ran up the tree with it. He probably wrapped it around one of the top branches because we never saw it again. I wondered how I'd face Máire Chubaird when I returned home next time. Would she accept my excuse that "A monkey ran off with it"? I doubt it.

But it wasn't the stealing of my beads that decided me to get rid of Rami. It was something he did with my bananas. When nobody was watching, he pealed all the bananas in the basket, threw the skins on the floor and rubbed each banana on the wall as if plastering it. Within a short time, every centipede and idle fly in Lafiagi was crawling about my room. It took James a day to scrub off the mess. My flirtation with monkeys had come to an abrupt end. Rami had to go. Sometime later I thought I recognised Rami monkeying about in the lorry-park. He looked hungry and in need of a banana. He made a great fuss of me. I am sure he regretted what he had done with my bananas. His mother had never told him not to play with his food or to think of the starving children in Africa.

I was soon to leave the Emir's palace and move to the new

Principal's house on the school compound. By then, James had found a lorry going to Biafra. We were all sad to see him go. Soon afterwards the Emir died and the women of his harem were divided out among his male relatives. The new Emir got Nangipe, Umaru's Wife Number 9.

There is no plaque on the wall of the Emir's palace to say that once upon a time a foolish Christian missionary lived here. He made no convert or even tried. He saved no souls. Nobody could ever call him a Crusader who planted the Cross in a Muslim land. But I didn't have to. My monkey did it for me. On top of the tallest mango tree in Lafiagi, I believe there hangs a crucifix, planted there by a playful monkey named Rami. I'm sure Máire Chubaird would be proud of him.

In front of the Emir's palace. Riding out with the Emir, under the umbrella and on white horse preceded by a flunkey bearing the Emir's staff of office, to celebrate the Muslim feast of Id. For my first year in the palace, this white horse was my only means of transport. It was permanently tethered to a post beside my door and attended to by Baba Doko, (Master of Horse), a former leper.

While waiting for my house on the school compound to be completed, living at the Emir's Palace provided an interesting diversion. At the start, I had only the Emir's white horse for transport. When I had settled in, the Emir would invite me to accompany him on a ride around the town, or to attend local ceremonies, such as Muslim naming - equivalent to our Christian Baptisms- marriage celebrations

and the like. Since the promised transport of my initial contract looked unlikely to materialise, Bishop Mahony took pity on me and bought me a car out of my government salary. Once thus mobile, I was often called upon in the middle of the night to take a girl to hospital, either somebody in labour or someone dying as a result of a back-street abortion. Unfortunately, I was always roped in too late and few of my passengers survived. Sexual mores in Lafiagi were fairly lax. A bucket of water from the well was three kobo and the girl who brought it was four.

I was always on very friendly terms with the Emir and at night, he sometimes came to my room where we shared a bottle or two of Guinness. His various wives often came to my place to borrow tea bags or sugar. I was on first name terms with all of them. When the Emir was away I filmed freely inside the harem. The wives thought I was just 'taking pictures' and were very comfortable with my presence. Later on, I acquired a portable electrical generator for the school and one of my first acts was a public showing of my film in the palace courtyard. This was attended by the Emir's entire household, many of whom had never seen a film. To their surprise and perhaps embarrassment, they discovered that my camera had also recorded sound. People knew I understood a smattering of Yoruba but not Nupe. Judging from the audience reaction that night, I suspect there were many things the Emir's wives regretted having said on my camera. In any case, the Emir and his retinue laughed so much that I thought they'd fall off their stools.

KAYAK ON THE NIGER

I did a bit of night school carpentry in my youth and would have liked to have built a currach but I did not have sufficient time or a good enough excuse to justify the time it would take. Moving to Lafiagi gave me that excuse. The currach posed the problem of finding and training a willing crew, so I thought I'd start with something simpler like a kayak that only needed a crew of one, i.e. myself. Somewhere or other I found plans for building a kayak and I discussed the matter with Fr. Mick McCoy, an old missionary friend who worked in the bush not far from Osi and who visited me regularly when I worked in those parts. Mick was a carpenter and supervised the building of churches

and schools but my idea of a kayak appealed to his imagination, especially as he figured that the bishop might not like the idea. He was a skilled carpenter and he knew from the plans that building it would not occupy much of his time. I explained to him that I wanted the kayak covered with tarred canvas, like the Aran currachs.

A second year girl student showing my DIY kayak to a visitor from VSO.

On Aran, landing a currach on the rocky shore of Bungabhla in the rough seas, risked tearing the skin and causing a leak, which was not uncommon but any damage could be repaired in a few minutes. All you needed was a piece of canvas soaked in tar, a box of matches, and in no time you could repair the tear and row back into the waves.

One day news arrived from Ilorin that my kayak had arrived there and as I had not yet got the promised transport (except for the horse), I took the first mammy-waggon out of town heading for Ilorin. My old friend and colleague Fr. Paddy Beausang happened to be in Ilorin with his pickup truck and offered to drive me back to Lafiagi with my kayak. This whole business of the kayak did not impress bishop Mahony who was still worried about his pennies. I am sure he considered it frivolous and not proper missionary work. But I needed some diversion. Paddy and about everyone who saw it were convinced that this contraption of mine would never float. About half an hour from our destination, we came to a tributary of the Niger and stopped to check the bridge before crossing. Being the end of the rainy season the river was in flood and fast flowing. While stopped, the idea suddenly struck me that this was as good a time as any to test-launch my ship before I made a fool of myself before the townsfolk of Lafiagi. It would also put Beausang's doubts to rest. The thought that there might be crocodiles did not occur to either of us, which was just as well. We parked the truck and launched the kayak in the fast flowing stream. It manoeuvred well, which emboldened me to let it run down the rapids below the bridge. Unfortunately I had not allowed for submerged trees – no such dangers on Aran. One invisible sharp splinter cut the canvas like a knife. The canoe suddenly filled with water giving me just sufficient time to head for the far bank and grab a low lying branch. The kayak was light as a feather and by perching on the stern and with the help of the overhanging branches, I was able to empty the water. The stern now bearing all my weight, the rest of the kayak poked out of the water at an angle of sixty degrees. The river was just narrow enough to enable us to hold a shouted conversation between the two banks.

"No Paddy, there is nothing wrong with the kayak. Just a temporary mishap." Said I up to my neck in water.

In the circling eddy near the far bank I proved to Paddy that I could still manoeuvre the kayak and with a bit of ingenuity might manage to get it across to the other bank where he waited with the truck. I thought I could swim if I had to. We devised a plan of action. Paddy went down river to the next bend in the rapids and was ready to grab me when I swept past. Success was not guaranteed so we were both relieved when our plan worked. We sat for a while on the bank watching the fast current and contemplating what might have been. We considered ourselves lucky. I never expected to have to patch my kayak but my patching system worked well, even better than on Aran. Here in the hot sun we needed no matches. Using the tar-soaked canvas that McCoy had thrown in as an after-thought, I was able to repair my kayak in minutes. Paddy and I decided not to tempt fate any further.

Over the next two years, I spent many pleasant and intriguing hours in this kayak paddling on the river Niger and exploring the surrounding regions. At first people thought it flimsy and a bit of a joke and were sceptical that it would float. I am a good swimmer and not only did my kayak float but I soon learnt how to summersault in it and in time I converted the local sceptics – about the only conversions I had in Lafiagi.

SNAKES AND SCORPIONS

During my time at Lafiagi Secondary School, several of my students got bitten by scorpions and snakes and this caused me to take more than an academic interest in both snakes and scorpions. A bite from a scorpion is very painful but not life-threatening for a healthy person. The pain, I was told, could kill anyone with a weak heart, or an elderly person. My first experience of a scorpion bite involved a fourteen-year-old boy. I heard the screams in the distance and I ran to see what had caused them. The boy had been bitten in the sole of his foot. A group of his classmates were holding him down on the ground as he screamed. Someone sat on each of his hands and legs while another fetched a blade from his desk and scored the sole of his foot around the bite until he bled profusely. In this way they hoped the poison would escape, which it must have done, because the boy was soon limping about and in a few days was fine. The next was more scary. The piercing screams of my cook almost hurtled me out of my bed just before dawn. He had come into my kitchen to prepare my breakfast. I thought he had been speared by my night-watchman whom some people thought to be mad. My cook was an elderly man and I thought this was the end of him. A few students held him down while they bled his foot and I then drove him to hospital where the nurse gave him an injection. He was back at work next day – which is more than I could say for the watchman. He was killed by one of the Emir's lackeys for drinking his palm wine and topping up the container with water. His body, we were told, was thrown into the Niger. The students told me his ghost was seen around the school for weeks afterwards.

In order to enable the school to stay co-educational, I had to build hostels for the girls who came from outside town. At first they had proved fair game for the Lafiagi men folk and too many of those staying in the town became pregnant. Near my house, a dozen thatched round huts housed about thirty girls. Shortly after the watchman was killed and in the small hours of the morning, thirty or so screaming girls, all wrapped in their bed sheets (to protect them from mosquitoes) came pounding at my doors and windows. Someone had seen the ghost of my watchman and group hysteria had quickly taken over. The terrified girls spent the rest of the night in my house sleeping as best they could in whatever spare nook they could find. When my cook came at dawn, he calmed them down and hunted them out.

It was a different story with snake bites. Ever since my experience of watching a man die of snake-bite in Osi, I was scared of snakes. There were plenty around Lafiagi. I once found a cobra under a towel I had casually thrown on my bed. Most of the snakes around Lafiagi were spitting cobras but the most dreaded one was called locally *Sye Waterana* or Good Bye Tomorrow. Anyone bitten by this snake never again saw the dawn. The fear of this snake was such that, immediately they killed it, the locals cut off its head and buried the lot several feet underground. So it was no wonder that whenever a snake was spotted there was immediate panic that disrupted the whole school. People grabbed whatever utensil they could lay hands on – stick, *panga* or classroom chair and rushed after the snake, causing pandemonium. One of my ways of dealing with fear has always been to study the cause of it and I tried to train my students in this approach. I collected all the books on snakes I could find. My first lessons in science was about snakes – types of snakes, types of snake poison, how snake poison worked on the human body and how to deal with snake-bite. I had my carpenter build cages with glass panels at the front so I could store and view captured snakes. Whenever anyone came into my office the snake spat venom on to the glass. The proximity of the snakes gave my teaching immediacy and relevance. I was able to summon several first-hand experiences of snake-bite. It was easy to get the students involved with the subject; something you cannot always do in a physics or chemistry lesson.

I set about learning how to catch snakes. I got the students to spread the word that nobody was to kill a snake but they were to send for me and I would catch the snake and take it away. I had a special forked stick and string ready to catch the snake and put it in my glass cage. Soon, I assembled an impressive collection of live snakes in my office – enough to frighten the living daylights out of the Emir's retinue when he took them to visit me after a school board meeting. I never saw a bunch of old men shuffle so fast out of a room as they did that day from my office. Later after we had studied the snakes sufficiently, I injected them with formaldehyde to preserve them, mounting them in glass cases on the wall of the science lab. The largest snake was a spitting cobra which according the textbooks was within a few centimetres of the record for West Africa. It had swallowed a chicken in a house in the town and the people had sent for me. The cobra first goes for the victim's eyes, blinding its prey with a spit before injecting the poison with its fangs. The pain in the eyes can be relieved by bathing them in tinned milk but the sight is blurred for some days afterwards. If you neglect to treat the eyes, you can eventually go blind. Facing a spitting cobra, the first thing to do is to protect your eyes by placing your hands in front of them. A snake cannot jump.

The more knowledgeable I became, the more confident I got and after a while I was able to hold the snake by the head behind the fangs and direct its spitting harmlessly at the walls or on to a piece of glass where students could later study it. Because snakes cannot double back on themselves or spring at you, I was able to catch a snake by the tail, swing it about my head and throw it as far away as I could and then demonstrate how to catch it as it tried to slither off. I demonstrated this at morning assembly in front of the student body. At first there were gasps. But there was purpose behind my madness, but try as I might I never had a person volunteer to catch the snake. For them, a snake was like the devil. The more you learnt about it, the farther away from it you wanted to stay. To feed the snakes, I had the students catch mice. Enterprising students earned a few pennies this way. This gave us sufficient time to study the snakes in detail before I injected them with formaldehyde prior to mounting them in the lab. One evening there was panic when a snake escaped during feeding-time. We had to lock up my office and the adjacent storeroom until next day when sunlight made it safer to look for it.

In Lafiagi, I lived alone and had very few visitors. Nobody with any sense wanted to visit Lafiagi. My bishop, William Mahony, came.

He was a light sleeper and I gave him my bed in the Emir's palace knowing well that he would not sleep a wink. I took my camp bed and slept in one of the classrooms. The bishop could not wait to get back to Ilorin. Another most welcome visitor was a young missionary, Andy Donovan whom Bishop Mahony had appointed to work in our new parish with the Kamberi tribe at Ujiji. The place was even more isolated than mine. When I was a student at university, I had played in a hurling match against the North Mon and I was marking Andy. When going for a ball I slipped and got Andy's hurley stick full in the nose. He visited me in hospital. It was his first time coming into contact with our students and it was no coincidence that my broken nose brought him eventually to Ujiji, a place I had worked in periodically when I was based in Bacita. At the time of his visit to Lafiagi, I was dependant on the Emir's horse for transport, so we used Andy's truck to take my kayak to the nearby Niger where together we spent the afternoon exploring. We became good friends. During school holidays I visited him at Ujiji accompanying him in his canoe as he made the rounds of his various outstations. I was able to take a few Kamberi youngsters from his parish into my school at Lafiagi and this gave me an excuse to visit Andy every school holiday. One hears how the shape of Cleopatra's nose may have affected the contours of Ancient Europe but modern Ujiji has the shape of my broken nose to thank for its progress.

After a while, my interest in snakes petered out and I informed the locals I had enough snakes unless they spotted a very rare one. Otherwise I was becoming a full-time snake-catcher and would have no time to teach, let alone get on with the business of living. I did not have the same interest in scorpions. They were too like the crabs at home on Aran. However they were bad news and an ever present danger as my old cook would no doubt agree. In the mornings I always examined the floor carefully before I put my feet out of bed.

Until my kayak arrived the only exciting distraction for me in Lafiagi was riding the Emir's horse. The Emir was aware of this, I think, so he set aside a horse specifically for me to ride. At first he gave me a tame-ish one but when he saw how I liked to gallop, he put aside a more spirited white mare for my use. I liked riding. I did a lot of it in my youth on Aran where the scope to gallop was limited. Here in Lafiagi I could gallop for miles to my heart's content. The only limitation was the stamina of the horse. At first I used the sandy beach-like banks of the Niger tributary near the town. Then, I got bolder, waded across the local river and went full gallop along the narrow pathways that led to the Niger. I think the horse liked the gallop as much as I did. I always returned home covered in sweat and exhausted as did the horse. The Emir and his chiefs were pleased that I had found a local activity of sufficient interest to keep me in town and I was soon asked to accompany the Emir and his retinue in the various rituals that took place in and around town. There might be around twenty horsemen in these groups. It was an opportunity for the local chiefs to show off their horses and riding skills. Nupe horses are trained to dance to the beat of drums. Local notables keep horses for that purpose only, and a well-trained dancing horse is a trophy and status symbol. The Nupe steer with their knees and use the reins only to have the horse dance and prance and stand on its hind legs. It took some getting used to. Once you got to know them, Nupe horses were very biddable.

One day as I had crossed the local tributary and was giving my horse time to shake itself dry before climbing up the steep bank. I intended, as usual, to gallop the seven miles or so to the Niger. Ahead of me wading the river was a local chieftain on a speckled stallion. When the stallion saw my white mare, emerging from the water, it neighed and became very agitated. It must have taken a fancy to my mare (or they may have been old friends). Whatever the reason, as soon as it reached the bank, the stallion took off along the sand with its elderly rider struggling to control it. Then suddenly it neighed frantically, turned round, jumped on its hind legs throwing its rider. It galloped straight for my white mare. There ensued what I can only describe as a horse-fight with both horses almost upright on their hind legs, belting one another with their front feet and biting one another. My mare seemed to win but in the tussle, it reared so far on its hind legs, - which in my ignorance I helped it do by mistakenly pulling at the reins- that it fell backwards. I managed to jump clear.

When it got to its feet again, I was quick to jump back into the saddle and for the next hour I had the most fantastic gallop I ever can remember. I had to cling on to the mane for dear life. With the stallion chasing behind, we jumped over fallen branches and ditches until, almost exhausted, we reached the vertical bank of the Niger where both horses paused for a think. I was afraid to touch the reins any more. The rider-less speckled stallion had kept pace with me all the while, like one sees in the Grand National. It was no match for the Emir's horse in speed. Fortunately, both animals considered the fight was over. Of course the story got back to the Emir and, that night, we talked about it over a few of my remaining cans of Guinness. I think the Emir was pleased that I had escaped unhurt. I don't know what, if anything, the episode did for my reputation for sanity in the community but it did no harm at all to my reputation for horsemanship. Both the Emir and I knew that I had a lucky escape. The Emir graciously blamed the other rider who happened to be a family member. After that he gave me a different horse.

Lafiagi was a low-lying flood plain and locally regarded as an unhealthy place, so it was not surprising that I soon became very ill with malaria, double pleurisy and amoebic dysentery. For too long, I had been living on my own in Lafiagi and not taking care of myself. It was the first time in my life I felt really ill, hardly able to crawl into bed. At first I thought I'd fight the illness but when I found myself only getting worse, I dragged myself out of bed and crawled to my truck and drove cross-country over a narrow seldom used road to Bacita.

I was seeing double most of the way but it was no double vision when a huge ape crashed across the shrub land and knocked itself out against the bolts of my front wheel. Normally I'd have managed to drag it to the next village where the meat would have nourished the hungry villagers for a week or more.

This time I did not have the strength, so I drove on, stopping briefly at the next village to let them know what had happened. I am sure the beast was in the pot before evening-time. When I arrived in Bacita the Sugar Company Doctor attached me to a drip and sent me off immediately in the ambulance to Ibadan 200 miles away. The doctor at the hospital gave me an injection. He said the drug was experimental. I did not realise just how experimental until I woke up in the small hours in a panic. The walls of my room were closing in on me. I ran around closing the windows in case I fell out. When that did not assuage my panic I went under the cold shower. I tried prayer but finding it no help, I turned to a mantra frequently uttered by our wonderful English teacher in Balinafad, my boarding school.

The teacher, an elderly missionary, Fr. Bush Heaney was fond of quoting Macaulay's *Lays of Ancient Rome*. Thomas Babington Macaulay was a cynical apologist of colonialism as a 'do-good' institution, while at the same time using it to feather his own and his family's nest:

For how can a man die better
Than facing fearful odds,
For the ashes of his fathers
And the temples of his Gods.

The mantra worked as it must have done for Heaney himself when he was a missionary in Africa. The wording might not get me anywhere near Paradise but it kept me sane until dawn came and with it help. In the morning when the doctor was summoned he explained that the drug did not work (as if I did not know). He warned me that what I was now experiencing was Cold Turkey and that the feeling might last for weeks. Mercifully it only visited me a couple of times in the form of depression, something very foreign to me.

After three or four years on the missions, missionaries were allowed six months home leave. This was as much to help them recover their damaged health as from any form of compassion. In earlier centuries, missionaries were left abroad for too long and many never made it home.

Shortly before I left Lafiagi for my overdue break in Ireland, Bishop Mahony had sent me an assistant in the person of Tim Carroll, a likeable young missionary. The idea was that Tim would take over from me when I went for my six months' overseas leave, which was already overdue. I suspected that the bishop's sleepless night in the Emir's place had convinced him that Lafiagi could easily drive one to madness, so he figured that sensible Tim could keep an eye on me. Tim's main interest in life was linguistics and if you wanted to make his day, you gave him a Nupe irregular verb to play with. Occasionally he accompanied me on my trips to Ilorin learning his Nupe vocabulary as we travelled. On the hundred mile stretch of road between Lafiagi and Ilorin, there was only one roundabout and for want of something more exciting to do, I always took this roundabout the wrong way. I could never figure out why this used to upset Tim. Later when Tim was appointed first bishop of Kontagora, which contained the Ujiji area, I thought I might have accidentally hit on a fool-proof predictive test for future bishops. I called it 'The Roundabout Test': cheaper perhaps than reading the entrails of Vatican chickens.

I had looked forward very much to my home leave but when the time came, I was exhausted and too ill to travel. I dreaded arriving home to Aran as an invalid. For that reason I spent several weeks in Bacita recuperating. For the first and only time in my life I understood what depression was like. As soon as I felt well enough, I contacted my old friend Paddy Beausang and he drove me to Lagos airport. It felt like a black cloud was accompanying me all the way home. I was in dread of it following me for the rest of my life. Unexpectedly, it lifted as soon as I landed at Kilronan pier in Aran and saw my brother Thomas there to meet me.

8

MY FIRST LEAVE HOME

Home on Aran, it took me a couple of weeks before I was able to walk the short distance from Bungabhla to the church at Onacht village. I pretended I was ok but I am sure the locals saw through my bravado. My heart was as heavy as my body was reluctant to move. Over my three years in Africa I had, by the flickering light of an oil-lamp, scribbled down some of my feelings about life and about my work but home on Aran a great feeling of meaninglessness came over me. I felt weak and ill. As I struggled against a westerly gale to walk home after saying Mass in the church in Onacht village, unfamiliar and disturbing thoughts kept crowding in on my mind.

The following week I was ordered by my superiors to give a retreat to a group of black-clad nuns perched on the edges of their seats in a convent somewhere on the mainland. If they only knew it, the good nuns had every reason to perch on the edges of their seats. I had not given a retreat before and I never saw a bunch of people that looked less in need of one, especially from the likes of me. I remember the occasion well because I made such a hames of a ritual called 'Benediction'. Only when I went to put away the monstrance did I discover that I had never put a Host in it. It was my first time doing 'Benediction' and I got all the sequences wrong. Furthermore, even if I could sing, I could not think of the proper hymns to intone.

For the rest of the week in that convent I expected the nuns to call in someone in a white coat to take me away. Instead, the nuns were very kind to me and lent me a typewriter on which to print out the thoughts that had invaded my head. I was having a crisis of Faith and the effort of committing thoughts to paper helped me banish the depression for good.

THE RETURN OF THE MISSIONARY

The narrow road wound itself like a frayed ribbon along the edge of the cliffs. Sturdy stone walls pinned it to the ground as if to stop the winter gales carrying it away. Here and there along the roadside and dotted among the rocky nooks stood whitewashed cottages acting like kingpins pegging the wavering ribbon more firmly to the barren hillside. And at the bottom of the hill, beside the sea, lay Onacht village with its stonewalled church brooding over the gurgling bay.

Onacht church is my home church just as Bungabhla, a mile further west, is my home village, the bleakest village of the Aran Islands. Nestling among the grey rocks at the bottom of a steep cliff, the village sits squatty at the end of the island road, its eleven houses clinging like limpets to the bare landscape as if trying to hide itself from the hostile elements. It is a quiet place disturbed only by the murmur of winter sea periodically punctuated by the wailing call of a sea bird or by a dog baying at the moon. Like the morning mist that sometimes creeps in from the Atlantic, a strange peace often hovers over the village and hugs the wild shoreline. It is this peace that I found so refreshing and indeed inspiring each time I come home, especially after the humid heat of Africa.

It was my first day home and as I walked along the road to Onacht church to offer Mass, the wind was at my back pushing me forward. It hurled huge raindrops after me, some of them missing their mark to splutter against the limestone walls or skid hissingly on the dull grey flagstones. A westerly gale was in the making. Huge waves swept in from the Atlantic, rolling dourly eastwards towards the Irish mainland. Already, angry breakers were baring their teeth against the edges of our island's jagged rocks as if impatient to eat into our few remaining fields and devour our very homes. It was almost night time.

Onacht church was empty and getting darker. It had no electricity. The red light flickering near the altar gave a semblance of life, warmth and even refuge. I enjoyed the lone quietness of the church. I needed it.

As I started Mass, two lighted candles gently pushed back the darkness from the altar and shut out vision of the world outside. Only sound penetrated the circle of light and wild nature's choir provided us with music. Often in Africa I have said Mass alone. And I felt alone too. But here in Aran, salty rain replaced the sweat on my forehead and I did not feel alone any more. The breakers falling on the shore ground out a slow rhythmic beat, rolling solemn music into our silent church. And winter's gale blew over the island and whistled its wailing hymn all around us like some gigantic stereophony.

I did not feel these sounds a distraction and the mood of the Mass followed me home as I pushed myself up-hill and through the gale westwards along the meandering road. By now night was pitch dark and the sea, by the sound of it, was angrier. Peering into the night, I could make out the white lips of the breakers as they spat their kisses at the shore in the age-old love-hate feud of land and sea, eternal partners in an undying war. By now the gulls and other sea birds had taken to the shelter of their homes in the southern cliffs and all sensible people too had gone indoors. Rain had stopped. Wind and sea kept up their lamentation, a weirdly overlapping duet, occasionally made more piercing by the screech of a stray cormorant caught out, like myself, in the storm. As I progressed westward over the hill, a faint light showed in some island houses and the moon was starting to peep warily over the western horizon, casting a pale ghostly polish on the wet countryside and giving a sickly feeling to Galway Bay.

Good-bye Nigeria. I was home in Aran once more. Rounding the bend of the road facing the Atlantic, Eeragh Island lighthouse flashed its bright beam into my face. It pierced the wet empty night of the sea, checking if the world was still there and casting a cold knowing eye upon life.

Up to then we had no running water or flushing toilet in our house in Bungabhla. I decided to remedy that situation and to build a kitchen, a toilet and septic tank. It was hard manual work. I had first to make the blocks and then take a ferry in and out to Galway to fetch the plumbing material. The challenge helped me recuperate.

Gradually I felt my old confidence returning. I am convinced the manual work helped me.

Half way through my official leave, I had a letter from the Emir of Lafiagi asking me to hurry back. The staff in the school, he said, were on strike. In Africa, teachers expect to be paid for correcting their students' examinations but I never subscribed to this practice. I felt that testing was part of the teaching for which one got paid anyway. Tim Carroll, as acting Principal, did not want to set a precedent by changing my system of doing things, so the Emir thought I should cut my leave short and return to the school to settle the matter. The result was that I used the return part of my air-ticket and took the next plane back to Nigeria without ever visiting the Society's headquarters in Cork. The Emir himself met me at Lagos airport. Returning so precipitously was one of those mistakes one makes. First I was not fully recuperated but worse still my superiors at our HQ in Cork had expected me to visit them to pay my respects. Shortly after arriving back in Africa, I had a letter from Fr. Carr, my Provincial Superior reprimanding me for departing Ireland without consulting him. He told me that he was relieving me of my position as a missionary in Ilorin Diocese and appointing me to the staff of the Society's HQ in Cork as Provincial Communications Secretary and editor of the Society's periodical, *The African Missionary*. I was reminded that I was under obedience and summoned home immediately, ordering me to report to HQ as soon as I felt well enough to travel. I am sure it was meant as an act of fraternal kindness, for which I should have been grateful. But I wasn't. I had indeed suspected that once my health started to fail, my days in Lafiagi were numbered. I hoped that I might have had some say as to where I was sent.

I did not expect to be re-assigned away from the Missions. My commitment to priesthood was very much tied up with improving the world, which at that time I saw as a continuation of my missionary work in Africa. I did not expect to be assigned home. My effort to fly under the radar and return quietly to my mission in Africa had backfired. It was with great sadness therefore, that I reluctantly handed in my notice to the Emir of Lafiagi. I believe that he too was not too happy about it, nor were his ten wives, though I only had occasional contact with them after I had ceased living in the harem.

PART II
AFRICA TO ARAN
ABANDONING THE CHASE

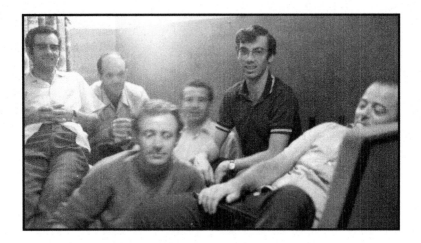

A Band of Brothers: Ilorin Diocese 1970. Andy Donovan, Paddy Beausant, P O'Toole, Vincent O'Leary, Brendan Lawless, Kevin Cassidy.

9

AN ENEMY IN CAMP

I spent six months in Lafiagi after I handed in my notice. It gave me time to tie up all the loose ends and make sure the school was running smoothly with the new Principal that I had recruited. Tom Todd was a physics and maths graduate from Queen's University in Belfast; he had the type of qualifications the new school needed, qualifications rare as hen's teeth in Nigeria. I had hoped Tom would settle into the job before I departed for Ireland. I briefed him on all the intrigues and on the people to watch, like the EO and Alhaji. They were guaranteed to instigate trouble. Unfortunately after about a year in the job, Tom found both the climate and the intrigue too much and handed in his resignation. He was succeeded by an African graduate who within two years wandered off with the content of the school safe. After that I lost contact. But by then I was far away in Ireland and having my own problems with the *Dia Beags* of the Institutional Church.

If one's aim is to bask in public gratitude, one does not work for a community project. I would not expect a 'Thank You' note from the old men who missed out on a second or third wife because I took into my school the young girls for whom they had paid dowries; nor would I expect to be lauded by the poverty-stricken parents who benefited from these dowries. When word got out that I was leaving Lafiagi, many of the town's folk came to my house to express their gratitude. The Emir and his household presented me with an African garment and insisted I wear it and ride around town one more time with the Emir and his retinue. I felt already sufficiently rewarded and fulfilled by the success of the secondary school project, not to expect anything extra. I did not expect Alhaji Audu, the building contractor, to come and kiss me Goodbye. Nor his son in law, the EO. My official departure from the town was delayed by some weeks because I fell ill again. Most people, including Alhaji, thought I had already departed for Ireland. One night, shortly after dusk, there was a knock on my bedroom window. When I opened the door I found the Emir's nephew whom I had once befriended and helped with his studies. He had a reasonably senior post in the Local Government Office in town. He came after dark so that nobody would notice him or blame him for leaking Alhaji complaints about me. He risked being sacked by the EO. I was touched that he would take such a risk. In Lafiagi, at the bottom of all official correspondence, it was customary to give a list of the important personages to whom you sent a copy. Alhaji's complaint about me was copied to all the note-worthy people in the state, including myself. I did not take much notice of that because in Lafiagi, though the custom was to add a long list of 'Copy To' people to your letters, you only mailed those who agreed with you, blaming the postal service for the non-delivery to the others. Here is Alhaji's letter:

Alhaji A. K. Audu,

General Contractor, Lafiagi.

13th September, 1972.

The Chairman, Board of Governors,

Lafiagi Seconday School, Lafiagi.

Building of 3 Classroom Block and Store

I am writing to explain myself full before you, members of the Board of governors, Sole Administrator, the Representatives of Civil Service associated with the set up of Lafiagi Secondary School about the refund of £153. 6s.6p. being levied against me by Fr. O'toole, the outgoing Principal of Lafiagi Secondary School. It appears the Fr. O'toole had had some ill prejudice against me in person since the inception of Lafiagi Secondary School. Besides the obstacles he placed against the success , my first contract work in the school, it had been his hand work that accounted to my handing over the classroom to him for decoration only. Fr. O'Toole had committed me to inordinate expenses over the work by tearing away all the ceiling and its supporters for the three classrooms, without signing my agreement with me. That had cost me the following amounts:

About 30 ceilings @12/6	£28.15s
50 tie-rods @1/6d each	£3.15s
Advance to Principal's carpenter	£50.0s
16 gal emulsion paint @£2/10s ea	£40.0s
4 gallons gloss paint @ £2.15/-	£11.0s
6 doors condemned @£6 ea	£36.0s
Blackboard steps	£4.15s
Total:	£174.5s
Retention Money:	£200.0s

In addition to above, the contract was awarded to me on Government cement controlled price of £16 per ton whereas it as only available at £27 per ton at Lafiagi. I bought 21 tons. Of cement for the project cost me £567.0s instead of £336.

I would like to add that the contract experience I had gained so far, building of 3 classrooms and store, I made would cost more than £5000.0s if valued by a Government Quantity Surveyor, but on this I had to sacrifice the money realised about £1,000 from other jobs .

In conclusion, I would like to express that the Principal Fr. O'Toole has special prejudice and hatred against me since he came to this School. Otherwise all allegations levied against me most of which are black and white in his custody have been settled amicably.

If Fr. O'Toole had not disliked me, there are other contractors whom he claimed to be more competent that are putting up faulty buildings at the school and that are never reported. For example, one contractor put up 8 foot high Science Block instead of 10 foot high which had its roof blown off by Mr. Todd for repair. This is a case which is never reported.

The Principal Fr. O'Toole had done a lot to elevate the educational standard of Lafiagi/Pategi Division but I very much regret to say that his actions sometimes are not in the interest of the people he claims to *serve but on what he personally wishes to be done.*

I am making this statement, not as a Contractor but as my understanding reflects of his activities.

I have the honour to be,

Sir, Yours faithfully,

A. k. Audu

CC.-

Fr. OTtoole, 2. The Sole Administrator, Lafiagi'pategi Division, 3. The Inspector of Education; 4. Various Representatives of the School Board and State Ministry of Education.

On the following day, before leaving Lafiagi for the last time I had the pleasure of responding to Alhaji's letter and copying his complaint and my own response to all the people on his 'CC' list – many of whom I knew to be critical of Alhaji's work. As one does when working on a community project, my correspondence was carefully referenced and available for inspection at any time. The salient points in my reply, dated 14th September 1972, stressing that I did not hate Alhaji or anyone else in Lafiagi, that as Principal, I had been appointed custodian of his community's money and that none of his enforced refunds went into my pocket. Also I was able to point out that much of his trouble arose because of his shoddy workmanship and that it was the Military Governor, after his official visit to the school, who had ordered the work to be re-done. I mailed my letters in Bacita next day to insure they were not intercepted in the Lafiagi post office where the EO had his spies. This perpetual warring got to one in the end and I could sympathise why my two immediate successors walked out after such a short stay.

I drove out of Lafiagi before dawn. I never heard from or saw anyone from Lafiagi again. My old Ibo cook, by then working elsewhere, wrote asking for money for his grandchild's school fees which I had been paying for some time.

About a dozen years ago while I was teaching at the University of Dar es Salaam, I was contacted by a Public Relations Officer working for Taite & Lyle Sugar Co. in London, England. The company had opened a sugar plantation at Lafiagi and employed many of my former students. A group of Nupe people were attending a training course in London. Among them were two young women by name of Umaru, daughters of the Emir of Lafiagi. They had spoken kindly of me to the PRO and had wondered if he might contact me and give me their greetings. The PR man told me the girls' names but I could not recall whether or not they were among the ones offered to me as 'little wives' (*yawo kekere* in the Yoruba language) by their ambitious mothers. The PRO assured me that both had grown up to be very attractive women. By then I was already married to Mary O'Hara and had no need of another wife be she big or little.

10

SUMMONED TO HQ

A frica is no place for an invalid, so when I was fit enough to travel, I followed my Provincial's instructions and headed home. Officially I had become the Province's Director of Communications and editor of the Society's magazine, *The African Missionary*. It was not a welcome appointment especially as it was where Fr. Joe Donnelly and others like him held court. I felt I was walking into a trap, a sort of lions' den. In Africa I relished working with a band of similarly-minded brothers. In Cork, rightly or wrongly, I felt everything I did was under scrutiny and unappreciated. I had no comradeship here or sympathy. I felt isolated. In Ilorin, my bishop and my colleagues had much faith in me and in my capabilities. I did not disappoint. In Cork it was the opposite. I did not disappoint them either – a sort of Pygmalion effect over which I seemed to have little control. However, I cannot blame or would ever wish to blame anyone but myself. Recently I had occasion to study my correspondence of that period and I cringe when I think of how immature I really was. Nor did I help the cause of my own eventual beatification by constantly referring to one of my superiors as 'Joe God'. I hadn't yet read Robin Myers' book *Saving Jesus from the Church*, though, had I done so, it would have helped me understand things better.

Just as I did when appointed to any new position on the missions, my first task on taking up my new post in Cork was to map out my territory, with 'Here be Dragons', 'Here be Snakes' warning signs. The snakes at Blackrock Road were invisible but the pit-falls were plentiful for someone as politically naïve as me. The Church is a gerontocracy, not a democracy. Having spent centuries promoting the philosophy of 'The Divine Right of Kings', it found, like the Muslim religion today, theocracy much more to it's taste. A convinced theocrat can only be a 'reluctant democrat'; vote as you like provided you vote as *I tell you.* It is difficult to debate with God or with someone who thinks he is God. This was my considered view and here is my little road-map:

The Society's provincial headquarter in Cork had three sections.

The central block. This housed "Promotion" or what used be called "Propaganda". This block included the office of the Society's magazine, The African Missionary of which I was editor. I was also nominally Provincial Director of Communications, an anachronism, since those in charge at the time viewed 'communication as a one-way medium that did not allow for dialogue.

There was the south wing – the pantheon that housed retired or sick missionaries. For me these were the heroes of our Society and I spent some time visiting their rooms listening to their stories which I found fascinating. Only a few were old. Most were sick. They bore their crosses bravely. There was, as one would expect, the occasional disgruntled person, one of whom referred to the place as Dinosaur Alley. I saw no dinosaurs there.

Then there was Feltrim, (Here Be Dragons), a stand-alone house inhabited by the Provincial Superior and his club. He appointed me but his coterie who equated reverence and submissiveness with loyalty, did not approve of me. I felt caught in a trap not of my making. To me this was a joyless place best avoided by those not craving the wallop of a crosier. I was considered lacking in the necessary gravitas to enter here, which was just as well or I might have been flattered enough to remain on in the Society and would now be ending my days on a treadmill in Dinosaur Alley in Cork instead of living on Aran. What depressed me most was the feeling of infallibility that clung to the place and the impression I was given that I had nothing constructive to contribute or ever would. At the time I was searching for meaning. There was none to be had here.

When I first arrived, it took several meetings in Feltrim to convince my superiors that one needed some training in order to edit a magazine but I stubbornly persisted which did not endear me to an establishment accustomed to rule by diktat.

After I finished my journalism training, I spent two years as editor of the *African Missionary*. Though nobody noticed, I felt that I did a good job. I persuaded many well-known people to write for the magazine. My argument was that the appearance of such well known media faces in our magazine gave our missionary endeavour support if only by implication. My superiors thought otherwise. For them, all media people were tainted and those who associated with them suspect. I got tired of dissent and eventually, I concluded that what my superiors really wanted was not an independent editor but someone to issue their press releases. It was the early 1970s and, as yet, the need for democracy or transparency had not penetrated church leadership to any depth.

Though I enjoyed editing the magazine, in order for me to work effectively, I need to feel I am part of a team. This could not happen in Cork and after two years I found myself doing the unthinkable – parting company with my brethren and going it alone in the world. This was a very painful decision for me to make and not something I ever expected to have to do. I think it was Aristotle who said that a man is happy when he knows he is happy. I was happy in Africa and I knew it. I was not happy in Cork and I knew it. I am not a loner but I can function well alone if I have a meaningful task. I need to be among friends who appreciate my work. This was not the case in Cork. I felt I had nobody I could rely on for advice.

Now at the age of seventy five and looking back over my life, I can be thankful for having had such a fulfilled and happy life. Mine was indeed a fortunate life. I can identify three significant events for which I am grateful: the first was in 1964 when I became a missionary priest aged 26; the other was in 1976 (aged 38) when I ceased being a priest and finally, 1985 (aged 47) when I got married.

With regard to leaving the priesthood, I had no qualms. I had given of my best years for a good cause, freely and willingly and cheerfully. Fr. Larry Carr, my Provincial Superior, and I spent an hour walking in the garden discussing my next step. He suggested that since I had never worked in a parish, I should do so for two years before making any final decision about priesthood. Carr was a kind and discerning man whom I can thank for allowing me to study journalism – which must have gone against the grain with some of his advisors like Fr. Joe Donnelly, a staunch believer in the Grace of State theory. Traditionalists in the Church believe in what they call Grace of State, a belief that if your superiors appoint you to do a job, God will give you the grace or wherewithal to do it properly. To me it seemed like an excuse for incompetence. I've never subscribed to the theory. In order to prepare me for the editing job, I first did three months at the Catholic Communications Centre in Dublin. There I trained to produce TV programmes but very little of the type of journalism I really needed in order to edit a missionary magazine. Then I worked with an Irish language programme called *Féach* on RTE-TV. This told me much about journalists and how they operated but again not what I needed for my job. From there I got on to the RTE Producers' Training course. Finally I did three months in the News Room at the Irish Times newspaper. If nothing else I made very good contacts, many of whom wrote articles for me when I became editor of the magazine. While at the *Irish Times*, the newspaper published about a dozen feature articles I wrote and this in itself bolstered my confidence. I still keep in touch with some of the friends I made during that period of my life.

Maeve Binchy, the writer and novelist, allowed me to publish a short story of hers; Brendán O'h-Éithir another, and Áine Ó'Connor, another popular RTE journalist wrote a monthly column. Writer John B Keane did a regular series of articles for me. I sought to make the magazine relevant to younger Catholics. For this I got a young priest, Páraic Standún to do a regular 500 word column for me – a move that infuriated the tin-pot gods in Feltrim. I knew Páraic and saw that he had his finger on the pulse of young people. He was not afraid to speak his mind. While training at the Communications Centre I first got to know Fr. Dermod McCarthy, a good priest, whose friendship I have enjoyed ever since. Dermod is one of those multi-talented people whose presence and ready wit can enhance any gathering.

But lest I appear ungrateful, Cork was not all bad. In order to escape the gloom of HQ, I had a small sailing boat which happily took me out to sea whenever the clouds on land got too thick. When our Society's much loved Superior General, a Fr. Monde, a Dutchman, came to retire, the Irish Province decided to present him with two weeks' holiday in Ireland. Fr. Carr asked me to show him My Ireland.

So together, Fr Monde and I travelled through Connemara visiting my friends the Mannions in Rosmuc and elsewhere. Fr. Monde also accompanied me to Aran on a trawler from Ros a Mhíl. En route he showed the Aran fishermen how the Dutch swallowed their herrings whole. He stayed on Aran for a week. He enjoyed himself as did I. Our conversations cheered me. He expressed sadness about all the idealistic young men leaving the priesthood but especially that most of them did not even consider applying for a dispensation. It was a novelty for me to think that Monde would even be interested in hearing my view on anything. In Cork I had come to accept that I had nothing of worth to contribute. Fr. Carr had a doctorate in Canon Law from Rome and when Fr. Monde and I returned to Cork, Carr naturally wanted to know how our trip went. When asked what I thought of Monde. I said:

"I wish we had more people like him. He is an inspiration."

"But," said Carr, "his filing system was in an awful mess when he left office." I am sure this was the Canon Lawyer in Fr. Carr speaking – or perhaps his Roman training.

My unguarded rejoinder was:

"In a little file you shall see me and in a little file you won't." What Christianity was all about according to the Vatican Curia. Tidy files.

It consoled me that the church as represented by the likes of Monde was more in line with the Church as I saw it.

After agreeing with Fr. Carr that I'd work in a parish for a while before making any final decision about priesthood, I felt reassured. I recognised that I needed a transition period. I was not happy leaving, letting go of that Ideal that had been lighting up my life for so long. I still felt that becoming a priest was the best thing I did in my life. Up till then, all my time as a priest I had worked in a sort of technical capacity either as a teacher, administrator or editor. I had little experience of working with believers at a parish level – in what the traditionalists called 'the care of souls'. I was not sure if I believed 'in the care of souls' or in the possibility of saving any soul, even one's own – if that. I would have liked to have returned to Africa as a missionary but since that was now unlikely, I turned to my Plan B. Still hooked on working in the 'Third World', I was keen to return there eventually, one way or another. I had been doing a bit of research and decided I wanted qualifications in Adult Education, something I had taken a fancy to over the years. I wanted to work next in South America and for that I'd need to learn Spanish, which also excited me. I had taken up reading the works of Paul Tillich (1886-1965) and of Ivan Illich (1926-2002), the author of *Deschooling Society*. Illich had become a sort of hero of mine until I met him in Chicago and then I went off him. Too locked into his own conclusions, like Joe God in Feltrim, infallible.

I had also become enamoured of the work of noted Brazilian educationalist Paulo Freire, who, I found, regularly taught in Toronto. I wanted to take courses from Freire in Adult Education, which was, I hoped, to be my passport to the Third World next time round. I was in touch with VSO and its Canadian equivalent, CUSO, organisations that I had worked with periodically in the past. At this stage, I am sure that, had I asked the Society for funding in order to study, they would have been quite willing to help but I was determined that from now on I'd make my own way in life and be obliged to nobody. I was very grateful to the Society for much of my early education. As Principal of a Government School, I had a reasonable salary in Nigeria but, like all missionaries I handed all my earnings back to the Society. Now, after my discussion with Fr. Carr, I was committed to working in a parish in Toronto for two years and for this I received my keep and an 'honorarium' in lieu of salary. I was not afraid of work, be it intellectual or manual. Organisations like my own Society had disappointed me and I wanted to study the reason why such otherwise well-meaning organisations did not meet my changing needs.

Many of the American Peace Corps people that I knew came to Africa full of enthusiasm and good-will ready to set the world on fire but soon found that they had to return home for more matches. I was now in need of more matches. My missionary Society had had in the past plenty of committed and talented volunteers but perhaps through lack of vision, or even neglect, had, over time, let many of them slip away. Why? I never found a satisfactory answer to this question or indeed to my own particular dilemma. While collecting my thoughts for this memoir I had occasion to review the correspondence I generated while based in Cork. With the benefit of hindsight, I would have done things differently now.

Purists will say I did not pray hard enough or become humble enough or sufficiently obedient to established authority. God knows I tried. The critics may be right but I am grateful I got out when I did before the recent tsunami hit the institutional church and tarnished the reputations of so many of my good friends, if only by association. Missionary Societies are founded and inspired by visionaries. They are killed off by control freaks. With hind-sight I now see that much as I wanted to be a good priest, certain 'priestly virtues' escaped me or perhaps were not in my nature or in my power to maintain. Here I have to admit that I had failed and had perhaps finally got myself, however clumsily, and perhaps by default, into the wrong 'little file' on the desk of *Dia Beag*. For now, anyway, *Dia Beag* ruled OK. One thing I definitely discovered: the God who made us is much greater than the gods we make. As regards vocations to the priesthood, this period in the Church was like Egypt of old, seven years of plenty. The attitude was: "There is plenty more where it came from." This is what the tinker girl at Knock Shrine once told me when I asked her to stop tossing her baby up in air in case she dropped him on his head. But I was impatient to find meaning in my life again, and perhaps foolishly, I could not wait. I had only vague plans and for a while after leaving, I just hung around marking time and hoping these plans would morph into something more concrete, which in due course they did. It did not keep me awake at night. Nothing does.

PART III
LIFE BEGINS AT FORTY

On Lake Victoria.

11

THE DREAM BLURS

Not since my 1952 decision, at the age of 14, to become a missionary had I felt it necessary to give any thought to the direction my life was taking. Not even when I was asked to leave the seminary because of my supposedly rebellious attitude, did I doubt the direction my life was taking. Now in 1975, over a period of a few months, for no very important reason, I began to lose faith in what, up till then, I had considered the great project of my life. After about ten years in the priesthood, my years of schooling and the education that comes from experience coalesced to give me a different understanding of my reality. By then, aged 35, I had acquired a fair amount of self-knowledge and I was fully aware that I had always been happiest when following a 'cause' or being part of a movement. Till now the missionary call provided the impetus and gave meaning to whatever I did. What brought about the change is complicated and I don't yet fully understand it myself. I have to believe that people change with time and experience and that I was now a different person from the person I was in 1964 when I became a missionary priest.

To be a good priest one needs almost super-human commitment and a very strong faith, not just in God and His Church, but in the existing ecclesiastical structure. I had no problem with doctrine. It was Chesterton, who wrote about 'the safety of the frame' and how the neophyte is obliged to stick to the rules so that in his ignorance he does not fall off the cliff-edge. However, once full knowledge is achieved, many rules may be circumvented because now the reason for them is understood. I had by now seen how the whole system worked – or didn't work – and I felt the sense of freedom that knowledge and understanding brings. As an historian, I had seen how the Roman Church was prepared to risk the unity of Christendom by the way they treated the Eastern Churches or indeed the Celtic Church before the synod of Whitby (664AD). For the sake of fixing the date of a Church feast-day and the style of a monk's haircut they were prepared to cast the whole Celtic Church into schism. Also, they would have stalled the whole modern missionary movement if they had their way.

With the passage of time my philosophy had undergone some change and I no longer felt the same commitment to priesthood or to the system that I did in my youth. I was now confident enough to plough my own furrow without seeking the approval of anyone. I had not yet decided what to do with the remainder of my life but I felt I had sufficient skills and determination to be able to earn a living outside the ecclesiastical structure. I did not feel trapped in the system as some might. I've always regarded myself as a 'volunteer'. I never felt cage-able. The concept of working for an abstract God always proved a bit difficult for me – like being employed by one of Plato's Ideals. I felt more comfortable with Jean-Jacques Rousseau's type of Social Contract and when I thought this contract had been breached, I felt free to leave. The idea of marriage had not as yet occurred to me. If I had given it any thought, I would have felt that giving up one commitment for another more burdensome one was not a smart move.

I was wary of falling in love – in fact afraid of it. I had many friends, both male and female, but whenever one got too close my first impulse was to put a continent between us. Sure, I wanted adventure – danger, travel, volunteer work in the developing world. I did not consider that tying myself in marriage knots was a desirable form of adventure. I was still living in the jet stream of the missionary rocket, not yet realising that very soon, by the very laws of physics, if not spirituality, I'd have to curve out of that orbit or find myself a new propellant. I was like those revolutionaries one reads about who, when they finish fighting one war, must needs find another or die. I met one of those people once, Ernie O'Malley, on the Aran Islands. He had fought in the war of Irish Independence and had written about it (*On Another Man's Wound*) but when that cause expired he could not resist getting involved in other revolutionary causes, as my cousin Éamon O'Toole explained to me after I spent one long evening in the company of the pair of them drinking in Seán a tSiopa's pub on Inis Oirr where Éamon was then teaching. I sat with them sipping my lemonade until closing time. In my youthful innocence, I only half understood what they were discussing. I did not drink alcohol then but O'Malley was one of my heroes and I had just read his book.

After discussing the matter of leaving the priesthood with my provincial superior in Cork, it never occurred to me to consult a psychiatrist or much less so, a spiritual director. I had no faith in either. Perhaps it was my Aran upbringing that conditioned me to try to solve my own problems first before bothering my neighbour with them. I had been told in the seminary that this was a trademark characteristic of mine –one to which I readily admitted. People expect one to suffer from all sorts of mental turmoil when leaving the priesthood but I didn't. It was winter and I took myself off to Aran for two weeks to think. I talked to nobody but to the raging sea. I walked endlessly along the rugged shore and the cliffs. Jumping over walls and rocks knocked into line whatever painful ideas were bothering my head.

Two things helped me to sort myself out: One, I felt that in my life up to then, I had not wasted my opportunities to do good and, two, I had never been bitten by the bug of wanting to save souls. After a fortnight walking the crags I had concluded that one phase in my life was over and that a new, unknown phase was about to begin. By the time I left Aran my mental bags were already packed. After that, meaningful activity and the passage of time healed me so that when several years later I decided to make the final break with priesthood, all I had to do was to grab my bags and go. I recommend the process. Cheaper than drugs or drink.

This was where I was at when I first met Mary O'Hara. Like many of my contemporaries at university in Ireland in the late 50's, I had fallen in love with her music. We felt that it showcased a hitherto neglected area of our Gaelic culture and heritage and she made us proud. Since marrying Mary, seminary colleagues take pleasure in reminding me that whenever it was my turn to play music in our student community room, I always played a Mary O'Hara album. Like everyone else at the time, I had read in the papers that Mary had disappeared to become a nun after the death of her young husband. Then out of the blue, one night, in Dublin in 1974, I was watching *The Late Late Show*, a very popular television program on RTE-TV. Like everyone else in that room, I was gripped by her story and thrilled to hear her sing once more. Ill health had forced her from her monastic fastness and here she was, taking up where she had left off 13 years previously. I was fascinated, not just by her singing but also by what she had to say.

When I have a problem, I like to make decisions immediately so that I can put my problems behind me. Mary is different. She likes to postpone making decisions perhaps in the hope that she'll never have to make any. Her most immediate influence on me was to make me postpone making any decisions about my future.

While awaiting my Canadian visa to come through I was temporally working in a parish in England. I was spending a couple of hours each day doing a door-to-door parish census. It was very stimulating work but it was frustrating too, coming up as I did against all the prejudices and hostility of the lapsed and the malcontent. I view organised religion as something that should help people attach a meaning to what happens to them in life and if, as happened to many, they have found the Church a hindrance, there must have been some misunderstanding. The Church is a community of believers, not just the office-holders appointed by Rome. Membership is a voluntary commitment. Threats and fear have no place in this arrangement.

When I came across Mary, I knew her only as Mrs. Selig, a widow who lived in a small cottage on a local farm. Each Sunday she cycled to Mass on a borrowed ancient war-time bicycle and on one of those occasions she mentioned she needed some help to move furniture and asked if I knew of any reliable people. I offered to come along with some friends and we fixed a time. After a game of squash with my friend Seán Trodden, a British Navy officer, we drove to the cottage expecting to find the widow waiting. But knock hard as we dared without breaking the door down, there was no response. We could hear music coming from inside. Somewhat annoyed at the wasted journey, we started to drive out of the farmyard and as we did so, the upper window of the cottage opened and Mary looked out.

We stopped the car.

"Did you not hear us knocking?"

"No, I'm sorry."

She came running downstairs, opened the front door and invited us in.

"But, what were you doing that you couldn't hear us? We almost knocked down the door, " I exaggerated.

"I was practising."

"Practising what?"

"Practising the harp."

There was a long pause while I studied Mrs. Selig more closely and then it dawned on me.

"Do you have any other name besides Mrs. Selig?"

"Yes, Mary O'Hara"

Seán and I helped place her furniture where she wanted it and she made tea for us. Apart from some paintings on the walls, and two harps and some books, the cottage was almost bare. That was April 1975.

Over the next couple of months before I left for Toronto, I got to know Mary better. She told me she was restarting her career as a singer but needed to organise herself better. It amazed me to see all the work she had lined up. One week she'd be in New York, next week in Germany, next week in the north of Scotland – all scribbled on scraps of paper scattered about on her desk. I offered to put it in chronological order for her and it covered several pages.

"Work comes my way sporadically by word of mouth," she said. "I have no manager or agent. Perhaps I should."

"But you must have had an agent or manager when you last sang."

"Yes, sometimes, but that was 13 years ago and he does not do that work anymore. Anyway, he could not stand my lack of organisation."

I asked her if she had any brochures, press-kits or hand-outs and she said "No".

Apart from two harps, there was not a single item in her house that proclaimed what she did or had done.

"You must have some of your recorded albums, then. How many were there?"

"Seven, but I don't have a copy of any of them."

"Are they still available?"

"I think so."

"Well, why don't you go to the music shop in town and find out? And if they are still available, please order a copy of each."

I borrowed a box-full of reviews – all staggeringly positive – originating from all over the English speaking world. The celebrated music critic Paul Hume of *The Washington Post* claimed that "she raised to a new high level the art of folk-singing." Another newspaper, *The Washington Evening Star* praised the "exquisite purity and delicacy that almost defies description.... Only a poet could avoid gaucherie in describing, song by song, Mary O'Hara's recital.... I have little doubt that she will soon be heard in many halls throughout the land: and I have every confidence that if we are lucky enough to hear her decades from now she will sound as wonderfully fresh as she did on first hearing." With such material, it was not difficult to prepare an impressive press-kit. It was to prove much more difficult to persuade Mary of the need for up-to-date quality photographs. I was so confident of the worth of what I produced that I ordered 300 copies at my own expense and I looked forward to seeing Mary's face light up when she read my piece. Alas, I was to be disappointed. I could see her face drop as she read through my masterpiece. Finally she said quietly:

"Thank you very much but I'm afraid this won't do. It is too glowing. It is like blowing one's own trumpet."

"But that's what press-kits are. You are not the one making these claims. You let the critics speak."

"No, I really cannot do it, I'm sorry."

I was very disappointed. I explained that I was only trying to help. I did not tell her I had 300 copies in the boot of my car. I persuaded her to take the copy with her and show it to her friend Bryan Guinness and if he said it was no good, then she could bin it and we'd forget the whole thing. She agreed.

A few days later she telephoned to say Bryan thought the publicity material was good, in fact very good, and just what she needed. She asked me to print some more. I told her I had 300 printed and in the boot of my car.

"But what would you have done if I said I did not approve of the material?"

"I'd have binned them," I said and I meant it.

With the press kits to hand, my friend Seán Trodden and I set about planning a charity concert on which to hang publicity and obtain up-to-date reviews and possibly some radio and TV exposure. We organised several charity concerts. I remember one for Shelter to collect money for the homeless and one to collect money for some pet project of my own in Africa. I mailed press kits to BBC radio and TV, to the organisers of Arts' Festivals, to potential managers, to music critics making them aware that she was back and performing once more.

Slowly we started getting results. The charity concerts produced excellent reviews, one from *Folk Review* (UK) claiming that "Mary O'Hara is simply without peer." I broached the subject of finding a manager to Mary - a matter of necessity in my view. Mary's views on this were contradictory. Yes, she needed some work in order to live but mightn't a manager get her too much work and work she did not relish. The thought of public performances had always filled her with a measure of dread. Logic, however, prevailed. Mary agreed to set about re-establishing communications with her old media contacts. My own recent brief association with the media in Ireland had given me some insights into this area that I would not otherwise have had. One of the first engagements I set up for her was recital of all-Gaelic songs in Halla Rónáin, Inis Mór, Aran. It was my home place and people still remembered Mary singing on Radio Érin in the 50s.

I started reading the newspapers and especially music publications with renewed interest. One name of a possible manager that kept cropping up was that of Jo Lustig. A controversial figure for some but a powerful champion of the artistes he managed. Early in 1976 Mary was invited to take part in a concert entitled The Best of Ireland at Carnegie Hall, New York and among the other participants were The Chieftains, a group of traditional Irish musicians managed at the time by Jo Lustig. It was the ideal opportunity for Mary to further her enquiries. As it happened, she sat next to Jo on the plane to New York and after returning home it wasn't long before Jo rang to discuss management possibilities. Mary was somewhat wary, especially as everyone she consulted, including The Chieftains, warned her against him. I seemed to be the only person that encouraged her to sign up with him. Later, when Mary's association with Jo turned sour people were able to say, "we told you so", but I've never regretted my advice. I liked Jo and felt very disappointed when later on, the two did not see eye to eye. He did much to promote Mary and her work. One of Mary's main concerns had always been that her work might try to take over her life. Unfortunately, this can happen when you hire a manager but I did not know that at the time.

It did not seem strange to me that I should help Mary. I helped many people. I had spent my life helping people. It was what priests did – help people. It was the nature of their calling.

Before leaving England, I had a telephone call from Mary enquiring if I knew of a good dentist. She said that she had only one session with a dentist during her twelve and a half years in her monastery.

"A singer must look after her teeth," she said, "it's very important."

I agreed it must be important but I did not know any dentists, but I would find out for her. I'd ask around among my friends. I was busy packing for Canada.

In a couple of days she telephoned again. Had I the name of a good dentist?

"Yes, yes, yes, I have in fact," I said, absent-mindedly, as I there and then thumbed through the yellow pages on my desk. I had completely forgotten to make enquiries.

"Here he is," and I read out the name of someone I pinpointed in the telephone directory.

It wasn't many days before Mary was back asking to know who on earth recommended that dentist. I had to admit I got the name from the Yellow Pages.

Silence at the other end of the phone.

"I'll find one myself."

She did just that.

It could have been the end of our friendship.

CANADA

In Toronto I worked in the parish of Corpus Christi, on the lake shore and I loved it. I've always felt at home, as it were, near water. I found the people in Toronto friendly and caring. I was in excellent good health, had endless energy and enthusiasm and had fallen among congenial people. When not busy with parish work I spent winter evenings teaching myself to ice skate on the frozen tennis court. A couple of times I accompanied parishioners to their cottages 'up north' fishing on the ice. You dug a hole, you fished and drank a lot of rye and water. Summer evenings I spent sailing on Lake Ontario with parishioners who needed an experienced crew member. Boat owners were competing for crews. On summer weekends many parishioners went up country to their cottages in the woods but the weekend was my busy time in the parish. It was all so very different from Africa and Cork. Like a perpetual holiday.

One family that particularly took me under their wing was the Doherty family. Their teen-age children opened my eyes on many aspects of life in Canada. In winter, they lived only for their ice-hockey, a game in which they failed to interest me. For me it was enough to learn to ice-skate well. The parents, Hugh and Gerdi Doherty treated me as if I were one of their own offspring. They helped make Toronto an exciting place for me. Away from the parish, their house was my second home. We've kept in touch over the years.

I remembered the Dohertys when, a decade or so later, I first took my pupils in Slough ice-skating. They gathered with glee to watch their 'old' teacher fall flat on his face on the ice. Instead they saw him whizz around the rink backwards, like a toy wrongly wound up. Their eyes bulged. It was my little joke.

Around this time too, I got friendly with William Kurelek, a painter of Ukrainian origin living in our parish. At the time William had just finished a book of paintings for Niagara Falls Art Gallery (1975) which he called The Passion of Christ. William or "Bill" as his wife and family called him, was suffering his own passion battling as he did with severe depression. The pair of us talked aplenty – or rather, I listened. As part of his healing process he decided to paint a mural of the Last Supper on the wall of our side-chapel at Corpus Christi. He asked if he could include me. It was at about this time that I had concluded that there was no future in priesthood for me. Having failed to make it into the Pantheon of the real Saints, I considered it only poetic justice that I appear in this painting as one of the apostles. The wall and the painting are now covered in protective fibreglass just in case someone resents my too-easy path to sainthood and feels like throwing a pot of paint at me. Perhaps at last I may be able to exclaim with Horace: *Exegi monumentum aere perenius.*

On Lake Ontario, 1976-

Tuesday was my day off in the parish. As long as I can remember, I've left a little corner or space in my life for experimentation - doing things that were not the normal run of duty, exploring areas about which I was curious but often ignorant. I suppose one could view it as a sort of 'play corner' where I experimented with new ideas, attempting things I found challenging. In teaching for example, one quickly masters one's own subject. The challenge then is to do different subjects or expand one's own subject beyond the bounds of necessity. Such experimentation kept boredom at bay but also added some excitement, an element of risk to a life that otherwise bore no risk. When I had settled into the parish, I gradually occupied myself with other interesting work. Most Tuesdays (my day off) I left town early to work with a music promoter who lived 40 miles up country. He managed a group of musicians and had a show on the local television network. Another concert promoter I got to know was Richard Flohil, who booked international acts.

Observing how these people worked sharpened my own promotional skills considerably. I found all this experience invaluable in view of my self-appointed task of promoting Mary in Canada – my corner for experimentation at the time. For the same reason I made it a point to acquaint myself with every entertainment programme on TV and with every music column in the newspapers. I took an interest in every Irish act that came to town and helped with its promotion. One day I was in class when I got an urgent phone call from an agitated Flohil.

"Have you heard of an Irish folk group called The Bothy Band?"

I had to admit I had never heard of them but then I did not claim to be an authority on folk musicians, Irish or otherwise.

"Well, Pat", he said, "it seems I've booked them into the Horse Shoe Inn" or some such place, "and I had completely forgotten about it. They are on tonight and there is not a single ticket sold."

He offered me fifty complimentary tickets if I could mobilise people to go to the pub and listen. In fact I think he even said I could buy a few drinks and he would refund me. It seemed as good a diversion as any from analysing Ivan Illich's deschooling theories. All my colleagues in the Master's class thought the same and also attended – Ghanians, Nigerians, Kenyans, Hong Kongians, Canadians, Brazilians, Panameans and I'm sure many other nationalities. The condition was that they'd cheer and shout and clearly demonstrate that they were enjoying the music – which they did, some to excess after a few drinks. Next morning the reviews in the papers were ecstatic. This unknown band had a volatile and international cult following! For the remainder of the week you couldn't get a seat. Richard was ecstatic too and my stock rose.

There were generally four of us resident at Corpus Christi parish – the pastor, Fr. Fournier, to whom I was an assistant, and a second assistant priest who was using the parish as a residence while studying at the university. One of those was Rex DeFour, a cheerful and bright young Trinidadian studying for his Masters at the Ontario

Institute for Studies in Education (OISE), now part of the University of Toronto. Rex spent every spare minute he had either playing tennis or squash, to which he introduced me. He had observed how fast I touch-typed and was pleased when I offered to type his term papers. In fact it was paining me to watch him type with his one finger and my less than altruistic offer freed both of us to play more squash.

Rex was aware of my Tuesday activities and of my healthy appetite for work and when, with his professor, he landed a government contract to carry out some educational research as part of a Royal Commission investigating education, he asked if I'd be interested in joining them as the third member. They needed someone who could type, analyse data and write. It was just what I wanted. As the grateful 'outsider' I ended up doing most of the analysing and I wrote the final report, later published. I knew that I was doing more than my fair share of the work but I enjoyed it and it brought me into contact with people with whom I would not otherwise have had the opportunity to associate. It was a serendipitous experience which whetted my appetite for further study.

It was during this time too that I got to know Marshall MacLuhan who was a member of the parish and lived two blocks away from the parochial house. I had read his *Global Village* and he was very helpful with an essay I was doing at the time on *The Medium is the Message*. I forget how I first got to know him but it may be that I baptised one of his grandchildren. After that I was a frequent visitor to his house. He'd pour me a glass of whiskey and we'd talk. A committed Catholic with an interest in anthropology he quizzed me on my African experience and especially my work with the Muslims. My Aran upbringing also interested him. I suspect that everything interested him. I was aware that he was famous (having seen him on the cover of Time or Newsweek) but his fame was never a barrier. He invited me to attend his lectures at St. Michael's. I had read some of his books before I met him. His encouragement also spurred me on. I now regret that I never got around to attending any of his lectures. He died in 1980, just as I was finishing my doctoral thesis.

I had committed myself to two years parish work but already towards the end of the first year I was veering off in other directions - but only on Tuesdays, my so-called day off! My plan for studying Adult Education and move to the Third World took a knock when Paulo

Freire (1921-1997) died unexpectedly. I decided nonetheless to pursue the Adult Education plan and on one Tuesday in April I visited the top floor at OISE which housed the Adult Education Department. Having typed Rex's various papers and seeing nothing too daunting in them – in fact I enjoyed reading them, I thought I'd do a Masters on my Tuesday off. The people at Adult Ed told me it was already too late to register for the coming September.

"Come back next year, but earlier please," the young girl at the desk blithely advised me.

I felt I did not have the luxury of time on my side. In the lift going down, while humouring my despondency, I said hello to a white-haired gentleman who had entered at the 12th floor. He immediately engaged me in conversation:

"You don't belong to this place, I can see from your accent" he said and he started to quiz me about who I was and what brought me to OISE on this fine April day.

"Oh, I was visiting Adult Ed enquiring about doing a Masters. You see, I want to go back to work in the Third World and I figure a Masters in Adult Ed would be my passport. But they tell me it is too late to apply for this coming year."

"Nonsense", he said, "if you are the right person it is never too late."

Before we had reached ground level he had prised a lot of information out of me about my background, education, work experience and probably general attitude.

"If you come back up with me to Ed Admin on the 12th floor, I'll start things moving. We are looking for people with experience such as yours in Ed. Admin. If you wanted to, you could still take half your coursework in Adult Ed."

EDUCATIONAL ADMINISTRATION

I found Professor Alan Brown, head of the Department of Educational Administration, to be a supportive friend for the rest of my stay in Toronto. Under his guidance I was to do, not just a masters but a doctorate in Educational Administration. But first there was the tricky matter of getting accepted after the deadline for applications had expired. I had to find transcripts of my earlier studies, a double first from the National University of Ireland. Worst of all I had to find a reference and the only professor from whom I could get a reference was Dr. Seán O'Tuama with whom I had clashed in my last year at college.

Seán had, in my view anyway, wrongly assumed that I stubbornly refused to insert vowel accents (*sína fada*) in my Gaelic scripts. One day in class, while in a bored mood, I argued against the whole idea of *sína fadas*, probably more aggressively than I intended. "If you know Gaelic, you don't need them; if you don't know Gaelic they are meaningless." O'Tuama took this personally. Before the final exam results were announced, Professor Hogan, the history professor telephoned me congratulating me on a first in history but lamented that Professor O'Tuama was intent on denying me a first in Irish because of my attitude to *sína fadas*. "Bloody *sína fadas*", I said. I explained to Hogan what had happened in class with O'Tuama and claimed I was only having fun. Anyway it seems O'Tuama's heart softened and I ended up with a double first. Now I was to crawl back to the same O'Tuama begging for a reference. I told Brown the story and he said he would take that into consideration when the reference arrived.

Some weeks later Professor Brown telephoned me at home and asked me to come and see him. I was filled with foreboding as I approached the 12th floor. He sat me down. I was sure O'Tuama had sunk my prospects with his *sína fada*. Brown read out for me a glowing reference. The bit I treasured most was his claim that I was a person of independent thinking "uninfluenced by received ideas or doctrines". I've kept a copy of that 'confidential' reference with me since and my only regret is that I never had the opportunity to meet O'Tuama again before he died.

But there was now the problem of doing the masters. I was determined to abide with my agreement with my provincial and do my full two years at Corpus Christi, so I only had Tuesdays free and if a funeral happened on a Tuesday I had to do it. A part-time Masters took 3 years and I did not have that much time to spend. The difference between a part-time and a full-time was the number of hours of lectures per week. Below a certain number of hours one became part-time automatically. So, I decided to register full-time, which meant taking every lecture available, no matter what subject, as long as it was on a Tuesday. With a couple of late night lectures thrown in, it became a great juggling act rising at dawn and driving into college to attend the earliest lecture available. As a full-time student I also qualified for various research grants. By the end of each Tuesday I was banjaxed, though very educated, having sat in on subjects I had no interest in except for the fact they happened on a Tuesday and helped me make the quota of hours necessary to qualify as a full-time post graduate student.

However, the rest of the week was fairly relaxed and thanks to my fast typing, I got all my coursework in on time. One professor wondered why I was taking a seminar in Labour Relations in Canada when by my own admission I had no interest whatsoever in either trade unions or indeed employers. He assumed, I think, that it was part of some Trojan Horse project by the Catholic Church. I assured him there was no such project because at the time I was only marginally involved with the Catholic Church, hanging on by the skin of my teeth. Towards the end of the Masters programme I was asked to join the department's doctoral programme and as I had by then completed my two years at Corpus and was living in an apartment in town, I was free of the Tuesday imperative with no funeral to distract me. I still had two papers left to complete for my masters (M.ED) but the Head of the Department promised to waive that requirement. Once I got my doctorate, he said, nobody would be interested in my Masters. Anyway, he said I could get it once I submitted the required papers. Come to think of it, I never did submit them.

I found the doctoral programme very stimulating. There were about twenty in the doctoral class, all of very diverse backgrounds and nationalities. Most of us were also involved in some form of paid research called 'studentships' which helped us make ends meet. My own research involved travelling all over Eastern Canada – the Maritimes, Nova Scotia, Newfoundland, Cape Breton and Prince Edward Island – interviewing pre-selected politicians and local authority administrators. It entailed flying out of Toronto, hiring a car, driving for days interviewing busy, often reluctant people who were not always friendly. But gradually I won people's confidence and taped our conversations for later analysis. The locations were varied - pubs, people's homes, offices, cars and a few in the houses of parliament – wherever people felt comfortable. The research was later published as a book entitled *They Politick for Schools*. It deals with how an individual's belief system affects educational decision-making. The experience proved very useful for my own doctoral thesis that was also based on interviews with elected local government officials.

For the rest of my time in Toronto I shared a two-bedroom high-rise apartment with Paddy Flatley, an old friend since boarding school days in Ireland. Paddy was a priest, a former missionary, now teaching at a local Catholic school. A care-free individual, he was very good company but because of our different schedules we saw little of one another during the week, more like ships passing in the night. I rose regularly at 5.30 a.m., played an hour's squash at the local court immediately it opened at 6.45, showered and breakfasted at the apartment, did some work and drove into college when the rush-hour had finished. I found I worked much better in the early morning, especially after a hard game of squash. Lectures and seminars took up the rest of the day. I was often out of town on seminars or doing research, the bread and butter of student life. I had many friends in town and if I had an early lecture I'd stay in town overnight to avoid the morning rush-hour into college. One travelled light. It was a busy but for me a thoroughly satisfying life-style.

Because of my own particular background, I took a special interest in how organisations worked and did not miss any opportunity to study them. At one seminar it was explained that within organisations, first-class managers picked better brains than their own so that they'd learn from them whereas second-rate managers picked less intelligent people than themselves so that they would not be challenged. Perhaps this was the reason why self-selecting institutions that placed loyalty above competence, did not seem to prosper. In a restricted gene pool, the Peter Principle is more likely to take effect. According to this theory, people in certain types or organisations are systematically promoted to the levels of their inefficiency; these incompetent managers then promote only those who present no challenge to them. Over time the quality of management within an organisation deteriorates.

Gradually I felt I was getting to the root of what was bugging me about my life up to then and about my Church defined as just the office-holders. QED? Not quite. One of the first lessons we were taught in the noviciate was that the qualities most appreciated in a church leader were sanctity and spirituality - qualities that I, for one, did not claim to possess. For a fleeting transitory moment in the past, I did desire them, but the feeling wore off quickly. The Holy Spirit, we were told will make up for what is lacking in the properly disposed members of the Church (the 'grace of state', theory) and in the end God will write straight with crooked lines. Time is on His side. So, Church organisations cannot be compared with secular society. There was nothing askew in the church to which I belonged – just that something was wrong with me. I was in the wrong place. I was neither submissive enough or holy enough. Not fit for purpose. It would be wrong to say that I was disillusioned with the Church. It was I that did not fit. My search had come to a satisfactory end. My discovery had set me free.

In the eyes of the Catholic Church I was still technically a priest. I was on good terms with my former colleagues and with what Canon Law would term my 'religious superiors' but I was taking orders from nobody but myself, nor did anyone presume to give any. At one stage my religious superiors suggested I apply for laicisation, a common enough procedure, but when I received the forms I felt I could not in conscience sign them without perjuring myself. They required me to admit several things I did not believe to be true. I believed my calling to the priesthood was genuine. It was real while it lasted. Yes, I did have some problems with authority, but who doesn't! I sent the forms back unsigned. A former religious superior wrote reminding me of the episode in the seminary when I was held back from Orders and told to leave. That alone, he said, would satisfy the legalistic minds in Rome. While I believed I had a vocation, my superiors in the seminary didn't. Case closed.

Generous university holidays permitted annual visits home to Aran. I had told my family several years prior to it happening that I planned to leave the priesthood and they seemed to accept the inevitability of it. Only my youngest brother, Michael, enquired any further:

"Are you planning to get married or something?" he asked one evening as we all sat by the fire in the kitchen. I could honestly answer that I had no plans to get married and he then wondered why I should bother leaving. I said something to the effect that there is not necessarily any connection but I don't think he was convinced.

It is a common perception that people leave the priesthood only because they wish to get married but in my experience that is not necessarily the case. People leave because of a crisis of faith or because they are dissatisfied with authority or disillusioned with the work they are doing and then, because remaining celibate makes no sense outside commitment to priesthood, they get married. It is easy to conclude they left in order to get married - like the ivy and the dead tree, cause or effect, the chicken and the egg. This celibacy thing has distracted people from what priesthood is about. Eventually, I came to the conclusion that I would never again recapture my earlier commitment, that I had in fact ceased trying, and that the best course of action was to make a clean break.

I wasn't particularly concerned about dispensations especially after studying and rejecting the official documentation sent to me from Rome. By this time I had got to know a number of capable and attractive women with whom I felt I could have happily shared my life had I so wished. I had come to see sex not as the terrible sin the church sometimes claimed. It was just a discipline necessary to maintain a celibate priesthood, which itself was only introduced in the twelfth century in order to prevent the clergy passing on church property to their offspring. A case of making a virtue out of a necessity. But it takes time to reject one's training and at this period in my life, I was still unwilling to kick over the traces. Just as training one into the church's view on celibacy takes a long time, shedding such conditioning was also a slow process, not something to be discarded over breakfast the morning after. For me marriage was a serious contract and I did not feel ready for that yet.

Around this time I had a meeting with my new Provincial Superior, Fr. Con Murphy, a classmate of mine at university and in the seminary. He knew my history well. He invited me to return to the SMA fold and offered me the post of a more meaningful editorship of *The African Missionary* and a welcome return to Cork. In one stroke he forgave me my past and wiped away any excuse I might have had for wandering off. I slept on the advice considering it seriously. Once a new generation was in power in Feltrim, and I had some meaningful role to play, I felt no great compulsion to part company with the Society. I might very well have stayed on. Con had read my mind and called my bluff. Much as I liked Fr. Con, I believe that one must keep moving forward. It would have been wrong for me at that stage to double back. When I met Con next morning I had decided not to return Cork.

I felt that the dream could no longer be resuscitated. That part of my life was over and done with. Con suggested that in that case I should apply for laicization which would dispense me from priesthood. Shortly after our meeting I received another bundle of documents from Rome suggesting I apply for a dispensation from priesthood. This time, because the documents came through Con, I studied them carefully, trying to see the reason behind each signature required. Rome likes everything in neat files. It was not my mother who had the vocation or my teacher but it was me. I did not find celibacy an unbearable burden, I was not in any way deviant. I had no problem taking responsibility for everything that had happened in my life, even my stupid mistakes – of which there were some. If asked to explain my particular ailment I'd have answered:

"Worn out by petty organisational feckdoodling."

You will not find it in any medical dictionary but it may be located under the heading: Hierarchical Institutions. It was obvious that the file-pushers in Rome needed an excuse to scribble a few comments like, "This guy should not have been ordained a priest" on my file and close it in order to make space on their shelves. What happened in my life did not concern them much as long as the file looked tidy. I sent the forms back leaving most of the spaces unsigned , but as advised, I sent a covering letter outlining what happened to me in the seminary and let the pen pushers in Rome come to their own conclusion, which would be that I had no vocation. I disagreed, but that did not matter.

Within a month I received a letter in lovely classical Latin. My Latin was a bit rusty by then. I have never read through the document fully but I presume it is my dispensation.

Back in Toronto, course work over, I was busily working on my doctoral thesis. Mary's work kept intruding periodically because she was having managerial problems with Jo Lustig and was busy writing her autobiography. I felt a responsibility here, being the only person among her acquaintances who had encouraged her to sign on with Jo in the first place. It was my understanding that a central plank to the agreement between them was that Mary's repertoire would not be interfered with but before long it became clear that Jo was determined to make his influence felt in this area. He claimed her material was too ethnic. Mary has a very independent mind. Because she is not interested in money or fame, it is difficult to persuade her into doing what she does not want to do.

The strain with Lustig was causing a rift between them. Mary would telephone me to complain about Jo's latest atrocity and without fail Jo would be on the phone a few minutes later asking if I would talk sense into this impossible woman. It was becoming ever more difficult to steer a path between the two irreconcilable positions. I felt that a little more give on both sides could save the situation but neither was prepared to compromise. Jo liked to talk "big money" and this did not impress Mary which, understandably, annoyed Jo. For Jo, business was all about money. For Mary, life was different. Jo talked film contracts for Mary if she'd agree to live in America for a year. "I could 'break' her there. It's where the money is" he would shout at me over the phone, as if I were the singer he was trying to kick into line. Mary could not see the larger picture and Jo would not make allowance for the particular.

The final straw was the autobiography. Mary's publishers, Michael Joseph, were keen that Mary write it herself; she said she was far too busy right then to do it, so Jo insisted on organising a ghost writer for her. I am sure this had more to do with safeguarding his commission than for any other reason. Mary sought the advice of her old monastery, Stanbrook Abbey, which recommended she get a lawyer. They put her in touch with a friend of theirs, Michael Rubenstein, a well-known London literary lawyer. I was in The Algonquin in New York spending a few days with Leon and Jill Uris with whom I had become friends on Aran some years previously when Leon was doing an article on Ireland for Harpers magazine and researching for his book *Trinity*. I took a call from Mary rerouted via Toronto. She told me about engaging Rubenstein and I knew it was the end of the relationship with Jo. I was just off the phone when Jo rang, he too having traced me to the Algonquin. Uris saw that I was upset and was wondering what was going on. When I told him he laughed.

"Tell Mary she is safe in the hands of Michael Rubenstein."

In a famous London libel case Uris lost and was fined a ha'penny. The opposing lawyer was Michael Rubenstein. I rang Mary to tell her.

One unexpected result of all this was that over this period Mary and I had kept in regular contact. A deeper relationship I was not prepared to contemplate at the time, nor was Mary, I believe. The Atlantic between us suited us both.

In 1980 I completed my doctoral studies. Professor Brown, my mentor during much of my time in Toronto, was keen that I find work in academia and the idea was not unappealing to me. Over my years in Toronto I had participated as a speaker in many of Brown's educational and management seminars, I felt myself to be a confident public speaker and teacher and I liked the university environment. But, to the annoyance of Brown, my itchy feet had returned. I hadn't fully got my hankering for the Third World out of my system and I had been in regular correspondence with Canadian Universities Services Overseas (CUSO), the UK's Voluntary Services Overseas (VSO) and others. Apart from what was in my head, I had no bothersome baggage, no particular pensionable ambition, no desire for fame or fortune. I decided to take a year off and wander – a sort of sabbatical – before returning to academia.

It was at this point that Mary O'Hara made a new entry into my life. In 1980 she had just ended her acrimonious 3-year contract with Jo Lustig and had just published a best-selling autobiography. She was now contracted to do more books and had signed up to record several television series that required much research and was scheduled to do concert tours in Australia and New Zealand as well as the now frequent concerts in the UK, Ireland, Canada and USA. As I had been responsible for finding her Jo Lustig, she now wondered if I might not search around for another suitable manager for her. It soon became apparent that working with Mary might provide much of the challenge, travel and adventure that my itchy feet needed. Also the 'between-management' hiatus made the invitation even more attractive and I soon found myself spending my sabbatical working with her. Brown was at first furious with me and told me so.

"You are giving up a promising academic career to become harp carrier for Mary O'Hara," he scolded. It was several years later, by which time Mary and I were married, that Brown with his own new wife in tow, stayed with us at Rivendell, our home in England, and he apologised for his remarks. By then he had concluded that I had not wasted my talents and there was nothing to forgive.

A SABBATICAL

My 'sabbatical' working with Mary continued. I found interesting work to do while trying to find her another manager. I tried my own hand at 'artiste management' setting up concert tours, negotiating with venues and musicians and television and recording studios. There was much varied activity to ward off boredom and idleness.

I travelled with Mary everywhere. I was not the only person accompanying her – there were her PAs Sarah and Sue and the other musicians and 'roadies' that make up every concert tour. I felt I was able to make good use of my research and other skills and managed to enhance Mary's work if only by shielding her from the hassle that is of necessity associated with such a fraught life-style. I did not have the negotiating clout of a long established professional manager but we figured that in the end Mary ended up with a reasonable reward for her efforts, perhaps a larger slice of a smaller cake but less tension. We found that we worked well together in a notoriously difficult situation and when we decided to marry in 1985 we had come to know one another's weaknesses and shortcomings very well indeed.

Summer, 1985.-

I would have liked to have got married in my home island of Aran with my family and friends around us but, as in the case of her first wedding, Mary was keen to keep our wedding private. At the time that would not be possible on Aran, or indeed anywhere in Ireland or England. The media would have had a field day. Mary felt one's wedding is so important an occasion that it should be shared with as few carefully chosen people as possible. That was not my view but I understood her point. With her first wedding she had the very reluctant blessing of the Church because Richard was not a Christian. There was no such problem in our case since we were both practising Catholics and I had received the necessary laicisation but as with all Catholic weddings there are many regulations regarding domicile and the reading of banns that did not fit in with our peripatetic life-style at the time.

Mary was touring much of the time but since engagements were planned a year or two in advance it was not difficult to arrange to be married in Canada in the town of Bramalea, 30 miles outside Toronto. Paddy Flatley, my old flat-mate from my Toronto days, officiated at the wedding. Matthew Freeman, Mary's Musical Director and pianist (we were in the middle of a Canadian tour) was Best Man. Mary was given away by Ray Byrne, an old friend of ours with whom she often stayed. His wife Joyce was Matron of Honour. The only other guest was a good Canadian friend, Dr. Russ Kempton with whom I had spent some wonderful times on frozen James Bay in the Canadian Arctic where he was working among the Inuit. The wedding was on September 17th 1985, slotted in between a concert in Stratford, Ontario and a book signing in Toronto the following morning. The wedding reception was at The Doctor's Livery in beautiful Lunenburg. The only other thing I remember is that we all laughed a lot, for what particular reasons I still don't know. It started when the priest found that Mary's ring did not fit her finger. I had left my new 'wedding suit' hanging behind my bedroom door in England. Luckily the priest had an extra suit that fitted me. The ceremony started two hours late because Mary too had left her wedding dress at a Toronto apartment and I had to drive back to fetch it. We had already driven the six hours from Stratford picking up our wedding rings from the jeweller on the way.

Immediately Mary had completed a few more engagements we flew off to Puerto Vallarta in Mexico for our honeymoon. En route we stopped off for a couple of days in Tucson, Arizona where Mary had a concert and where we had time to visit a jeweller to make sure the ring fitted her finger.

12

TRANSITION & NEW LIFE

I started managing Mary O'Hara's work in the early 1980s. There were many and varied aspects to her work: touring, writing, television programmes, making recordings. Much of it involved new skills for me but I like learning new things. Time passed very quickly. Our marriage in 1985 did not necessitate any significant change in our life-styles.

Mary's career was flourishing. However, she had never enjoyed being in the limelight and sometimes hinted that one day she'd retire from performing - sooner rather than later. With that prospect in mind, I decided to return to teaching. I'd always wanted to return to teaching at Teacher Training level but in order to do that I needed some experience teaching at primary school level. For that I needed a professional teaching qualification. While still managing Mary I obtained a Post Graduate Certificate in Education (PGCE) from the University of Southampton, a town within easy driving distance of our home at Rivendell Cottage in Hampshire. We planned to put the management of Mary's work in the hands of Johnny Manns, a London-based agency that we had come to trust. But before that I decided to get back into teaching first. I did not find the PGCE course at Southampton too demanding and I was determined not to miss any classes. I remember catching one 10 a.m. class after arriving at

Heathrow from Boston. It was part of the thrill. After graduating I had the offer of several posts but I accepted one at a primary school not far from home. The Principal was Catherine Brock, whom I knew to be a superb class-room teacher. She promised to teach me everything she knew and she was true to her word. She gave me the opportunity to teach the whole range of class and age groups in her school. I baulked at infants.

Ms. Brock's ran an efficient school. At that time, computer use and IT skills were new to UK primary schools. Though I did not have specific responsibility for computers in the school, I soon found that the little expertise I had in this area was constantly called upon. It was a case of "In the kingdom of the deaf, the one-eared is king". I developed an interest in computers as a powerful teaching tool.

After two contented years with Ms. Brock, I decided to move up a couple of classes and applied for a post in a combined school in Slough, a town on the outskirts of London and about an hour's drive from home. A combined school consists of infants, primary and part secondary. It was my first such application and was delighted to be called for interview and offered the post. I was appointed Head of Upper School and put in charge of IT and Design Technology for the whole school. Here, I had much greater scope than in Ms. Brock's school and the IT and Design Technology element made sure I was open to new and interesting cutting edge teaching technology. By now also I had been accepted for a Masters in IT at the University of Reading, a town half way between where we lived and Slough.

Berkshire Local Education Authority was facing up to the shortage of IT teachers by funding Masters' courses for primary and secondary schoolteachers and hiring replacement teachers for those willing to study. An unexpected bonus for me. From then on, I devoted my time to study and to teaching, while Johhny Manns managed Mary's work. Because I could not now accompany Mary on tour, she gradually cut down on her concert schedule and in 1994 she decided to give up singing completely, while her voice, as she puts it, was "still at its best." In the meantime I had settled into teaching children and forgot I ever wanted to teach teachers. Therefore, when I was offered a post as Deputy Head of a school in Hampshire not far from where we lived, I enthusiastically and, as it turned out, foolishly accepted it. By then I had calculated I could handle all aspects of teaching. But I was mistaken. I still had much to learn. I visited the school and was blinded by the pristine and up-to-date state of their IT and Design Technology facilities. In my eagerness to accept the post at Knights Enhim, I had failed to notice that the school was classified as 70% Special Educational Needs (SEN), mostly behavioural. As Deputy Headmaster, I was also responsible for IT and Design Technology throughout the school and this excited me immensely. Unfortunately, I soon found that pupils with such severe behavioural problems could not be trusted near a computer (their first instinct was to tear it apart). Hence the pristine conditions of the equipment. Nor could pupils be allowed the simplest implements such as compasses or saws or knives in case they stabbed one another. This curtailed teaching. Before I went to teach at Knights Enhim, I did not know that such schools existed. Because almost all activity in the school was devoted to controlling pupils' behaviour, there was very little teaching with the result that, over time, any staff foolish enough to have stayed had become deskilled. True, I had always left a corner of my life for experiment but this was not the type of experiment I had in mind. After six months of futile effort to teach, I had to admit I had failed and I reluctantly handed in my resignation. It was a bitter and humiliating lesson but it had its silver lining. After leaving Knights Enhim, I took up supply teaching. The skills I had picked up at Knight's Enhim stood me in good stead whenever I was asked to teach in a school that was out of control. In the end my experience at Knights Enhim turned out to be a fruitful one. I learnt new teaching skills and became more confident and calculating in my teaching.

While at Knights Enhim, I had come to hate teaching but I found the supply teaching afterwards very stimulating. One week I might be teaching Desk Top Publishing to a class of fourteen year-olds in the town of Basingstoke in Hampshire; another week Design Technology to a difficult group in a deprived area in Reading, or, as in one instance, several months teaching A Level religion at a Catholic Comprehensive. In this latter case the disruptive pupils had caused their young teacher to have a nervous breakdown. It had been his first teaching appointment. I now felt a sort of euphoria about teaching. This was my state of mind when I arrived home one wet Friday evening, poured myself a glass of wine and studied the Times Educational Supplement, a favourite week-end reading of mine. Mary and I had planned to spend our Christmas holidays in Mombasa, Kenya. On my way home from school, I had also picked up some holiday brochures about Mombasa, Kenya. Reading them gave me a new hankering for Africa. In the TES that week there were a number of advertisements for teaching posts in Nairobi, Kenya. In order to see her reaction, I decided to sound Mary on the idea. Her response was immediate:

"Why not?"

"But," then she pondered, "what would we do with Rivendell ?"

"Let it, perhaps. Or sell it. It's only a house." I suggested.

And that was how in 1996 we found ourselves in Nairobi, with me teaching Physics and Maths. I was meant to be Head of IT, but as there was no electricity in Nairobi for most of the time, I was fitted into whatever vacant slots that were available until such time as the school managed to order electrical generators from the UK. This African sojourn was to become the most enjoyable and dangerous adventure of our married lives. What started out as an idle plan for two month holiday ended up as a six year adventure and there were a couple of occasions when it was to lead us almost to the brink of death.

13
DÉJÀ VU OF SORTS: REDISCOVERING AFRICA

Back again in Africa. I was thrilled to be working with Africans once more. For anyone who loves Africa, the widespread corruption that has been causing the continent to go backwards instead of forward is disappointing. Until recently, anything connected with brand Africa smelt of death, hunger and corruption. However, a new breed of African is emerging. When I taught journalism at the Tanzania School of Journalism (TSJ), research showed that most households were headed by women who put food on the table and kept the fathers of their offspring in beer. Recent research (*New York Times* 11/10/2012) shows that some of these women are at last breaking through in the international market and making Africa proud.

I now believe that young Africa may have found another way to bypass corruption through Information Technology. The technology proved too complicated for politicians to find a way of organising their slice of the cake. Africans are smart, intelligent people and once freed of the shackles of corruption, I believe that they will make that leap forward, assisted by the new technology. It is encouraging also to find honest African politicians like Jane Banda in Malawi setting the pace. During our six years stay in East Africa, wonderful things happened to us and we met wonderful people. I find it encouraging that, belatedly perhaps, the prosperity that has escaped Africans for so long may at last be knocking on their horizon.

TEACHING PHYSICS AND MATHS

My early years in Africa had left me with an unquenchable thirst to return. Unlike West Africa, Nairobi has a moderate climate due to its geographical location - about 100 miles south of the equator and at an altitude of 6000 feet above sea level. We rented a three-bedroom house in Lavington, a respectable suburb of Nairobi but also bordering a sprawling slum. Our one-acre plot was surrounded by a 15-foot high concrete wall and sturdy iron gates. The place was guarded night and day by four huge dogs, a night-watchman and a day-time watchman. The ever present danger and the need for constant vigilance was our first shock. Friendly as individuals were, one felt in potentially hostile territory all the time.

Once classes started at Peponi, we pre-occupied ourselves on week-ends by camping. During the first week, we found ourselves with a bus-full of excited students heading in the direction of Mount Kenya. For anyone used to teaching in England, the students of Peponi were models of civility and good behaviour. It was Mary's first camping experience and she took to it like a duck to water. Our first outing with the school children included swimming in a river high up the mountain and, a lot of climbing in a tropical environment where we had to be continually on the alert for snakes and exotic animals. Our worst encounter on that first trip was with ants when some students inadvertently stepped on them. The ants crawled inside their clothes biting their way up the body. Dunkings in the cold mountain stream failed to dislodge them. Eventually the students had to gather in little private groups, strip, and pick off the ants one by one. From that time on Mary and I went camping on our own almost every week-end. Friday afternoons, Mary would pick me up from school and we'd head straight for that week-end's camping destination, sometimes by the shores of Lake Naivasha or by a small waterfall in Nakuru National Park or farther afield. Umpteen times we stopped the car simply in order to savour the sight of exotic wild animals – zebras grazing along the side of the road, giraffes gazing at us as if they were the tourists. This was such a delightful contrast to

Nigeria. We felt care-free and foot-loose and for that reason we sometimes took foolish risks. One of those was venturing into the dense bush where, unbeknown to me, there were wild buffaloes. We did not know then that buffaloes are regarded as the most dangerous killers in Africa, more so than the lion or hippo. I suddenly found myself facing one of those fierce creatures on a narrow bush path. We stared at each other; he immediately went into the 'charge' position and grunted. Out of sheer terror, I did the right thing: standing utterly motionless, like a stick insect. The buffalo's eyesight is poor, sensitive only to movement. Apparently the trick is to do just what I did - remain ramrod still so that one almost becomes invisible to the buffalo. A buffalo hunter explained to me that I had had a very narrow escape. Later on we were to hear of people tossed in the air and gored by buffaloes. Then there was the unforgettable time of camping by Lake Naivasha, just beyond the area set aside for camping. Well before dawn we were awakened by the distinct sound of a group of hippos grazing around our tent.

I was hired as IT coordinator at Peponi but Kenya, at the time, was suffering from prolonged power cuts. Computers required electricity, so instead of teaching IT, I found myself teaching Physics and Maths until the electricity problem was sorted out. Physics had been my favourite subject in school but knowledge of the subject had advanced considerably since my time in college and this meant my having to burn the midnight oil to catch up. It also meant that for the first few months or so, even our camping trips were overshadowed somewhat by my need to study and prepare my lessons. It was the type of challenge I relished. None the less, it seemed incongruous to sit in our tent by Lake Naivasha, wild animals all round us and me swatting up on my lessons for the following week and studying physics text books by hurricane lamp.

It was six months before an electricity generator arrived from England and I was able to settle into my job as Head of IT. This was exciting and challenging work, especially trying to take the teaching staff with me when I decided to computerise the students' end of term reports. I had never worked in such a well-organised school or with such a disciplined group of students. For a teacher used to places like Knights Enhim, it was a sheer delight to work in this environment. In this school, founded, owned and run by the Kenyata family, pupils were polite and eager to learn. Teachers were motivated to teach. Parents took an active interest. Unlike in England, educating children here was a joint project between all those involved. The school placed a high emphasis on games. In my school days I excelled in athletics, so I felt confident about sport. At Peponi each member of staff had to specialise in one sport and everyone had to know how to play and referee a cricket match. In my interview for the post I pretended I was knowledgeable about cricket. In fact, I had no interest in the game and knew nothing about it. This soon became very obvious. Occasionally I was given the duds to coach but the students were very kind to me and covered up for my lack of knowledge.

As I've mentioned and from the start, in spite of the atrocious roads, Mary and I travelled constantly during our free time – and there was plenty of it. Travelling in Kenya was hard work, often adventurous, even dangerous, but never monotonous. One always had to be prepared for the unexpected, be it the bridge down or the fatal accident. Mammoth potholes seemed to open up over-night out of nowhere. You had to be prepared for any eventuality and never leave the house without the necessary emergency equipment – tow-ropes, spares, blankets, first aid and HIV kit. Even so, you had to time your travel so as to reach your destination before night-fall, the hour when robbers were most likely to strike. For easy get-away, they favoured vehicles with four doors and a boot and it was with this in mind that we chose our vehicles. Robbers sometimes spilled nails on roads leading to certain towns and if you got a puncture, you were advised just to drive on regardless. Arriving at a destination without mishap was an achievement calling for a celebratory drink.

SMA MISSIONARIES IN KENYA

Wherever one goes in Africa there are Irish missionaries and Kenya was no exception. I knew my old Missionary Society was in Kenya and I was keen to meet up with my old colleagues once more. With that in mind, one of my first actions on reaching Kenya was to visit the Society's seminary in Nairobi. In spite of my wandering away from the fold, I always felt admiration for missionaries and felt I still belonged to the Society. It was gratifying to find my colleagues giving me and Mary such a warm welcome and I was certainly glad to see them. At that time two former class-mates were based at the seminary, Paddy Harrington, a former Superior General of the Society and later to become bishop of Turkana. There was also Con Murphy, an old friend and former Provincial who was responsible for having me apply for my dispensation from the clerical state. We spent many pleasant hours in the seminary in Nairobi conversing with the brethren and (in my case) catching up on the latest developments in the Society. Mary and I had a standing invitation to meals and even to stay. Paddy Harrington had a degree in anthropology from the University of Western Australia, a Masters from the University of Washington and a PhD in Social Science from the Gregorian in Rome. Con Murphy had a masters in counselling from Boston College. Both men when in charge of the Society, had initiated the custom of sending promising students to study in places other than Rome and this enlightened policy was gradually bearing fruit in the Society. With the right policies and capable people in charge, it is surprising how fast an organisation can reform itself and recover from past mistakes. In my seminary days, students were students and the priests were referred to as 'The Gods' and the chasm between them was immense and strictly maintained. Here in Nairobi, students and professors mingled and took their places in the queue for meals and sat wherever they found a seat. Once I sat beside a philosophy student who was scheduled to leave the seminary next day. Over the meal he told me that he felt he had no vocation and having discussed it with his superior (sitting on the other side of me) they decided that he should leave. He told me that he was grateful for the good start that the Church had given him and that he was now going to build on that and be a good member of his church wherever he ended up in life. In my own seminary days, if a student decided to leave or was sent away, he was whisked off early in the morning and put on the train before any of his friends found out. Contact with colleagues still in the seminary was frowned upon and anyone who kept in touch with those who left was suspect and regarded as 'disloyal'. Very like the immature behaviour of school children: "I'll not be your friend, if you are still his friend". I treasured my new-found contact with my colleagues and felt that if I ever had a problem, they would be there for me.

When leaving for Kenya, rather than selling our old VW car in the UK we decided to ship it to Nairobi. The saga associated with importing this vehicle, getting it taxed and insured, could be an introduction manual to Africa; pompous officialdom's fondness of red tape, form-filling and petty corruption. After months of inexplicable waiting, we were notified that our red car, nicknamed Marco The Red Dragon, had finally arrived in Mombasa. I took a day off school and Mary and I travelled by the night train to Mombasa to collect Marco. This train was a quaint but unreliable relic of colonialism. It looked as if it had escaped maintenance since colonial times – as had the rail track. It was said that if the driver took the brake off in Nairobi the train would automatically run downhill all the way to Mombasa and that was what it felt like too. We had a reasonable supper on the train – smartly dressed waiters attended to all our needs – but afterwards we were advised to lock ourselves inside our cabins and wait there till the train arrived at Mombasa at dawn.

Forewarned about possible snags, we had fortunately booked ourselves into a very smart beach-front hotel. In the few days our car was waiting in Mombasa it had developed some 'missing parts' and was not yet in a safe condition to be driven the 120 miles up-country to Nairobi. We arranged to leave it with mechanics and return another time to pick it up. We had not enjoyed our down-hill train journey all that much, so, we shuddered at what it might feel like as the train chugged its way back up hill the 700 miles to Nairobi. We were on the look-out for alternative transport home and when we saw in the hotel foyer an advertisement for a 'luxury non-stop' coach to Nairobi, we booked it.

The bus was scheduled to leave at seven next morning and to arrive in Nairobi at three in the afternoon. It was ideal travel time for us. It would also enable us to reconnoitre the route we hoped to be taking with Marco. We set out for the coach station early, only to be told that the coach was full – no matter that we had booked and paid for our seats. We could see the coach parked in the yard but there was no record of our booking and no sign of any other passengers or a driver. Luckily we decided to hang around and keep an eye on 'our coach' in case it decided to move. Mid-morning and unannounced, what seemed like a driver turned up. We were told to hop aboard. Half a dozen other passengers joined us in the almost empty bus. As we drove out of Mombasa, the driver stopped to pick up more passengers, pocketing their fares as he went along. We sat just behind the driver in the seats that I thought safest in the bus. There were no seat belts.

After leaving Mombasa, our so-called 'non-stop' bus to Nairobi, gathered speed. Creaking and swerving here and there, taking in both sides of the road and picking up anyone and everyone heading in our direction. At one road-side stop the driver picked up a bag of green leaves which I recognised to be *khat*, a marijuana-type stimulant taken by long-distance drivers in Kenya to help them stay awake. In Nigeria drivers chew kola nuts but here it was *khat*. Chewing the green leaves had other side effects besides keeping the driver awake. Every so often our driver dipped into his bag of *khat*, put a few leaves into his mouth and offered passengers some. About four hours into the journey, the green leaves began taking their effect and the driving became noticeably more erratic. As evening approached, the driving became even more hazardous. Our driver raced other drivers to see who'd reach a pot-hole first. Watching on-coming vehicles kept us glued to the edge of our seats because one never knew which side of a pot-hole either vehicle would take, or what decided the drivers' decisions. There was no rest as one was constantly vicariously doing the driving. The rules of the road seemed suspended and understandably favoured the larger vehicle. It was only as we approached Nairobi and the dual carriageway and the police roadblocks that our driver drove more carefully. By the time we reached Nairobi we were all on first-name terms. There is something worse than the slow train to Mombasa – the road back to Nairobi.

As it turned out, we got to know the road from Nairobi to Mombasa well because it needed several trips back and forth before we finally took possession of Marco our Red Dragon.

SAILING DOWN THE COAST ON AN NGALOW

On one occasion while in Mombasa to collect Marco, we took a taxi along the coast for about thirty miles and stayed at a hotel recommended to us by a friend. It was election time and President Moi's ruling party had organised the killing of opposition supporters in the Coast area, thus causing many tourists to cancel their bookings. Locals depending on tourism suffered most. Police roadblocks had increased enormously, some demanding bribes using any number of bogus excuses. It was then I discovered the disarming effect of Mary's smile and ready laughter. The African has no defence mechanism against laughter. He joins in and before you know it you are cheerfully speeding away from the roadblock, your supposed crime forgiven or forgotten. On this occasion, we had become friendly with two fishermen who made their living taking tourists out to the reef in a battered-looking outrigger with a large even more battered-looking sail. It was a traditional-type boat, what the locals called an ngalow, made from a hollowed-out tree. Mary and I discussed the plight of the suffering locals and thought it was our duty to try to help in our own small way. We came up with a plan. We'd cancel the taxi and return to Mombasa on the ngalow. The boatmen jumped at the suggestion and promised to get us to Mombasa in four hours. The few tourists we confided in, thought the idea hair-brained. Anyhow, next morning, after breakfast, as we marched down the beach with our minimal luggage, we met several of the hotel guests who just shook their heads making no secret of the fact that they thought us daft.

"They will rob you and dump you overboard," one opined.

The boat looked even more flimsy when we got into it. The sail seemed much more tattered than the one we remembered from our trips to the reef during the previous couple of days. Anyway, by now it was too late to give in to our misgivings. We boarded the contraption with plenty of quiet reservations. The boat tacked across the tall waves as it slowly wove its way out towards the reef and then, just as our confidence was returning and we were looking forward to crossing into the deep water beyond the breakers, the long pole that the younger man used for pushing us got trapped in the rocks. For a while the momentum carried the boat on towards the breakers, but as it was a necessary part of the boat we had to retrieve it somehow. As the boat turned sideways to the breakers, our navigator jumped overboard to retrieve his long pole.

There followed a period of confusion and navigational uncertainty as we tossed and turned and for a while, there was a possibility that we might be swamped by the breakers. The thought came to me but I was not sure if our swimming skills were sufficient to save us. There were no life jackets aboard or anything to hang on to if we overturned. The older boatman whom we presumed to be the skipper, finally managed to drag his navigator and his pole aboard and we faced the oncoming waves with renewed vigour. Crew and passengers were all smiles once more. We made a successful passage over the reef. Once beyond the reef, we sailed on down the coast with flying fish splashing about us and one falling inside the boat narrowly missing Mary. It was not always plain sailing but we were in good spirits and Mary's ready laughter had the usual therapeutic effect on everyone. Both our boatmen spoke English well and chatting about the conditions of their lives so intrigued us that the hours at sea slipped by unnoticed. We did not even notice that the tropical sun was burning our skin. The promised four hours was more like six but, like everything else in Africa, one learns to build such things into one's expectations. Had there been fewer holes in the sail, we might have shaved several hours off our voyage, but who would want that? It was money well spent. Having reached Mombasa, we dived over-board, the crew carrying our things ashore. We sat for a while on the shore chatting with the crew and then we walked up to our hotel while our ship sailed back home up the coast. Idyllic.

Shortly after arriving in Kenya, we had invested in a tent and two sleeping bags with a view to going camping every weekend. We soon found that Marco could not manage the rough terrain or the potholed roads. We bought a Land Rover. With its 'roo bars', it resembled a fortified tank and scared off the *matatu* (the African equivalent of local buses) drivers whose normal method of getting their 'right of way' was to rev up and charge our small Marco. It seemed that road users in Kenya made up the rules of the road as they went along and we found that otherwise aggressive drivers had great respect for a Land-Rover bristling with iron bars. *Matatus* plied the streets of Nairobi in search of passengers, flitting hither and thither, pouncing with speed upon any prospective traveller with a ready fare. Nairobi traffic seemed permanently grid-locked and was not a place for the timid. Few white women in Kenya ever drove but Mary actually enjoyed it.

Just as our red VW was called Marco, our Land Rover became known as Lazarus because of its survival from its one spectacular crash. Now with Lazarus we gradually started to explore the more distant countryside, places within a couple of days' reach of Nairobi. One of our first memorable trips was to Lake Baringo, about two days' distance from Nairobi. Most lakes in this area of Kenya are saline and some are soda but Baringo is fresh-water and has crocodiles, hippos and several hundred species of birds and fish. We arrived at Lake Baringo after dusk, later than planned. We had considered setting up our tent by the lake but a friendly fisherman warned us about the danger of doing so. Hippos come up from the lake in the cool of the night to feed and become aggressive if one gets between them and their young. Instead, the fisherman suggested we accompany him to an island on the lake that catered for tourists. We transferred our cold-box to his canoe and off we went. Under cover of darkness, the rhythm of the oars as they dipped into the water reminded me of Aran. But here on Lake Baringo the sound, mixed in with other tropical noises, made it all seem magical.

In the uncertain darkness, it felt like a long time before the island finally came into view. Then, all of a sudden, there it was, looming above us. At first it looked menacing and eerie, a cragged spur of jagged rock rising steeply out of the waters of the lake. We followed the fisherman to the top, up winding paths lit with paraffin lamps. We picked our steps carefully. High up, out of reach of the lake midges, we found awaiting us a cool breeze and the loveliest of sleeping quarters. Hidden in the nook of the rock, there was a thatched hut. A man-servant served us supper. It was difficult to believe that our exalted perch was 1000 metres above sea level and situated right on the equator. It was even more exciting to wake up in the morning, the sun shining through the gauze curtains and to see from our bed the lake shimmering far, far below us. There were crocodiles basking in the morning sun, hippos too.

We breakfasted in a different hut perched on an overhanging ledge of jagged rock. As it was Sunday and we needed to reach Nairobi before dark, it was with some reluctance that we meandered towards the jetty, late morning. To our surprise we saw a young African swimming. The boatman assured us that it was quite safe to swim. Mary was tempted to do so and I dared her jump in, which she did, while I kept a close eye on the distant crocodiles. I knew she wanted to be able to say that she swam in a lake with crocodiles. She did not risk staying long in the water, nor would I have risked it, no matter what the boatman said. Crocodiles spend much of their time in the water submerged and can sneak up at one unnoticed.

School holidays in Kenya were frequent and lengthy. After we felt we had explored enough within striking distance of Nairobi with our camping, we decided to explore farther away. We made a few exploratory visits to Mombasa, staying at different locations, seldom at hotels. Soon we discovered our favourite hide-away on the coast, a place called Mweni Cottages, twenty miles south of Mombasa, not far from the Tanzania border and on the shores of the Indian Ocean. It consisted of thatched huts for rent. Situated along the shore, each hut had a bedroom, sitting-room and kitchen with fridge and cooker. A house-keeper/cook was part of the deal.

Towards evening a fisherman would visit each hut carrying the day's catch in a basket on his head and, with the help of the cook, Mary would select the night's supper. During the day, young girls visited each hut, bringing locally grown vegetables. Again the cook helped Mary haggle until they arrived at an acceptable price. Our days were spent reading, swimming or walking the reef when the tide was out. I went scuba diving and Mary snorkelled. Not once did I manage to persuade her to don the scuba diving gear but she joined me to swim with a school of dolphins. Snorkelling was as far as she would go. We both enjoyed snorkelling, feasting on the sight of the multitude of different coloured fish and tropical flora. Though she is a very good swimmer, Mary lacked the courage to scuba-dive finding it claustrophobic. After I described coming up against a shark on one of my dives, I knew there was no hope of ever persuading Mary to scuba-dive. Then one day while at the bottom of the sea, my oxygen tank developed a problem and I had to make an emergency ascent. That ended any discussion of Mary ever scuba-diving.

In Kenya security is a perennial issue, as indeed it is in most of Africa. The hut was well protected with shuttered windows and iron bars everywhere, which seemed odd as any enterprising thief would not need even a ladder to reach up and put his hand through the thatched roof. On the first night we had an intruder. In the small hours we were awakened by a terrific racket coming from the kitchen, the sound of pots, pans and plates thrown about. Having extricated myself from the mosquito net, I grabbed the cutlass that we always kept by the bedside. We listened while the sound continued unabated. It took a while for me to muster up enough courage to push open the creaking kitchen door. Inside, staring at me with huge innocent eyes, was a little bush baby, beautiful to behold. He had crawled in through the half open window and was investigating the food situation. Neither of us had ever seen a bush baby before and we had to light the kerosene lamp and look up a book to identify it. It was with some reluctance that we set him free. The fright was very real but the capture of our would-be burglar made the few broken cups and plates worth-while.

ROBBERS STRIKE

Everyone warned us about the danger of robbers and it didn't take long before we discovered for ourselves. I had an appointment with a computer company in town and we parked as usual, paying the watchman the customary fee to keep an eye on our car while we were inside the building. I was driving Marco at the time and had hit a couple of pot-holes. On our return to the car, the watchman greeted us warmly but when I reversed out of my parking space I found I had no brakes which I blamed on a pot-hole I had hit as I drove through town. This was confirmed when the watchman pointed to the oil on the ground where we had been parked. He suggested we call a "mechanic" and we were very surprised at the alacrity with which four of the very species I needed appeared out of nowhere as if he had anticipated our needs and had them there ready and waiting for us.

Without a word, one of them dived under the car and reappeared almost immediately with a contraption of tubing dripping with oil. I recognised it as the brake-fluid system. The 'mechanics' offered to fix the damage and demanded money to go to the garage and purchase new fittings but I insisted on accompanying them, knowing that there was no VW garage in Nairobi. We then did what Africans generally do and found a welder. Job completed and after much haggling over price, the three 'mechanics' accompanied me (the fourth having stayed behind with Mary by our immobilised car) heading in the direction where we left the car and Mary. We were marching in single file and nearing destination when I was suddenly jumped by robbers. I did not see or hear them coming – just that I came to lying in the ditch choking. My three 'mechanics' were standing over me shouting "we saved you from robbers."

In my confusion, I had my doubts as to who were the robbers and who were the saviours, but lying half-conscious at the bottom of a Nairobi gutter was not the best position from which to argue. The 'mechanics' helped me to my feet and eventually we reached the car where the unsuspecting Mary was waiting, still in animated Swahili conversation with the fourth 'mechanic'. As mechanics go, the speed with which they reconnected my break-fluid system, made it obvious that they had plenty of practice in this type of work. Mary paid them whatever money she had left in her purse, I having been relieved of mine, and promised to return with more on the morrow. As we drove off, I saw in the rear view mirror that the so-called mechanics were paying off the watchman who must have complained that he was not receiving his proper share. Obviously, he could not ask us to intervene. It was clear that he had facilitated the thieves in their work of cutting my break-fluid pipes while we were parked. We hurried home. I explained to Mary what had happened; I poured myself a stiff drink and had my bruised neck seen to.

Using Nairobi as a base, we continued to spend our weekends visiting different parts of Kenya. This email sent to a friend in the UK captures some of the colour of our travel at this period:

Monday, June 02, 1997 5pm

Dear Tricia,

Just returned after a 550 mile round trip to Tsavo and Amboseli National Parks, both bordering Tanzania. Today, as we returned home in the evening sun, Amboseli, with Mount Kilimanjaro as backdrop, looked magnificent. In all, on this particular safari, Mary drove about 400 miles in the Land Rover. She is getting used to the heavy gears and, I think, enjoying the driving. We hope this newly acquired means of transport will take us anywhere we want to go in Kenya.

This evening Mary drove all the way back from the foot of Mount Kilamanjaro (120 miles), much of the time through rough terrain, a land teeming with elephants, giraffes, wildebeest, monkeys – you name it. Several times we had to stop to let animals get out of the way. A kick from a giraffe has been known to shatter windows and reshape vehicles, so one is warned not to get within kicking distance. They might also drop something unpleasant on you. This morning we stopped to let a group of elephants cross our path - As Mary was at the wheel, she was all for reversing out of the way but we stayed put and the elephants ignored us and just passed in front of us as if we did not exist - about six adults and several less than one year old. If they can walk under the belly of an adult they are under a year old. They were joining a herd of about 50 -70 other elephants on the other side of our path. We've watched them and each day they seem to do a circuit of several miles that takes in a swamp, which they wade through, and a leisurely walk, during which they constantly eat grass. An elephant has to eat several tons of grass each day. Much of it is dropped behind in the form of dung, a lot of undigested grass which (when dried) the Maasai use to light their fires. The Maasai do not use matches – just rub two pieces of wood together. They showed us how it is done. Yesterday we saw two lions up a tree. Then they climbed down and, with their two young offspring in tow, joined the male who was sunning himself by the side of the path. He seemed less interested, as if busy contemplating something else and he moved farther away each time a youngster started playing with him, pulling his tail. I think they all had just eaten, a fact understood by the grazing zebras, who seemed relaxed and not over anxious about the possibility of their being next on the lion's menu.

We spent the Friday night in Tsavo West National Game Park, (reputed to be the largest in the world) which at one time, twenty years ago, had over twenty thousand elephants. This time we only saw a few though we saw several hundred in the next park (Amboseli). Saturday morning it was a 4-hour drive across very rugged landscape. We had to wait an hour for an armed guard to accompany us sitting on top of our Land Rover, weapon at the ready. We only got out of the car once, something we were forbidden to do anyway and something the guard wanted to make into a big bribe-able issue. We wanted to photograph about a dozen giraffes that stood in our path. Giraffes are a curious lot, examining us and our cameras very closely. One sometimes wonders who is studying whom. Close-up, they look like one of God's designs gone wrong. Anyway we were not ambushed, as the soldiers at the roadblock predicted we might be - the reason for the compulsory armed guard. I personally did not see the point since the Somali bandits would find the soldier's automatic weapon a much more useful item than anything we carried. Even our Land Rover, in this road-less rock-strewn wilderness would not be much use to them. Anyway the armed guard is government policy. Apparently, some travellers were ambushed in this area last year. Ours was a very rough journey, much of it in first or second gear. The one hostile-like action was a group of Maasai warriors running towards us with spears but they only wanted to sell them. Tourists consider such decorative spears souvenirs. I bought one for 300 Kenya shillings - about £3.50.

All the best for now,

Pat

LAZARUS CRASHES OVER A BRIDGE ON THE ROAD TO MOMBASA

As time went by and we had exhausted the available safe camping sites inland, we were evermore attracted to places like Mweni Cottages on the coast. The journey from Nairoibi to the coast and back was dangerous – once we counted ten fatal crashes. A journey that normally should take six hours could take up to twelve and more, depending on any new crashes. A few times we had to seek overnight accommodation en route because it was never safe to travel at night. By August 1997 we had spent a year in Kenya and felt we were experienced Africa travellers. We had got stuck in the bush, we had broken down, we had been robbed, our food had been stolen by monkeys, we had camped in lonely places – we assumed we could handle anything fate threw at us.

The idea of a weekend at Watamu Bay, north of Mombasa, en route to the famed island of Lamu, was entising, so we set out from Nairobi before dawn. Lazarus was loaded up and prepared for all eventualities, or so we thought - jerry cans full of petrol, bottles of drinking water, emergency equipment and the inevitable sandwiches. On long journeys we took it in turn to drive, each spending two hours at the wheel. On this occasion we passed evidence of recent very bad road accidents and, as we neared our destination without mishap, we were beginning to count our blessings. Mary was driving. I sat cross-legged on the passenger seat, studying a map. Fortunately, as we neared Mombasa, I had put my safety belt on. This saved my life. It was a long straight road – a narrow ribbon of tarmac flanked by two strips of loose shingle one on each side. Beyond it, was dense tropical vegetation. When driving, one always tried to keep the two inside wheels on the tarmac while approaching drivers likewise made room for us to pass. We were some 50 miles out of Mombasa; it was just after midday on a straight stretch of road when in the near distance we spotted a large lorry approaching, heavily laden and taking up the whole width of the tarmac. He ploughed on making no allowance for us. To avoid a head-on collision, Mary had to drive off the road. Suddenly she found herself facing a narrow one-lane bridge. Luckily there was no other vehicle coming against us on the bridge. But by now she had lost control of Lazarus. The barriers along the sides of the bridge had long ago disappeared, ripped off possibly by out-of-control-vehicles such as ours now was and, as Lazarus lurched from side to side, it kept missing the abyss by inches until, in one final lurch, it toppled over. A lone iron bar protruding from the bridge pierced the front of Lazarus and helped flip it over on to its roof dropping it in the undergrowth at the foot of the bridge some twenty metres below. The thick thorny undergrowth broke our fall. It was the dry season, so the river was empty of both water and crocodiles. Miraculously, neither of us was hurt. I briefly passed out as we plunged over the bridge but came to when we crash-landed. There we were strapped into our seats upside-down. I recall each of us asking the other:

"Are you OK?"

Neither doors nor windows would open. I kicked out the shattered windscreen and there was just enough space for both of us to squeeze through. I had to crawl back into the vehicle to retrieve our safari jackets containing our passports and cash.

Several people lined the overhead bridge, observing all this. From reading press reports of similar situations, I knew that they were not waiting to rescue us but to rob us. I cautioned Mary what to expect. It took us a while to negotiate our way through the sharp cactus and by the time we reached the road, a sizeable crowd of onlookers had gathered. Not one moved to help us. As good luck would have it, a school bus from Nairobi was passing. I knew the driver and flagged him down. I never had an accident in my life before and sought his advice on what to do next.

He advised me that my first step should be to summon the Maasai herdsman who was herding cattle down the valley and hire him to protect us and the crashed vehicle. Otherwise, he said that the vehicle and our belongings, even what we were wearing would disappear. First I settled with the Maasai, whose name we later found to be Julius and the bus-driver gave me a lift to the nearest police station twenty miles away.

Mary seated herself under the shade of an acacia tree and shared her sandwiches with Julius and a kindly woman who came to befriend her. I decided not to frighten Mary by telling her about the potential robbers. I was away several hours. In my absence, after a while, Mary noticed several shifty-looking characters coming up to Julius and arguing with him – they pointed to the wrecked vehicle and stared at her. She quietly removed any sign of wealth, such as rings and jewellery (we had a policy of travelling with very little) and trusted

Julius would not give in to the robbers. Robbers don't argue with a Maasai with a spear.

Finally after several hours I turned up with two policemen in tow. It had not been easy. The policemen wanted a bribe in return for their help. Then they needed money for petrol. The arrival of the police was not as much of a help as we thought. It seemed that their sole function was to see how much money they could extract from us. Short of putting a gun to our heads, they tried every ruse in the book and some not in the book. The comedy dragged on into the afternoon. Eventually a European driver stopped and offered us a lift back to Nairobi and we accepted his offer, having first arrived at a figure with the police to have the vehicle towed to the police station for the night. We promised to return on the following day to continue negotiations. Police in Kenya consider accident insurance money as something that should be shared, preferably with them. Manufacturing the evidence is taken for granted.

Deeply grateful for having survived intact, it was after midnight when we reached our home in Lavington. Even the barking watch-dogs sounded welcoming. Early next morning, after a fitful night, we set out once more for Mombasa, this time driving Marco. We first stopped at the hospital A&E to see to Mary's swollen hand but when it looked like we would spend the rest of the day standing in a queue, I, in my role as a doctor of sorts, pronounced Mary cured and off we went. Overnight we found that there had been several fatal accidents on the Mombasa road and we realised that any one of them could have been us. It made one feel humble and grateful to God, the protector of fools, drunks and drivers on the Mombasa road.

Arriving at the police station earlier than expected, we found that the police had removed the radio from the car and were in the process of removing other saleable parts of the engine. "To keep them safe for you," they explained cheerfully. Every phase of the crash report had to be carefully negotiated. However, once the police understood that, no matter how they phrased the report, there was no more money in it for them, things speeded up. In the end and to celebrate, I bought them a crate of beer. One who claimed to be a Muslim wanted something different, preferably cash, but I knew he was lying and, in order to tease him, I suggested he convert to some other religion if he wanted his share before the his colleagues finished the beer. I had already arranged with a tow truck in Nairobi to come and pick up the vehicle immediately – otherwise all of it might have disappeared into the 'safe-keeping' of the police.

At last we were allowed to leave the police station, but, by then, it was approaching nightfall and the police warned us of robbers along our route. They advised us to travel only in daylight and to spend the night in a local lodging, which they recommended - the only one within a distance of 50 miles. It was the most uncomfortable, mosquito-infested place we had ever slept in – not that we were able to sleep much with the multitude of mosquitoes that entered through the holes in our net. Dawn did not come soon enough.

Mary and I consorted very little with the expatriate community in Nairobi. There were however a few people whose company we appreciated. One congenial couple were the O'Mearas, who lived near Nakuru. Robert O'Meara was an accountant but earned his living painting the wonderful wild animals and African scenes of the Maasai Mara. His very attractive wife Fleur was from New Zealand. Robert claimed that the sale of his paintings had enabled him to educate his three sons at Glenstal Abbey, a Benedictine school in Ireland. We met these sons and they were such good company and a credit to both their parents and to Glenstal. We sometimes stayed with the O'Mearas at their charming cottage in the woods in the shade of Mount Kenya. We loved to linger over breakfast on their veranda, warding off the monkeys that tried to pinch our bread. There was pandemonium when a group of monkeys managed to lock themselves into our car and in their panic sat on the horn giving us all a fright, fearing robbers had arrived.

There was also Diarmud Davin and his wife Pity, a quiet dignified Kikuyu who was employed as a social worker in the Nairobi slums. Diarmud was a teacher and a colleague of mine at Peponi School. The couple lived not far from Mount Kenya on a plot of land inherited from Pity's family. Then there was Nicola McCutchen, a young teacher colleague of mine and her Dutch husband Jos, a horticulturalist who in due course took charge of President Moi's successful flower-exporting farms. There were also Joe and Elsie Emmett, recognised orchid specialists, long-time residents of Africa. We frequently visited their house in Nairobi and they ours. Once or twice we travelled up country with them. Joe was very knowledgeable about Africa, its history and wild-life. Both had spent their lives in Africa and we benefited from their experience.

After our accident on the Mombasa road, it was to be several months before Lazarus was fit to travel again. Having got accustomed to the Land Rover and Marco being unfit for travel, in the uncharted bush, we decided to invest in a new Suzuki 4x4. For some reason we never got round to christening it but it opened up new vistas for us during our final year in Kenya. As with Lazarus, we fixed the roof so that the passenger could stand up and view the wild life as we drove through the bush.

CAMPING IN THE MAASAI MARA

One of our earliest adventures with our Suzuki was a camping trip to the Maasai Mara National Park in the company of our friends Nicola and Jos. We pitched camp just outside the National park and spent a couple of hours before dusk exploring the area. We set up our two tents –separated by a huge mound of elephant dung – on high ground overlooking a bend in the river. For safety, we had travelled in convoy, Jos and Nicola in their own 4x4 vehicle, somewhat bigger than ours. We had heard that robbers had attacked and injured campers at this very site only a week previously so we hired a Maasai man to guard ourselves and our tents while we set out for a drive in the park in search of wild animals.

We were an hour's journey away from our camp when we were hit by one of those sudden tropical downpours that make you literally stop in your tracks; all we could do was sit it out in our vehicles and watch the dense rain cascade. The muddy red laterite roads turned into rivers of treacle but eventually, as the downpour eased, we braved the elements and headed for camp, following closely in one another's tracks. Floating off the road into the undergrowth was a risk we had to take but, eventually, we reached our destination safely. It was dark. The Maasai guard had had the foresight to collect some dry wood for a fire, so we were able to cook a meal. A trick I had learnt was to bury an empty beer can, fill it with kerosene and light it. It proved better than any fire-lighter. The rain eventually stopped and as always in the tropics, things dried up almost instantly. We chatted round the camp fire until the mosquitoes drove us inside our tents.

THE ATTACK OF THE BABOONS

During the night we were suddenly awakened by an almighty din – flashing lights, animal noises and the shouting Maasai. At first we thought it must be another robbery until the watchman explained that a troop of baboons had invaded the camp site and tried to get at the contents of our cold box that I had unwisely left outside our tent. The baboons damaged the lid of the box but the alert watchman prevented them getting at the contents. The morning light showed up bits of several broken cold boxes, evidence that we were not the first campers that the thieving baboons had raided.

It proved impossible to get back to sleep after the baboon raid, so we rose at sunrise to a truly magnificent morning, the humid air cleansed by the heavy downpour of the previous night. We stirred up the embers of our fire of the previous night and after a leisurely breakfast, prepared to spend the day exploring the park. With Jos and Nicola leading, we drove along the now hardened and dry laterite road. We followed some elephant trails but, finding no elephants, we returned to the main track. Mary was standing up in the back of the Suzuki with her upper body through the roof and watching out for signs of wild-life.

Rounding a bend, we suddenly came upon a large troop of baboons sitting by the verge, idly playing as idle baboons do. One huge Alpha male, twice the size of any of the others, detached himself from the troop, swaggered past Jos and Nicola heading for our vehicle. Seeing Mary, he leapt on to the roof of our Suzuki. Mary dived down into her seat crouching in the corner trying to make herself small, if not invisible. The baboon sat on the roof looking down at her as if inspecting what he had found. By now Mary was greatly alarmed, as were we all, but Mary in particular who seemed to be the focus of the baboon's interest. She tried to shoo him away, but instead, he jumped in beside her, grabbed her shoulders with his large paws and grunted into her face. Mary, on her part was struggling in vain to push him away. By now, poor Mary was convinced the end had come. There was very little any of us could do about it. My first instinct was to go for the cutlass that I always kept under my seat, but (as it happened , fortunately) I had given it away some days previously to a Maasai man who helped pull our car out of a stream. I'd be no match for this baboon. He was huge. I was still sitting at the wheel trying to think what to do and Jos and Nicola were running towards us. Some instinct told me to put the vehicle in reverse and as soon as I did so, the baboon took one leap and disappeared through the roof as quickly as he had come, leaving us all shattered but grateful. Simultaneously with my gear shift, Mary, by now convinced she was about to be savaged, gave a heart-felt cry to the Almighty for help. This coincided with my gear shift. There is between us to this day, an unresolved theological dispute as to which action caused the Baboon to exit.

We figured out where the nearest tourist hotel in the park was and drove there, treating ourselves to some stiff drinks.

KENYA CONTRACT EXPIRES

Eventually my two-year contract at Peponi finally ran out and though the school wanted to extend my contract, Mary and I felt that now was the time to experience other parts of East Africa. When school closed in June we headed straight for the coast where we spent the following two months living in near bliss in our favourite thatched cottage by the Indian Ocean, eating fresh fish, making the odd foray into the countryside and even out to sea. We had no more visits from the bush baby.

With Mweni so close to the Tanzania border, it was tempting to visit a country towards which I felt very partial since my university days when many of us who studied politics followed the career and experiment of the young Julius Neyrere and wondered how his particular brand of socialism called Ujamma, or self-reliance would fare in the New Africa or stand the test of time. Mary and I made many of our decisions on a whim. More or less on the spur of the moment one morning, we left our car at the airport in Mombasa and flew to Dar-es-Salaam for the day. We decided to stay the night and before departing the airport in Dar,confirmed our return flight for the following morning. In the morning, we came to the airport two hours before the flight was due to leave and was shocked when the check-in girl eyed us glumly and told us the flight had just left. We could see it rising up into the sky.

"But it couldn't have." I exclaimed in disbelief, "We are two hours early. We confirmed the booking when we flew in last night."

Obviously it made no difference. At that moment, several other angry passengers came running along, shouting at the unfortunate girl manning the Air Tanzania desk. One man claimed his luggage was on the plane, even if he wasn't. He had checked in and was left sitting in the waiting room when the plane, with his luggage on board, took off.

"I'm booked to fly on to London this afternoon. And the next flight from here to Mombasa is in two days."

The poor man was understandably in a proper rage, muttering about doing business in Africa, etc. etc.

We resolved not to join the irate passengers who threw abuse at the hapless girl at the desk but we decided never again to fly Air Tanzania. There was nothing we could do now but search for a flight back to Kenya. This type of behaviour, I had observed, was a fairly frequent occurrence in Africa. A government minister comes along in his motorcade with out-riders pushing all traffic aside. Without a word to anyone he commandeers the plane belonging to the national airline and orders the pilot to fly him somewhere. Passengers are ordered off and, in this case, the pilot was ordered to fly the minister and his relatives to Kilimanjaro. The girl at the desk confided to me later that it was a common occurrence. I asked her if I would get a refund and she shook her head saying.

"Of course, you can try."

We didn't even bother to try. It was several hours before we found a small plane going to Zanzibar from where we booked a flight to Mombasa.

Fortunately, my replacement at Peponi undertook to continue renting our place in Lavington. This pleased us as it ensured the continued employment of our staff, people of whom we had grown fond over our two years with them. We left Nairobi quietly. Muthoni, the matriarch of our household, warned us to tell no one we were leaving in case we might be robbed. We all decided to keep our departure quiet. As a parting gift we offered to fund the training of each staff member in a new skill of their choice. Muthoni could not think of any new skill but wanted us to buy her a plot for a house in her Kikuyu homeland, something beyond our budget. She had assumed we were very rich, that is, until one day I showed her a photo of our thatched home in England. To a Kenyan a thatched house wasn't much of a status symbol. Her father had been a local government policeman in the days before independence and she had seen him cut to pieces in front of the family by the Mau Mau. Given her background, she had little time for the politicians, many of whom were former Mau Mau or, for that matter, for men in general.

Gently spoken Reuben, our Luo gardener and day-time watchman wanted to learn carpentry. Muthoni told us his young wife and a child had died of typhoid. When he did not turn up for work one week Mary had Muthoni search for him in the slum where he lived. Eventually, he was located and they took him to hospital. He had typhoid. The doctor told them that if they hadn't found him he'd have been dead by morning.

Wycliffe, Reuben's half-brother, our night watchman, was much more taciturn. He wanted to become a lorry driver. We assumed we'd pay for his driving lessons and driving test but instead he wanted the money up front. To our surprise, he arrived next morning with his brand new driving licence, stamped and all. He'd bought it on the black market. Having now got his licence, he'd gradually learn to drive, literally bit by bit. He arranged with a Matatu driver to teach him. He would hop on to a Matatu at a street corner, drive a couple of blocks and hop off again. Next day it would be a different corner. After so many weeks of this he'd be an expert driver and with his fake driving licence he would soon join the others clogging the streets of Nairobi. In fact, while still our night watchman and before we left Nairobi, he had already started to drive a lorry, which explained why thieves were able to crawl past him as he slept while on night duty. They stole all the man-hole covers including that of our septic tank. We also set up Reuben's physically handicapped brother Job as a shoemaker. Job had been using primitive tools to repair the shoes of passers-by. Our kindness was meant to help him but instead, it only sharpened his taste for palm wine. This little venture proved a failure, even before we departed Nairobi. A drunken shoe-maker working under a tree proved too much of a temptation for robbers.

When word got out that I was finishing at Peponi, I was summoned to the Headmaster's office to meet the principal of Starehe, a secondary school for orphaned street-boys. The school was situated in one of Nairobi's worst slums and was founded by this very charismatic character whose name escapes me. By that time the school was several years old and had carved for itself a name as one of the best schools not just in Kenya but in the whole of Africa. The principal of Starehe, having heard I was leaving Peponi, was offering me a post as head of IT. I felt flattered. I offered to consult my wife and come back to him within a couple of days. It would mean volunteering to spend two extra years in Nairobi living in a very small tin-roofed house on the school compound. I had encountered some of Starehe's graduates in my work and admired them enormously. Mary and I were both very excited though somewhat apprehensive. We visited the school and observed how it operated and decided to give it a go and volunteer to work there without salary for two years.

My main fear was that Mary would find the living conditions too harsh. We had Jean Heitz, a Dutch friend, staying with us at the time and she accompanied Mary to Starehe to measure our dwelling for curtains. Up till then, the principal had been all over us but now that we had more or less committed ourselves, he suddenly distanced himself and was not nearly as helpful as Mary had expected. She found it difficult to cope with this sudden change in attitude. She telephoned me and communicated her apprehension. Luckily we had not finally committed ourselves. As some of the arrangements for working at Starehe had been made through the school's deputy headmaster, I telephoned him to express our disappointment and surprise. I gathered that this was not unusual, and that in the Headmaster of Starehe, we were dealing with a charismatic but temperamental individual. I told the Deputy that our offer was withdrawn. After my own past experience with autocratic bachelors, I did not want to go down that route any more. When God is one's immediate line manager the temptation to autocracy is understandable.

FAREWELL TO KENYA

At one stage we had considered driving home to the UK from Nairobi via Arabia. I had researched the route and the possible problems but after several visits to the relevant authorities in Nairobi, I concluded that the red tape would be too much.

After finishing at Peponi in June, we decided to spend the months until September in Myweni in our favourite thatched hut by the Indian Ocean. However, shortly before we were due to leave

Kenya, I was offered the Headship of a Moslem secondary school in Mombasa. This was an unexpected though exciting development.

The offer came from the Aga Khan Educational Foundation. I discussed the conditions over the phone but the official interview took place in a hotel near the airport on the day we were leaving for London. We met Mr Bin Yamu, the chairman of the Mombasa Aga Khan Education Board, and thrashed out the final details of my contract. Our residence was to be on the school compound in Mombasa but Mary, knowing Mombasa, was not comfortable with this and in order to accommodate her, the Board offered to house us in a property on the beach nearby. This, we both considered to be a touch of Nirvana. This was September and by mid October, two air-tickets would be sent to us in England and I would return to Kenya and assume my duties of Headmaster by mid-December. It was also agreed that if, for any reason, the tickets did not arrive, the deal was off. So, we departed Kenya on a high note, leaving most of our belongings stored in the SMA seminary in Nairobi along with our land-rover Lazarus, expecting to pick them up again by Christmas at the latest. But again we found that 'man proposes, God disposes'. We could not foresee that we were on the brink of our most exciting African adventure yet, something way bigger than living on a beach in claustrophobic Mombasa.

14
WELCOME TO TANZANIA

The prospect of two full years on the coast greatly appealed to both of us and our departure from Nairobi in mid-September 1998 was a quiet but happy occasion.

A HIATUS IN THE UK

Assuming Mr Bin Yamu would get back to me with the two return tickets to Mombasa, we spent the autumn of 1998 tidying up our thatched cottage in England, re-thatching it, and installing a new kitchen. But when by December Bin Yamu hadn't made good on his promise and the weather in the UK was becoming miserable, we found it irresistible when APSO, a branch of the Irish Government's Overseas Development Department offered me a post teaching in Dar -es-Salaam, Tanzania - at The Tanzania School of Journalism (TSJ), University of Dar- es-Salaam.

I was to teach post-graduates and supervise their theses. With regard to the TSJ job, along with suitable academic qualifications I was required to have a professional qualification in teaching such as my PGCE. My subjects were Public Relations and Advertising, core subjects for post-graduate students studying for degrees in journalism which would permit them to write for the local newspapers, something they were forbidden to do otherwise. Later on, my responsibilities were expanded to include IT and computer-assisted journalism for the undergraduates. Dar es Salaam is by the sea with the island of Zanzibar only a two hour ferry ride away. It was the ideal location for the likes of me and Mary. I signed up for two years, which, later on, we extended to four.

The arrangement with the Irish Government was that Mary and I would travel out together to Dar es Salaam in time for me to start teaching after Easter 1999. APSO had a strict schedule of initiation and language training for all newly recruited Development Workers (DWs) and their spouses. This meant a two-week Kiswahili course in Dublin before setting out for Dar, another two-week orientation course in downtown Dar-es-Salaam immediately after arrival, followed by a six-week Kiswahili immersion course in Arusha, a small town situated in the lush green foothills of Kilimanjaro, near the border with Kenya. On a good day, Arusha is about ten hours' drive north of Dar – depending on the condition of the roads and on the number of accidents en route. All driving times in Africa are proximate and best calculated 'on a good day'.

As often with Africa, things did not work out as planned. The Tanzania School of Journalism, pleading dire shortage of staff, badgered APSO to have me in place to start teaching in January. As I was to discover, organisation and planning was not TSJ's forte and, having presented myself at the school every morning at 8 a.m. during all of the month of December, I was one day summoned to the Principal's office to be informed that I would not now be needed until after Easter. The Principal, Mr. Moshiru said:

"You need not report for work every day. It will save us electricity."

I had been given an office with an air-conditioner. However, I felt I had lessons to prepare and I liked interacting with the students. Then suddenly without warning, one morning in March, without any preamble, the Principal called me into his office again and said:

"Pat can you start teaching the post-graduates?"

"When?"

"Tomorrow morning."

"Why the urgency now?

"Because they have just complained that their teacher for PR and Advertising has not turned up all term."

In fact the man in question who had government connections, and drew his school salary each month, was away on a scholarship in the USA. I knew it and everyone else was aware of it. But that was how things work in Africa.

Next morning I started teaching an eager class of sixteen mature post-graduates, about half of them women. All of them would have been funded by some government department. Two were army officers, one was deputy to the Premier of Zanzibar, another was an assistant to the Prime Minister of Tanzania and one woman was a well-known broadcaster on the national TV station. I insisted that I could not do my job without making the computers available to the students. Hitherto they had been locked away and available only to staff. It took weeks to negotiate this and the only way it could be arranged was for me to take on the additional post of head of IT, which suited my plans perfectly. I insisted that all students passed an examination in computer literacy before they could graduate. Included in that was touch-typing. I am a very fast touch-typist myself and that made sure that there was something at which I excelled.

By then, Mary had just arrived in Dar es Salaam. After completing her orientation course in Dublin, she successfully survived the Dar 'week-in-the-slum' course and the Kiswahili immersion course in Arusha. She then joined me in Dar. The University was contractually obliged to provide accommodation and transport but we were by now sufficiently experienced about Africa not to put our faith in such promises. We brought our own transport, Lazarus, from Nairobi and we were prepared to pay for our own accommodation as long as TSJ found it for us. My main concern was to find suitable accommodation for Mary. I had been prepared to rough it as I had done in Nigeria but I did not expect Mary to rough it.

Julius Nyerere, as part of his *Ujamma* socialism programme, had confiscated most privately owned properties in Dar and handed them over to government departments like TSJ, who immediately and automatically set about looting and vandalising them – easy come, easy go - stripping them of everything of value, including plumbing, doors and windows. As soon as I arrived, TSJ lined up several dwellings for me to inspect. After what seemed like days traipsing around Dar es Salaam, visiting one uninhabitable property after another, the hot sun and the rainy season took their tolls and we were all becoming a bit frayed at the edges. Six of us travelled in three run-down cars, each car taking turns to get stuck in the mud and needing a push. Mr Moshiru, the Principal of TSJ, began showing his frustration at my lack of enthusiasm for the derelict properties on offer. One day after having to get out to push his car through the mud one more time, he showed his annoyance and muttered:

"Dr. O'Toole, I expected a dedicated volunteer worker like you to put up with some suffering and inconvenience with regard to accommodation."

For the sake of Africa, I assumed, which annoyed me. Well aware of this mentality among many educated Africans, I straightened up and turned to him:

"Now look here, Mr. Moshiru. Let's get one thing straight. I came to Africa to share my skills with you, not to share your suffering with me."

That cleared the air and, in spite of himself, Moshiru laughed. (Later I heard him repeat my remark with amusement at meetings.) Now, I went on to explain that whereas I could put up with discomforts, I was determined my wife Mary, who in any case wasn't an APSO DW, should not be subjected to miserable living conditions. Over time, Mr. Moshiru became a good friend and over the occasional drink, he'd share his frustrations about African corruption with me. He supplied us regularly with passion fruit from his farm up country.

The house I eventually selected was situated near the main road, in an area known as Kinondoni B, a noisy sprawling mixture of dwellings, some fortified, some not. It had barred windows (with no glass) and was surrounded by high walls and iron gates. It had, of course, to be guarded day and night or it would have been looted. Unfortunately there was no garden attached. A garden would have been very welcome in the stifling heat of Dar, but the house was not far from the sea and within easy drive of TSJ, thus saving me the fumes and stresses of the snarling traffic jams that seem to plague every African city. Also I was keen to live among the Africans, not on the reservations so favoured by the ex-pats.

I arrived in Dar es Salaam driving a Kenya registered vehicle, which suggested to the police that I might be a potential source of income. Invariably wherever I drove, I was stopped and questioned.

They tested every avenue in order to make me part with some money. It is called *kidogo* (something small) in Swahili or bribe in English. The best was the 'one way street' trick.

"Sir, you're driving the wrong way."

"Why you think so?

"This is a one way street."

"But there is no sign."

"Yes, sir, back there" pointing in the direction from where I had driven.

There was no sign.

"There is, sir."

"Show me, hop in."

The policeman sat in beside me and we drove back up the street, the policeman pointing me to another street that I had not travelled.

"No, no. I did not come by that street but by this street here."

After finding nothing that resembled a one-way sign, the matter of the invisible sign-post was dropped.

"I will take you to the police-station."

"Why so?"

"Because," he imperiously intoned, "you have broken the law of Tanzania. You will have to go to court and spend the day there."

"I know the courthouse. I will enjoy my day there."

"How come you know the court-house?

"I take my students there. I teach journalism at the Tanzania School of Journalism."

I felt this did not go down well and there followed a lengthy silence as I negotiated the potholes in the rutted street. Then:

"I will take you to the police-station."

"Why so?"

"Because you have broken the law of Tanzania."

Inside the dark room in the police-station, I was put sitting in front of two female police-women who took my particulars and why I had been arrested.

"Because I broke the law of Tanzania."

I engaged in some light-hearted banter with the pair of bored police-women. To their amusement, I insisted on practising my best Swahili. Having been taught much of my Swahili by my students, I knew all the 'wrong' words to use. The police-women and myself had a very good laugh while awaiting the return of the glum policeman. After a long delay, the policeman emerged from the office of his superior. They had obviously had a conference and decided against arresting me. Now much emboldened after my cheerful conversation with the two women and believing I was now unlikely to be carted off to jail, I enquired: "You're bringing me to jail, sir?

"No, I'm setting you free."

"But why, sir, I have broken the law of Tanzania?"

"Because we cannot find the log book..."

There was a slight sequel as the policeman beckoned me outside out of earshot of the two police-women.

"Where are you going, sir?"

"T. G. Dobie, the Garage."

I'll take you there by a short-cut."

He sat in beside me and we had a very civilized conversation en route to T.G. Dobie, the garage. He understood well why I could not give him a *kidogo* but neither of us saw any harm in the price of two bottles of beer which was more than two days' wages for a Tanzanian policeman.

I had arrived in Tanzania at the end of the dry season, Mary joining me two months later. When the rainy season came, we found that two of our bedrooms flooded. It happened suddenly after each heavy rainfall and it emptied just as quickly. It was a design problem with the house that could not be easily rectified, certainly not by us, so we moved our bed to the front room where it stayed for the rest of our time in Dar. Waking up in a big bed draped in a mosquito net and surrounded by a quiet lake with the sound of trickling water is certainly a novelty. One of our visitors, Dermod McCarthy, christened our guest bedroom 'The Lake District'. In any case, by the time the first floods happened, we had become accustomed to our house and searching for another property was out of the question.

One of our first visitors in Dar-es-Salaam was George, our Maasai godson whom Mary had befriended in Nairobi. The Maasai move freely across country borders without travel documentation, and the police do not bother them. We gave George some money to help him set up a little road-side stall he had planned. When he was returning to Nairobi, I offered to drop him off at the bus station and was taken aback to find him emerging from our spare room decked out in an ill-fitting, shabby suit, shirt and tie and carrying a briefcase and wearing designer sunglasses - all completely unnecessary, out of place and surely uncomfortable on the long hot bus ride to Nairobi. But I said nothing in case it might offend him. It came as no surprise to hear some months later that his fancy dress attracted the attention of the police, as I expected it would. They stopped him at the checkpoint half a mile from the border and fined him heavily for not having travel documents (which the Maasai did not need anyway).

Foolishly he paid the fine from his wad of notes, returning the balance to his pocket. The temptation proved too much for the police who put him back on the bus only to remove him again before the bus crossed into Kenya, this time relieving him of all his possessions, his money, watch, designer sun-glasses and fancy tie, leaving him no choice but to hike the remaining 100 miles or so to Nairobi. This hike was no problem to George who was a long-distance runner and a hundred miles for a Maasai was like a morning jaunt.

After leaving George at the bus, Mary and I decided to spend the day at one of our favourite beaches. We were driving out of town when we saw a youth being chased by a mob shouting Olé which in Swahili means 'thief'. I warned Mary:

"They are going to stone him to death."

We stopped the car and watched the mob chase and grab the young boy. Holding him by his arms and legs, they carried him shoulder high back to the shanty shops from where he was fleeing. He was crying and pleading in Swahili:

"She gave it to me, she gave it to me."

He was referring, I assume, to a loaf of bread he had in his hand.

But his pleas for mercy fell on deaf ears. Some in the mob already had stones in their hands. We thought that by stopping to watch, our presence might deter them but, grimly resolute and ignoring our presence, they walked past us in silence bearing their captive to his death. There was nothing we could do except offer up a quiet prayer and drive on.

This is what happens when a police-force becomes corrupt and the community has no faith in the system or that justice will prevail. They take the law into their own hands to protect themselves.

MY MOTHER DIES IN DAR

During our six years in East Africa, family and friends from Europe came to visit. My mother, Bid Bhilla, came. She flew out with my brother Michael and his family. When she came to stay with us in Nairobi she was in her early 80s – with a heart condition but game for any adventure. That trip was a great success and she enjoyed herself with never a murmur when unforeseen hardships cropped up, like the time she was subjected to an extra 8-hour long diversion to Amboseli National Park. A little older now and once again, against the counsel of her GP back home on Aran, she was determined to visit us in Tanzania. I picked her up at the airport around midnight. Her flight had been delayed and we did not reach our home in Kinondoni B until 1 a.m.

At around dawn, Bid Bhilla died quietly in her sleep on December 23rd. As it was Christmas-time, a Muslim and Christian holiday, most government places had closed down. Were it not for the help of my post-graduate students, and of their local contacts we would have had a very difficult task preparing my mother's body for burial. People of all faiths and none went out of their way to help us. Those responsible for issuing death certificates, performing autopsies and any sort of documentation were all gone home 'up-country' for Christmas. One doctor was a hundred miles away when he was contacted and he returned to Dar es Salaam just to issue the death certificate, without which we could not have done anything.

We cremated my mother's remains on a big pile of scented wood in the Hindu crematorium near where Mary and I lived. My brother brought the ashes back to Aran for burial. First we put them in an empty ice-cream box and later transferred them to a little carved wooden box bought in Zanzibar.

This is how I described it for the family in an email:

Sunday, 24 December 2000
Dear Máire, Catherine, Enda, John & Thomas,

Mom has died. It was a beautiful Mass and afterwards she was cremated in the Hindu crematorium in Dar es Salaam – just up the road from where we live. We have the ashes (bones) with us here in the room as I write.

What a story mom has been telling all those Aran people in heaven. She's always enjoyed being one up on her neighbours – this time she's really done it in style. Nobody is likely to match this – getting themselves cremated in Dar es Salaam! Not Mary Tim; not anyone. The Irish ambassador to Tanzania and his staff attended the funeral Mass. The Tanzania Irish society was represented, my colleagues from APSO and at the university attended. The Muslim principal of the Tanzania School of Journalism where I teach and some students and staff came and helped carry the coffin. We all took turns at carrying it. A Swahili choir with drums and bangles sang lovely rhythmic Swahili hymns – the Lord is my shepherd, there is nothing I shall want. Mom would have been tapping her toes to the rhythm of the drums. There is definitely nothing more she needs or wants now or ever again.

When I was home in summer I broached with mom the subject of her coming to Tanzania. I told her it was a strenuous journey and that her heart was weak. Yes, she wanted to come. She would come. She was so much looking forward to it. It would have been cruel to advice anything other than promise a hearty 'welcome to Dar'.

"But remember mama," I said," if anything happens you'll be going home in a matchbox."

"I don't care. When you're dead, you're dead."

"OK, then", I said, "When I myself die, I want to be cremated."

I wanted to make sure she understood what I was talking about. She just replied:

"When you're dead you're dead, a mhaicín."

End of conversation.

Now she's dead and the 'remains' are cremated and, as I write, the bones, which we retrieved from the ashes, are here with me in an empty plastic ice-cream container. She would find that amusing. Another one up on her kind neighbour Mary Tim. Her ashes will be buried in Onaght graveyard beside dada's remains, after 'Month's Mind' towards the end of January. Michael will take them home. We cried when we found her dead and again at the funeral Mass. The priest asked me to say a few words. I thanked those who came and spoke a bit about mom. I found it hard to control my voice. But, our feelings were one of gratitude rather than sadness - grateful that she had a very full and satisfying life and a painless and peaceful death.

"I'm coming to see Mary and Patsy and then die," she told Ann on the plane.

It is what she wanted. You never expect your mother to die and it is always a big shock when she finally goes.

It rained when we were carrying the body out of the house. It rained as we drove along the coast road on the way to the mortuary. The Tanzanian doctor accompanying us remarked:

"In Africa it is said to be a sign of good fortune and of blessings when it rains."

There was a thunder storm during the Mass too – warm rain blew across the aisles inside the church, sprinkling the coffin and the congregation with drops of welcome soft, soothing tropical water. It rained too as the hearse drew out from the church on its way towards the crematorium.

A Tanzanian priest celebrated the funeral Mass. He gave a kindly sermon in English and said some words in Kiswahili. I don't know which of his words I understood least. After Mass, he came to the door to bid us farewell and was surprised we were cremating the body. Catholics don't do it here. I explained to him that it was ok.

For the past two years in Dar es Salaam, as I drove to work at the Tanzania School of Journalism, I passed the Hindu Crematorium. The place was significant only as the spot where I sometimes see a mongoose crossing to the banana plantation apposite. From now on the Sree Hindu Mandal Crematorium will have a different meaning for me. It was here yesterday evening, as dusk fell, that Michael, Ann and I picked my mother's burnt bones from the ashes of a funeral pyre.

When mom arrived in Dar-es-Salaam, her plane was late and all the luggage (not just mom's) had gone to Daruselem, a town of similar sounding name elsewhere. Mom worried that her heart medicine had gone astray. I assured her we could get replacement medicine in Dar. But in the end she did not need any. For the last several years she has been living on borrowed time. If she had lived another day she'd have been living in borrowed clothes as well.

She took two glasses of water when she arrived from the airport and went straight to bed. She shared a bed with Áine. It is a huge double – even quadruple-type bed favoured in Dar es Salaam. Electricity here is 8 hours on, 8 hours off and it is very hot in the house when the fans don't work. It is even more chaos on the streets when the traffic lights don't work, which is why the hearse was several house late for the funeral Mass. Mercifully, the night mom arrived the electricity had stayed on all night.

I got up at seven and peeped in to check on her. She seemed fast asleep. I peeped in later at about nine and listened to her steady breathing. I was glad that she was resting. She had a smile on her face and looked happy. I was content to let her sleep on.

Half an hour afterwards we heard Michael and Ann stirring in the next room. Suddenly Michael rushed in and said:

"Come quickly, we think mom is dead."

We all gathered around her bed. She was still in the same position, but now obviously dead. Her eyes were closed and she still had the smile on her face.

If I had not such good contacts in Dar, the days that followed could have been pure nightmare. Through my contacts we were able to reach officials at their homes and obtain the necessary death certificates and permits to have her cremated. Because it was the Christian and Muslim holiday, many government places were closed. What normally might have taken a couple of weeks, we did in a matter of days. My friendly contacts opened doors for us, even at the crematorium which was shut down for the holidays.

I had been looking forward to introducing mom to all our lovely neighbours. She'd have enjoyed sitting under the shade of the tall mango tree with Big Moma next door. The neighbours too were looking forward to meeting her. But it was not to be.

Much love,

P & M

VISITORS TO DAR ES SALAAM

When living in an exotic place like Dar-es-Salaam, it is not difficult to entice one's friends to visit. Our most important visitor was my mother. She had spent some happy weeks with us in Kenya and she very much wanted to come to Tanzania.

Apart from members of my family, another interesting visitor to our house in Kinondoni B was a good friend, Professor Adrian Hastings, a specialist on Africa. He spent a week with us, his visit coinciding with the TG4 filming. Another most welcome visitor was Mary's cousin, Jacqueline Kirwan-Haghshenas, who spent a month with us touring Tanzania's National Parks. On one occasion we were chased by a rogue elephant and I narrowly avoided overturning the car while trying to escape. Jacqueline's husband, a professor at Teheran University was unable to come but, at her request, we sent him a photograph of her posing outside a hotel called the Viagra Inn, hoping the mullahs in Teheran would not confiscate it. His absence gave us the excuse to spend an adventurous month with both of them in Persia later.

Over the years, Mary and I had made a point of meeting periodically in different parts of the globe with two very dear friends, Dermod McCarthy and Marguerite McCurtin. This time we decided our meeting place would be Africa. Mary and I took the overnight bus from Dar es Salaam to Nairobi to meet up with Marguerite and spent a month or so travelling in Kenya together. Later on, we were joined by Dermod to tour the Serengeti. Together, in awed silence, we watched the annual animal migration which is a sort of miracle of nature. We completed the adventure by taking a public bus from Arusha to Dar es Salaam, an endurance test in itself - a thirsty bumpy ten-hour ride. Later on we visited the island of Zanzibar together. I remember the visit of Dermod and Marguerite as a merry time full of fun and lots of laughter.

Towards the end of 1999, while we were still resident in Tanzania, TG4, an Irish television channel sent a team to Dar es Salaam to record a programme about my work. The arrival of the team proved an interesting diversion for all of us. What I associate most with these adventures is the generally easy-going atmosphere.

PLACES WE FAILED TO VISIT & A ROBBERY

Because of local wars, famine and floods, we failed to make it to Turkana in Northern Kenya or to Lalabela, in Ethiopia, two places we very much wanted to visit. We did spent a couple of memorable nights with our tent in a Maasai village. Mary was engrossed in doing some sketching but what I mostly remember is the intense almost unbearable mid-day heat. In the evening, the women invited us to watch them milking and in the morning we accompanied them on a long trek to fetch water from a dirty-looking hole in the bed of a dry river. We felt honoured when the very tall chief (with a tiny wife) invited us into his house. Risking giving offence, we decided not to take up his invitation to sleep there but instead set up our tent in the courtyard.

Just before we left East Africa for good, our house was broken into and we were robbed. The heavy pounding of the monsoon rain on the tin roof, allied with the familiar whirring of the ceiling fan, drowned out the sound of the armed robbers cutting the iron bars on the windows at the back of the house. As the rain abated at dawn, Leonard, our Malawian night watchman, tapped on our window frame (there was no glass in our windows, only mosquito netting) and urgently whispered:

"Mama, Mama, all is not well!" It was an African euphemism for:

"You have been robbed of everything."

We counted ourselves fortunate that we had not been shot as so many others had been. We later worked out that the watchman must have let the robbers in by the front gate and, once inside, the robbers used their acetylene equipment to cut through the one-inch thick iron bars on the kitchen window. We slept through it all. Leonard later claimed that the robbers had climbed over the wall at the back but the neighbours on examining the walls very carefully, found no footprints on the whitewashed bricks and came to the same conclusion as ourselves. We didn't blame Leonard for letting them in because, after all, I had told him never to risk his life resisting thieves. The owner of the house, sent some one next day to replace the iron bars in the window, warning us at the same time to move out of the house immediately since we were now targets. Student friends also warned:

"They'll come for your car tonight. Don't be seen driving around the town either."

I swapped cars with one of my post- grads. For the next few nights Mary and I stayed with various VSO friends, spending our last night with a bunch of dedicated missionary sisters outside of Dar. These sisters had been doing wonderful things for the local community, digging wells for them, paying school fees for their children, sharing what they possessed with the villagers. Their reward was being robbed at gun point while the police, summoned by the villagers, took whatever valuables the thieves had overlooked in the dark. It was a pity that we had to disappear like this because we wanted to celebrate quietly with Big Moma and our lovely neighbours. The most we could do was not to report the robbery, thus keeping our kind neighbours out of gaol. The local police, had they heard of the robbery, would have locked up our neighbours as suspects, knowing that we'd have paid money to have them released. One of my post- graduates picked us up at the sisters and dropped us off at the airport. We moved smoothly through customs until we approached Emigration. I saw with alarm that Mary's passport had expired by one day – a major disaster if the man at emigration noticed. It would have cost us at least a hefty bribe, if not a week in detention. I don't know how I could justify the bribe to my journalism students but, having seen the prison facilities in Dar, we certainly did not want to end up there. On the spur of the moment I decided to brazen it out. Mary would have to distract the man at emigration – overwhelm him with her grasp of Kiswahili. The ruse worked.

15

THE SALMON COMES HOME

MARY RESTRINGS HER HARP AND RESUMES WORKING

While in Africa, Mary kept her harp in its crate but now, back home, she restrung it with the intention of transcribing her songs with harp accompaniments.

When it was first suggested to Mary that she write down her harp accompaniments, she baulked at such an undertaking. During her singing career she never wrote down her harp accompaniments, preferring to memorise them. Now she found that she had forgotten many of her accompaniments so that she had to rely on muscle memory or listen painstakingly to her recordings. In order to commit her arrangements to paper, she taped her songs and asked a so-called music specialist to do the transcribing.

"Easy", said the specialist, "I can transcribe a few in an hour."

But the task proved beyond her, so Mary realised she'd have to set to and do it herself. She got a lot of help and advice from our friend Alan Tongue, Mary's former BBC television producer. I had noticed that the 'music specialist' was using a music program called *Sibelius*. I know nothing about music but I am reasonably competent on the computer. When we got home after watching the 'expert', I secretly ordered a copy of *Sibelius* and, just as secretly played with it in my attic study for several weeks. To me who can't sing a note and would not know a musical crochet from a hole in the wall, (ask Mrs Hehir), I knew I'd be laughed out of the house if I mentioned to Mary what I was up to. But, using the *Sibelius* manual and one of Mary's harp accompaniments, I gradually managed to put the song and the arrangement on to the computer and, even more importantly, succeeded in getting the computer to play it. So, one morning I played my song very loud and I soon had Mary at the door listening.

Puzzled, she enquired: where did you get that?

When I told her that I had done it myself, she looked at me in disbelief. Then she sat by me at the computer and we listened together. Her response was: "Magic!"

With Mary's help I soon learnt to refine my work and acquired a certain mastery of *Sibelius*. In the end we produced the arrangements for sixty songs, enough to fill five volumes of her songs with harp accompaniments. Mrs. Hehir would have been very proud of me. Which proves that if you live long enough, you can master anything.

HARP ON THE WILLOW

Mary retired from singing in 1994 but when she returned from Africa in the early Nineties , she started giving presentations, entitled *Travels With My Harp* which gave us an excuse to start travelling once more to places like Australia, Canada and the USA. In 2009, Boston College put on a special six-month exhibition of her work.

John Misto, an award-winning Australian playwright had written a play *Harp On The Willow*, based on Mary's life. It ran for thirteen sold-out weeks in a theatre in Sydney and later for eight weeks at the 1000-seater Comedy Theatre in Melbourne.

All this unexpected activity gave us both a new interest in travel, not that we had lost any of our old enthusiasms. Malcolm Cooke Productions produced Misto's play in Melbourne and invited Mary to appear at the end of each performance to give a short talk. Marina Prior, the foremost singer/actress in the Antipodes, played the part of Mary and opera singer Joan Carden played the Lady Abbess at Stanbrook. Mary's agreement with Misto stipulated that he'd never require her to see the play or read the script. She felt that this gave him sufficient carte blanche to write freely, not having to look over his shoulder wondering what Mary might say or think. This produced a somewhat comical situation with Mary giving a talk at the end of each performance in Melbourne and signing autographs afterwards with people asking her about characters in the play that she had never watched.

Our stay in Melbourne was one of the high-lights of our life together, thanks to John Misto's play and the generosity of Malcolm Cooke Productions.

Much as we looked forward to our visit to Australia, we almost didn't make it to Melbourne as this email to our English friends John and Darya Amor shows:

Melbourne, Oz

Dear John and Darya,

It has been said that if you look like your photograph on your passport, you are too sick to travel. The photograph on Mary's passport, though taken recently, makes her look relatively young, which caused the people at the Australian passport office to mistake her age which called for the ticking of just half a dozen boxes. Had they realised her real age, she'd have had to tick scores more boxes. We were over half way to Melbourne when they realised their mistake and this almost caused a disaster. We flew Emirates, almost missing our flight due to accidents on the M3. The plane was also delayed in Dubai, so we were very tired by the time we reached Bangkok, only desiring to get to our bed before we collapsed. A taxi took us from the airport to the hotel, a favourite place where we had stayed several times before.

At check-in, the very polite Thai girl bowed several times and mentioned some very urgent messages for us from Oz but in our eagerness to get to bed, we decided the messages could wait till morning. She also mentioned that at the request of the Australians, the hotel had arranged to send a doctor to our room immediately we checked in.

"What for?" I enquired trying to suppress my impatience, "It is sleep we need, not a doctor."

As nobody at the desk seemed to know the reason for the doctor, we concluded it was a mistake and cancelled the appointment. By then it was 8 p.m. Thursday night Bangkok time, Friday morning in Oz. We had been travelling for 24 hours and neither of us was firing on all cylinders.

Just as the porter opened the door to our room the phone rang. It was Anthony Blair, Mary's Oz agent speaking from Sydney.

"There is a crisis, Pat. Did you receive my messages at the desk?"

"Yes, Anthony, four separate messages. But I did not plan to open them till morning. What's the crisis?"

"It is about Mary's work visa in Oz. She will be refused entry until we sort it out. But no panic. We have come up with a plan. It's all in my fax and marked urgent."

"What's wrong then?"

"After Mary had already taken off from Gatwick, the Australian Immigration Dept. discovered she was over 70 and for that reason required a doctor's certificate in order to be allowed to work in Australia. This explains why we requested a doctor to go to your room immediately you arrived in Bangkok. He will issue the certificate that will allow Mary to enter Australia. You are ok."

I saw from the faxed forms that the doctor had to test Mary and tick about 150 boxes.

"But this will take hours", I protested "and we need to get some sleep."

"I'm sorry, Pat. Immigration has agreed that, given the circumstances, she need only tick half a dozen boxes or so. Have the doctor sign them. He listed the important boxes.

That Mary is in a good mental state.

That she does not have cancer.

That she does not have TB.

That she does not require a dialysis machine.

That she can if so required, return to the UK unaided and on her own. etc.

"Apart from the first," I joked, "we can tick those ok."

In the haze and with our lack of rest, I could see that this might be a lengthy operation and I was starting to wonder if I was in a good mental state myself.

"We have arranged for a doctor to come to your room and certify Mary fit to travel." He said.

This was the doctor's visit I had just cancelled. I had to return to the front desk to reinstate the cancelled visit. I tried to rebook the doctor from our room, but this proved impossible. Nobody seemed to know what I was saying and I did not know what they were saying. I needed eye contact and perhaps a bit of semaphoring with my hands.

At the front desk, everyone joined their hands, bowed and nodded "yes" to everything I uttered. It did not take a wizard to conclude that my Irish accent was not understood in Bangkok. Well, not at this hotel, they didn't.

Back at our room and several urgent calls later, Mary was waiting to get some much needed sleep and I felt the same – neither of us in a fit mental state to enter Australia. Time was running out. By now it was late Friday in Oz and Immigration closed for the weekend. We were scheduled to arrive early Sunday morning . Now the problem was understood. The desk called to say that the doctor would telephone me shortly.

The doctor telephoned and I took his call. Mary took a deep breath ready to answer the 150 questions required by Australian Immigration before they'd allow her off the plane in Melbourne. The Doctor's voice on the other end of the line sounded annoyed, for which one could not blame him in the least. It was a thankless task to ask of a doctor at 9 p.m. Friday night.

"You want a certificate? This very big job. I can't do it. It can only be done at hospital emergency. Now closed for week-end."

"Well, they told me from Australia that they had arranged for you to do it in the hotel room here."

"No. No. No."

"You asking me to lyte you a celtificate?"

"No, I'm not asking you to lie. Nobody wants you to lie. There is nothing wrong with Mary."

"I cannot lyte to you a celtificate."

"But doctor, I am not asking you to lie."

This went on with me trying to get a word in and explain the contents of the Australian faxes to the good doctor, while he kept emphasising that this job could be performed only by the emergency department at the hospital. Every so often when I thought I had got through to him that Mary was ok and that he did not have to lie about her condition, the good doctor would butt in with his mantra:

"I cannot lyte to you a certificate." Clearly showing I was not having any impact.

Mary, listening in all the time and waiting for her mental state to be assessed, remarked later how my voice was rising a decibel with each new mantra from the Doctor.

Normally I am a calm patient person but according to Mary the pitch of my voice was reaching 'take-off' point in the end.

"Doctor, I cannot understand this. Why should we want you to lie. There is nothing wrong with Mary. It is just a formality for Immigration. It must be normal practice for doctors to issue certificates, like for sick leave and so on."

I forget how the good doctor responded but by now he must have noticed that I was getting hyper and rattled. Simultaneously, I think, it must have dawned on both of us, that we were dealing with a pronunciation problem. Sheepishly, I apologised, blaming my dimness on lack of sleep and travel exhaustion. We immediately took a taxi to A&E at the local hospital. It was open all night and we took it for granted that it was only a matter of fact procedure that we would get Mary's sanity certified by morning.

By now it was Friday 10.30 p.m. in Bangkok and my sanity too was becoming a bit dodgy and might also require certification. As it happened the A&E could not certify the sanity of either of us. They had a policy, etc. etc, proving that certifying our sanity was not going to be an easy matter.

A young doctor explained that certification for Australian visa purposes was a lengthy procedure and was only done by a specialist unit at another hospital which was now closed for the night. It would open at 8 a.m. and to be head of the queue we'd need to line up at 6 a.m. We returned to the hotel and when Oz called at around midnight, I told them the situation and promised to be in the queue by six – something I had no intention of doing. They telephoned again at 5.30 a.m. only to find us still in bed.

From the start it was the mistake of Immigration in Australia and somehow they sorted it out while we slept. They were already in the soup with the media about their handling of some Asian boat people and concluded that it would have been bad publicity for them to have more newspaper headings saying Mary O'Hara arrested at the airport *and deported for want of a certificate of sanity. Most people get through life with no proof of their sanity. Me for instance.*

Much love,

Pat

Boston College decided to house Mary's papers in their Burn's Irish Library and wanted to put on a Mary O'Hara exhibition. Mary updated her autobiography which she called *Travels With My Harp*. It was published in 2012 and in the same year we sold our thatched cottage in England and came to live on Aran. For me the wheel had turned full circle.

Teaching can at times be a chore but an activity that, nonetheless, gave me great pleasure. However, teaching does not give one the same satisfaction as, for example, making a chair or building a currach or a house.

Shaw with his usual wit captures the difference: "He who can does. He who cannot teaches". The two subjects that gave me most satisfaction to teach were Information Technology and Design Technology, perhaps because they combined 'doing' with 'teaching'.

Recently while walking down the main street in Slough, I was stopped by a well-dressed young man in a smart uniform:

"Do you remember me, Mr. O'Toole?" He enquired.

Of course I didn't, which disappointed him. Immediately he volunteered the information.

"In Year 7 you taught us science and one of our projects was about 'Flying'. You used a Coca Cola bottle to fire a rocket over the roof of the school. Then, before we wrote up our project, you brought us to visit the RAF Museum near Birmingham. I have recently qualified as an RAF pilot and it is because of you. Thank you, Sir."

His name was Stephen Tobin and he did not realise that he had just handed me a great reward, the type that any teacher would cherish.

Then, out of the blue as I was putting the finishing touches to my memoirs and wondering to myself if my whole work in Africa and elsewhere had been a fool's errand, I had an email from a former student, who I understand is now a senior minister in the government of Tanzania. He had heard that I was not well:

30/08/2012

Dear Pat,

Thanks for everything and I hope The Almighty God will give you strength to overcome your illness. You have all our prayers. There are quite a few of your students that keep in touch and have good memories of you and of Mary. I will send you their emails in the near future.

A few years after you left Tanzania I thought I would again get into more education, only this time I went into Sports Management, so in 2005-2006 I did an Executive Masters degree in Lausanne Switzerland - Sponsored by the International Olympic Committee. Then in 2009 - 2010 I went to Greece for a Master's Degree in Olympic Studies - Specializing in Organization and Management of Mega Sports Events. I now do consultancies for FIFA and IOC. Your postgraduate course in PR provided the foundation for all these courses, thanks to you.

Give my regards to Mary and I'll look up her new book on Youtube. I believe she mentions her stay with us in Dar es Salaam.

Best regards,

Henry Tandau

Of all the email, the one from former bishop Tim Carroll of the Ujiji area is the one I treasure most. Thank you Tim. He is now Provincial Secretary and living at the Society's headquarters in Ireland. He had heard I was writing my memoirs and wished me well. He wrote:

Hi Pádraig,

I still remember the stories you told me about your time living in the Emir's Palace in Lafiagi.

As regards Ujiji in Borgu, it now has two priests in the Vicariate of Kontagora. I handed over the Vicariate of Kontagora to a Kamberi man bishop Bo'us Yohanna from Agwara parish.

The seeds you and others sowed have flowered and fruited. We built on foundations put in place by yourself, John Slevin, Nicholas Flavin, Andy Donovan, Kevin Cassidy and others.

Take care of yourself

Tim Carroll

BACK AMONG ONE'S OWN PEOPLE

Back on Aran among one's own people, one feels it having a rejuvenating effect on one's spirit. It may be an illusion, of course. Perhaps it is such an illusion that draws the salmon back to its roots. I certainly feel the pull of it. It may not work as magically as the poet Raftery described it. However, it works for me:

Dá mbeinn-se 'mo sheasamh I gceart lár mo dhaoine,
D'imeóch an aois díom is bheinn arís óg
If I were back living in the midst of my people,
Age would desert me and once more I'd be young.

My fellow islander and, likewise, an exile from Inis Mór, the great poet, Máirtín Ó Direáin, in his poem *Faoiseamh a gheobhadsa*, captured some of the pensive mood that sometimes steals over returned exiles like myself as we renew acquaintance with the island of our birth:

Faoiseamh a gheobhadsa
Seal beag gairid
I measc mo dhaoine
Ar oilean mara.
Ag siúl cois cladaigh
O Luan go Satharn
Thiar ag baile.
I will find solace/ For a short time only/ Among my people/ On a sea-girt island,/ Walking the shore/ Morning and evening/ Monday to Saturday/ In my western homeland.

There is a place on the low road near the shore in Bungabhla where I like to sit and think. The heap of regular flagstones piled up in the walls is evidence that there was a settlement here once – one or perhaps a group of stone houses called *clocháin*. They nestled in a nook of the cliff facing out to sea. I sit on the mound of empty sea shells accumulated over years, perhaps over centuries of habitation. I like to go there when the sea is stirred (*boga sa bhfarraige*). The deep slow-moving waves that started somewhere far out in the Atlantic travel around the north shore of Brannock Island to become the roaring breaker referred to by the locals as *an bhrachlainn*. I feel that over the centuries others have sat here like me, watching out to sea, as I do.

As I sit there deep in thought, a neighbour passes, driving a cow before him. He knows I am engrossed in thought so he does not disturb me.

"*Coinnigh do mhisneach, a mhac*" (Hold Fast), he mutters as he moves by.

There is no greater blessing an Aran man can wish on you than that you hold on to your courage.

In this landscape, not much has changed over the centuries. *An bhrachlainn* makes the same sound today as it always has done. I think of how blessed I have been in life. Though I have not yet figured out why I became a missionary, I still believe in *Dia Mór* and I thank Him or Her for bringing me back here to my roots towards the end of my sojourn on earth.

ABOUT THE AUTHOR

Pádraig O'Toole was born in 1938 on Inis Mór, one of the Aran Islands. In 1962, he graduated with a Double First from National University of Ireland College, Cork. After that he spent a spell in Africa working as a missionary and in Ireland as a journalist. He taught in Nigeria, Kenya, and Tanzania, also in the UK and Canada. He has post graduate degrees from universities in Canada and the UK. In 1985, he married the singer and harpist Mary O'Hara. After Mary retired from singing, they returned to Africa. Pádraig taught in Nairobi, Kenya and later at the University of Dar es Salaam, Tanzania. They now live on the Aran Islands.

Lafiagi, 1970.

CPSIA information can be obtained at www.ICGtesting.com
Printed in the USA
LVOW04s1457080615

441616LV00002B/483/P